AF361349

THE SUPREME MODERATOR OF CLERICAL EXEMPT RELIGIOUS INSTITUTES

THE CATHOLIC UNIVERSITY OF AMERICA
CANON LAW STUDIES
No. 369

THE SUPREME MODERATOR OF CLERICAL EXEMPT RELIGIOUS INSTITUTES

A HISTORICAL CONSPECTUS AND CANONICAL COMMENTARY

A DISSERTATION

SUBMITTED TO THE FACULTY OF THE SCHOOL OF CANON LAW OF THE CATHOLIC UNIVERSITY OF AMERICA IN PARTIAL FULFILLMENT OF THE REQUIREMENTS FOR THE DEGREE OF DOCTOR OF CANON LAW

BY

MAURICE J. GRAJEWSKI, O.F.M., M.A., PH.D., J.C.L.

THE CATHOLIC UNIVERSITY OF AMERICA PRESS
WASHINGTON, D.C.
1957

Imprimi Potest
THEOPHANE KALINOWSKI, O.F.M.
Provincial

January 14, 1957

Nihil Obstat
ROMAEUS O'BRIEN, O. CARM.
Censor Deputatus

January 11, 1957

Imprimatur
✠PATRICK A. O'BOYLE
Archbishop of Washington

January 28, 1957

DIVO PATRI NOSTRO SANCTO FRANCISCO
EIUSQUE
IN SUPREMA MODERATIONE
INCLYTIS SUCCESSORIBUS

TABLE OF CONTENTS

PAGE

FOREWORD   vii

PART I. A HISTORICAL CONSPECTUS

CHAPTER

   I. THE PRISTINE CONCEPT OF A SUPREME MODERATOR IN MONASTICISM   3
      A. PRELIMINARY NOTIONS
      B. THE ABBOT IN ORIENTAL MONASTICISM
        1. St. Anthony and the Monks of Egypt
        2. The Rule of St. Pachomius
        3. Basilian Monasticism
      C. THE ABBOT IN THE MONASTIC ORDERS IN THE WEST TO THE X CENTURY
        1. Pre-Benedictine Rules
          a. *Italian Monasticism*
          b. *French Monasticism*
          c. *Spanish Monasticism*
          d. *Celtic Monasticism*
          e. *African Monasticism*
        2. The Rule of St. Benedict
  II. THE OFFICE OF THE SUPREME MODERATOR FROM THE X TO THE XII CENTURY   22
      A. THE X AND XI CENTURY
        1. The Congregation of Cluny
        2. The Camaldolese
        3. The Carthusians
      B. THE XII CENTURY
        1. The Cistercian Order
        2. The Premonstratensian Order
        3. The Gilbertine Order
        4. The Military Orders
 III. THE SUPREME MODERATOR IN THE MENDICANT ORDERS OF THE XIII CENTURY   42
      A. THE FRANCISCANS
      B. THE DOMINICANS

PART II. A CANONICAL COMMENTARY

IV. THE AUTHORITY OF THE SUPREME
MODERATOR   59
  A. THE POWER OF JURISDICTION
    1. The Concept of Jurisdiction
    2. Commentary on Canons 196 and 197, § 1
  B. THE DOMINATIVE POWER
    1. The Nature of Dominative Power
    2. Commentary on Canons 501, § 1, and 1312,
      § 1 and 2
  C. THE AUTHORITY OF THE SUPREME MODERATOR
    1. The Nature of the Supreme Moderator's
      Authority
    2. The Extent of the Supreme Moderator's
      Authority
    3. The Determination of Competency of Su-
      periors

V. THE PERSON OF THE SUPREME MODERATOR
OF CLERICAL EXEMPT RELIGIOUS INSTITUTES
                                   81
  A. CANONICAL QUALIFICATIONS OF THE CANDIDATE
  B. THE APPOINTMENT OF THE SUPREME MODERATOR
  C. THE TERM OF OFFICE
  D. OBLIGATION TO ACCEPT THE OFFICE

VI. THE LEGISLATIVE POWER OF THE SUPREME
MODERATOR   89
  A. POSSESSION OF LEGISLATIVE POWER BY SUPREME
    MODERATOR
  B. THE POWER OF ISSUING PRECEPTS
  C. THE POWER OF GRANTING DISPENSATIONS
    1. Dispensation from the General Laws of the Church
      a. *Pre-Code Legislation*
      b. *Legislation of the Code*
    2. Dispensation from the Special Law of the Order
      a. *Pre-Code Legislation*
      b. *Legislation of the Code*

VII. THE JUDICIAL POWER OF THE SUPREME
MODERATOR   112

A. Pre-Code Legislation

B. Legislation of the Code

    1. Commentary on Canon 1579, § 2

    2. Commentary on Canon 1594, § 4

    3. Supreme Moderator's Judicial Rights and Duties

    4. Beatification and Canonization Processes

VIII. THE EXECUTIVE POWER OF THE SUPREME MODERATOR   125

A. Personal Aspects of the Executive Power

    1. Profession of Faith

    2. Residence

    3. The Definitorial Council

    4. The General Chapter

    5. Canonical Visitation

    6. The Decrees of the Holy See

    7. The Quinquennial Report

    8. Participation in the Ecumenical Council

B. Administrative Aspects of the Executive Power

    1. Authority over Provinces and Religious Houses

    2. Authority over the Members of the Religious Community

        a. *Admission to Novitiate and Profession*

        b. *Dismissal of Religious*

            1) The *Ipso Facto* Effected Dismissal of Members of a Religious Community

            2) Dismissal of Religious in Temporary Vows

            3) Dismissal of Religious in Solemn Vows

        c. *The Reservation of Sins*

        d. *The Prohibition of Books*

        e. *The Supervision of Studies*

        f. *The Affiliation of Tertiaries*

CONCLUSIONS   163

BIBLIOGRAPHY   165

ABBREVIATIONS   xiv

INDEX   177

BIOGRAPHICAL NOTE   181

CANON LAW STUDIES   182

FOREWORD

The hierarchical arrangement of the government of the universal Church has its counterpart on a smaller scale in the constitutional arrangement of authority within religious communities. Not much difficulty is experienced in perceiving the parallel existing between the jurisdictional position of the pastor, bishop and pope, and the offices of the local superior, provincial and supreme moderator of religious institutes. The historical evolution, however, of these offices does not follow the same pattern in both societies, since the ecclesiastical hierarchy developed from the universal papal sovereignty down to the localized authority of the pastor in his parish; the monastic hierarchy conversely grew from the limited jurisdiction exercised by the monastic abbots or priors to the eventual acknowledgment of a universal supreme moderator of the religious organization.

A twofold motive induced the undertaking of this study of the office of the supreme moderator of clerical exempt religious institutes. The first of these is the complete lack of a historico-juridical monograph on this subject in canonical literature; the second is the desire to write a complementary study to the two excellent dissertations appearing in the series of Canon Law Studies of the Catholic University of America, which treated extensively the office of the local and the provincial religious superiors respectively.[1]

Of the two parts into which this study is divided, the first will treat of the historical development of the office of the supreme moderator, while the second will furnish a commentary on the contemporary common law legislation affecting his office.

---

[1] Clancy, *The Local Religious Superior*, The Catholic University of America Canon Law Studies, No. 175 (Washington, D.C.: The Catholic University of America Press, 1943) (hereafter cited as *The Local Superior*); O'Brien, *The Provincial Religious Superior*, The Catholic University of America Canon Law Studies, No. 258 (Washington, D.C.: The Catholic University of America Press, 1947) (hereafter cited as *The Provincial Superior*).

Since the historical development of the office of the supreme moderator cannot be found in the universal church legislation or in the writings of the decretists and decretalists, the present study limits itself to the examination of the Rules, Constitutions and Statutes of Religious Orders to show the origin, gradual development and the extent of the jurisdiction of the general superior. In the first chapter selected primitive monastic rules of the East and the West will be examined for traces of the office of a general superior and the nature of his jurisdiction. The second chapter will be devoted to an analysis of the office of the supreme moderator during the great monastic reforms of the tenth, eleventh and twelfth centuries, which introduced a more abundant legislation and a more explicit determination of the extent of the jurisdictional power of the general superior. A detailed study of the special legislation of the Mendicant Orders in the thirteenth century will constitute the third chapter, since at that time the hierarchical organization of monasticism reached its perfection and, with very slight modification in the course of succeeding centuries, remains in effect in the canonical legislation of the universal Church.

The canonical commentary constituting the second part of this study begins with the fourth chapter which deals with the general concept of the authority of the supreme moderator. In the fifth chapter the legislation of the Code concerning the person of the general superior is delineated. The remaining three chapters comprise a commentary on the specific canons of the Code dealing with the legislative, judicial and executive powers of the supreme moderator.

To avoid needless repetition of matter which has been fully covered in the studies of Clancy and O'Brien, commentary on canons dealing with the rights of religious superiors in general or referring alike to all major superiors will be eliminated. O'Brien's study of the Provincial Superior, in particular, covers much of the authority enjoyed by the supreme moderator in virtue of his rôle as major superior. For this reason all aspects of government shared by the supreme moderator in common with the provincial superior are left untreated in this study. That accounts for the absence of a commentary on such topics, for example, as the administration of temporal goods and the coercive powers of the general superior.

No specific canons in the Code allot any power to the supreme moderator in these matters which is not already enjoyed by the provincial. The difference is only one of degree, not one of kind, for canon 502 grants the general superior a community-wide authority which is identical with the one exercised by the provincial in his restricted sphere of jurisdiction.

The writer wishes to express his sincere gratitude to all who had a part in making this work possible: to his superiors for the opportunity of pursuing the study of canon law; to the members of the faculty of the School of Canon Law at the Catholic University of America for their expert and generous assistance and guidance; to the librarians and confreres who have kindly proffered their help and encouragement.

ABBREVIATIONS

AAS—Acta Apostolicae Sedis.

ALKM—Archiv für Litteratur- und Kirchengeschichte des Mittelalters.

AOFM—Acta Ordinis Fratrum Minorum.

Codex Regularum—Holstenius-Brockie, *Codex Regularum Monasticarum et Canonicarum.*

CpR—Commentarium pro Religiosis.

CpRM—Commentarium pro Religiosis et Missionariis.

Dictionnaire—Helyot, *Dictionnaire des Ordres Religieux.*

Fontes—Codicis Iuris Canonici Fontes cura Gasparri editi.

Hefele—*Histoire des Conciles.*

Heimbucher—*Die Orden und Kongregationen der katholischen Kirche.*

Mansi—*Sacrorum Conciliorum Nova et Amplissima Collectio.*

MPG—Migne, *Patrologiae Cursus Completus, Series Graeca.*

MPL—Migne, *Patrologiae Cursus Completus, Series Latina.*

MOPH—Monumenta Ordinis Fratrum Praedicatorum Historica.

PART ONE

A HISTORICAL CONSPECTUS

CHAPTER I

THE PRISTINE CONCEPT OF A
SUPREME MODERATOR IN MONASTICISM

A. Preliminary Notions

It is commonly held by theologians and historians that the religious state is of divine institution, having its basis in the words of our Lord: "If thou wilt be perfect, go sell what thou hast, and give to the poor, and thou shalt have treasure in heaven: and come follow me." [1] Many of the early Christians answered this call of *of Our Lord till the Dawn of the Middle Ages* (3 vols., London, 1922), I, 1–33, for a detailed exposition of aseticism in the New Testament according to the teaching of Christ and his disciples.
grace by means of the practice of a private asceticism, as was manifested by the virgins and prophetesses at Caesarea. [2] Other examples of a fertile ascetical movement during the first three centuries of the Christian era abound in the writings of the Fathers and the Apologists. [3] These ardent Christians chose the more perfect religious state by observing faithfully, besides the common precepts obliging all the faithful, the evangelical counsels and many of the ascetical practices referred to in the Gospels, e.g., fasting and abstinence, retirement and prayer.

A very serious difficulty was encountered by these early ascetics in the manifold distractions which are inseparable from domestic and social life. Escape was, therefore, sought in the wilderness and the desert, where sanctity was easier to achieve because of the fewer distractions and temptations. Man, however, is a gregarious

---

[1] Matt., XIX, 21. The same injunction is also recorded in Mark, X, 17–31, and Luke, XVIII, 22–30. Cf. Pourrat, *Christian Spirituality from the Time*
[2] Acts, XXXI, 8–9.
[3] Cf. particularly the following works: St. Clement of Rome, *Epistle to the Corinthians;* St. Justin, *Apologia;* St. Cyprian, *De habitu virginum;* St. Methodius, *Convivium;* St. Clement of Alexandria, *Stromata;* Tertullian, *De virginibus velandis.*

animal by nature and needs the society and support of his fellow man. The hermits, consequently, sought out the company of like-minded individuals, and with the spread of their fame for sanctity came the inevitable disciples who wanted to profit from the guidance of holy men and thus laid the foundations of the later cenobitical or monastic life.

In the first two centuries of the Christian era no religious state in the strict juridic sense is found, for it was neither necessary nor possible. Its necessity was precluded by the prevalent spirit among the early Christians of living under the direct inspiration of the teaching of Christ and the Apostles in such a manner as to be, in a sense, practicing monks. Its impossibility is obvious since the religious state, which of its very nature presupposes divergent forms of life dependent upon the conditions of time and place, lends itself to a slow historical evolution before perfection is attained through the cumulative experience derived by the trial and error method.[4]

In the third century the first clear delineation of monasticism made its appearance in Egypt in two distinct movements. The first of these was the semi-eremitical system instituted and directed by St. Anthony (c. 251–356), who, after a long life of seclusion spent in the wilderness along the Upper Nile, undertook the guidance of a multitude of monks who were drawn to his neighborhood by his reputation for holiness. The second distinct system departed from the eremitical and semi-eremitical Antonian organization and is characterized by the cenobitical or conventual type of monachism. In this monastic framework introduced by St. Pachomius (c. 292–346), the monks lived together under a complete system of organization, no longer like a family under the rule of a patriarch or a father, but rather as an army under a strict discipline of a military character with all the machinery of a

---

[4] Heussi, *Der Ursprung des Mönchtums* (Tübingen, 1936), p. 67: "In Urchristentum gab es keine Mönche. Sie waren dort nicht nötig und geschichtlich nicht möglich. Nicht nötig, denn die Gemeindeglieder waren alle ganz weltflüchtig gerichtet, sie waren in gewissen Sinne alle Mönche,—geschichtlich nicht möglich, denn das Mönchtum als Stand setzt die Differenzierung der Gemeindeglieder nach dem verschiedenen Mass der religiösen Hingabe und eine längere geschichtliche Entwicklung voraus."

centralized government including a superior general, a system of visitation and the regular assembly of a general chapter.[5]

Unlike the office of the provincial, which is a distinctly non-monastic function,[6] the office of the supreme moderator of religious orders has its foundations in the very origins of this monasticism and has undergone a slow, but perceptible, historical development with the perfection of monastic legislation throughout the centuries. In its primitive stages it consisted in the simple acknowledgment of a general superior by a body of dedicated men, who looked upon him as the vicegerent of Christ in their community. With the spread of monasticism from the East to the West, the growth in the number of religious, the increase of monasteries and abbeys, and above all, with the multiplication of monastic rules, the office of the religious supreme moderator took on a more precise juridical nature.

The adumbrations of the office of the general superior in the first six centuries of the history of monasticism within the Church become more explicit with the monastic reforms of the tenth, eleventh and twelfth centuries, when the autonomous monasteries and abbeys surrendered many of their rights to the centralized government which was being gradually introduced to meet the demands of extraordinary expansion and necessary control. In the thirteenth century, with the founding of the first true Orders of Mendicants by St. Francis (1182–1226) and St. Dominic (1170–1221), centralization became an accomplished fact, and the office of the supreme moderator became a canonical reality in the modern sense of the word. Since that time ecclesiastical legislation has made it imperative for all communities of religious to organize their hierarchy of government along these lines, so much so that the present Code of Canon Law does not envisage any religious organization on the level of an Order which would be lacking a general superior customarily resident at Rome who would exercise supreme jurisidiction over the entire Order.

------

[5] Butler, *Lausiac History of Palladius*, Texts and Studies, VI (2 vols., Cambridge, 1898–1904), I, 234–235 (hereafter cited as *Lausiac History*).

[6] O'Brien, *The Provincial Superior*, p. 1.

B. The Abbot in Oriental Monasticism

1. St. Anthony and the Monks of Egypt

Of all the Christian monks who dwelled in the desert wastes of Egypt the most celebrated is St. Anthony (c. 251–356), who is generally reputed to be the first monk and is called the Father of Christian Monasticism.[7] After he had spent a long life in solitude and penance along the east bank of the Nile, St. Anthony was approached by other holy men seeking enlightenment in the spiritual life and insisting that he forsake his eremitical life and instruct them as a group in the ascetic life of which he was considered a master. He complied with their wishes and began to organize in a very loose fashion the first group of Christian monks about the year 305.[8] Thus for the first time in the history of the Church a venerable anchorite ventured to teach, advise and direct a group of enthusiastic followers by establishing among them a vague bond of union, based on a common life and a common superior.

No written rule was adopted but a degree of organized uniformity in their observances was obtained by the personal leadership of their founder and first superior. A collection under the title "Rule and Precepts" was made by the early disciples and is considered representative of the primitive laws governing the early monks.[9] Only rarely is mention made in this collection of a governing head of the community.[10]

St. Anthony, as the founder of this form of monastic life, was

---

[7] St. Paul of Thebes (ca. 234- ca. 347) is sometimes called the first anchorite. It is known from the *Vita S. Antonii*, written by St. Athanasius (295–373), that he himself was taught the way of asceticism by an old man living in retirement and was encouraged to perseverance by sympathetic companions with a similar vocation for the higher life. Cf. S. Athanasius, *Vita et Conversatio S.P.N. Antonii*, c. 3, 4, 8, 11, 12—Migne, *Patrologiae Cursus Completus, Series Graeca* (161 vols., Parisiis, 1857–1866), XXVI, 843–862 (hereafter cited as *MPG*).

[8] *Ibid.*, c. 14—*MPG*, XXVI, 863–866.

[9] *Regulae ac Praecepta S.P.N. Antonii ad filios suos Monachos*—Holstenius-Brockie, *Codex Regularum Monasticarum et Canonicarum* (6 vols., Augustae Vindelicorum, 1759), I, 4–5 (hereafter cited as the *Codex Regularum*).

[10] *Ibid.*, c. xxii—*Codex Regularum*, I, 4: "Addisce quotidie disciplinam a senioribus; nec ullum aggrediaris opus, nisi consulto Patre Monasterii." Also in c. lxv: ". . . nec respondeat Superiori."

looked upon as the undisputed general superior of the brethren. A semi-eremitic organization was adopted. The monks continued to live in individual cells, which were grouped together in such a manner that they could be of mutual assistance without needlessly disturbing one another. St. Anthony, however, encouraged the brethren to assemble at stated intervals to benefit from simple spiritual conferences on the governance of their daily life, common worship and the celebration of the Holy Mysteries.[11]

The only definite rôle of the general superior appears to be the regular holding of these conferences, the occasional visitation of outlying monasteries upon the invitation of the brethren,[12] and instruction by means of a personal example which encouraged imitation. His authority in the society consisted in a supremacy of greater spiritual wisdom. The organization remained a spiritual democracy ruled by way of a personal influence over those who voluntarily placed themselves under the control of the superior.[13] In this way St. Anthony, though he did not found an Order, was instrumental in paving the way for the systematically arranged common life which is the basis for monastic Orders in their more fully developed form.

2. The Rule of St. Pachomius

Unlike St. Anthony and the numerous other directors of ascetical groups which flourished contemporaneously, St. Pachomius (c. 292–346) inaugurated a distinctive type of religious life, which is known as cenobitism. He was determined that those who placed themselves under his exclusive guidance should be subject to his unquestioned authority, live under one roof and observe one and the same rule and daily horarium.[14] This momentous decision marks undoubtedly the very beginning of community life and the origin of monasticism in the strict sense of the word.[15]

---

[11] S. Athanasius, *op. cit.*, c. 16—*MPG*, XXVI, 866–867.

[12] *Vita S. Antonii Magni Abbatis*, c. xiii—Bollandus, *Acta Sanctorum* (65 vols., Paris, 1863–1902), II, 17 ianuarii, 496–497.

[13] Butler, *Lausiac History*, I, 234.

[14] Heimbucher, *Die Orden und Kongregationen der katolischen Kirche* 3 ed., 2 vols., Paderborn, 1933–1934, I, 77 (hereafter cited as Heimbucher).

[15] The words "monk" and "monastery" are derived from the Greek word "monos" (one) and hence properly refer to the one who lives alone or to

Since only a part of the Pachomian Rule of Life was committed to writing, it was therefore in a constant flux due to the changes incorporated according to the lessons derived from practical experience.[16] Pachomius was also fond of implementing his formal rule with many personal letters on points of discipline and administration sent to local superiors as the occasion demanded. This practice accounts for the many divergencies and discrepancies which appear in the subsequent editions of the rule.[17]

From the very origin of Pachomian monasticism a general superior possessed the supreme authority in the community.[18] During his lifetime St. Pachomius exercised these functions as a matter of course, first from his cell at Tabennis in the Thebaid and later while in residence at Peboou, which became the center of the organization.[19] When approaching his death he appointed his successor in the person of Petronius, thus eliminating the election of a supreme moderator in favor of personal appointment.

No limitations were placed upon the authority of the general superior, to whom absolute obedience was due at all times in all matters. He appointed the provosts or local superiors (*praepositi*) and transferred all religious, including superiors, from one convent to another according to his prudent judgment, in order to preclude all occasion for any bonds of attachment to arise and for the local superiors to become independent heads of convents.

---

the place where a single monk has his abode, and not to an individual living a common life or to a place where many are congregated under one roof, although accepted usage of the words usually has this latter connotation. In strict parlance, instead of the words "monk," "monastery" or "monasticism," one should use the more precise terminology of "cenobite," "cenobium" and "cenobitism."

[16] *Vita S. Pachomii,* c. 10, 16-17—Migne, *Patrologiae Cursus Completus, Series Latina* (221 vols., Parisiis, 1844–1855), LXXIII, 235, 239–241 (hereafter cited as *MPL*).

[17] Albers, *S. Pachomii Abbatis Tabennensis regulae monasticae.* Florilegium Patristicum, Fasc. XVI (Bonn, 1923), pp. 1–7; Mazon, *Las Reglas de los Religiosos. Su Obligación y Naturaleza Juridica.* Analecta Gregoriana, Series Iuris Canonici, Vol. XXIV (Romae, 1940), p. 24 (hereafter cited as *Las Reglas*).

[18] Albers, *op. cit.,* p. 4.

[19] St. Pachomius himself directed a confederation of eight monasteries. Cf. Bollandus, *Acta Sanctorum,* III, 14 maii, 310 and 316.

This common direction secured a unity among the Pachomian cenobites. Regular visitation on the part of the general superior preserved the purity of the Rule and offered an opportunity for the immediate correction of transgressions.[20] Besides making a personal visitation, the supreme moderator was wont to send exhortatory letters to the superiors of isolated convents with instructions which enjoyed the force of personal precepts.[21] From time to time Pachomius was accustomed to address his monks on such subjects as prayer, inspirational passages from the Sacred Scriptures, the Incarnation, the Passion and Resurrection of our Lord, and the like.[22]

A closer union between the convents was obtained through the semi-annual chapters held at Eastertide and on the thirteenth of August.[23] At these appointed times all the members of the Congregation assembled at the mother-house for the purpose of mutual edification and the reception of salutary recommendations from the general superior, who likewise took advantage of the occasion to make the necessary changes in the personnel of the monasteries. Nevertheless the function of these chapters always seems to have been merely advisory and the supreme power remained, in theory and practice, in the hands of the supreme moderator alone.

At the first of these general chapters held at Easter time, the spiritual side of monastic life was stressed with the solemn celebration of the grandest of the Christian feasts, the solemn reception of the Holy Eucharist and the baptism of catechumens.[24] The second general assembly was devoted exclusively to the temporal administration of the community. All the superiors were expected to render an account of their annual financial transactions to the general econome, who was the chief steward or business manager of the brotherhood.[25] Pachomius also mentioned in one of his

---

[20] *Vita S. Pachomii,* c. 52—Bollandus, *Acta Sanctorum,* III, 14 maii, 316.

[21] *Ibid.,* p. 320.

[22] *S. Pachomii Abbatis Tabennensis Regula ad Monachos,* c. 27—*Codex Regularum,* I, 27; *Vita Sancti Pachomii Abbatis Tabennensis,* cc. 40 and 46 —*MPL,* LXXIII, 258, 263-264.

[23] *Vita S. Pachomii,* c. 52—Bollandus, *Acta Sanctorum,* III, 14 maii, 316.

[24] *Epistola Patris Nostri Theodori,* c. xii—*MPL,* XXIII, 99–100; Ladeuze, *Étude sur le Cénobitisme Pakhomien pendant le IV siècle et la Première Moitié du V* (Louvain, 1898), p. 286.

[25] *Vita S. Pachomii,* c. 52—Bollandus, *Acta Sanctorum,* III, 14 maii, 316.

letters that at this second chapter the brethren were obliged to the mutual forgiveness of personal injuries and the settlement of any quarrels or complaints that perhaps had arisen in the course of the year.[26]

Human nature being peccable even within the monastery, St. Pachomius was compelled to encourage the observance of his Rule by inflicting penalties upon transgressors.[27] None of the subordinates questioned his exercise of this punitive power, for they considered it as a necessary aspect of his supreme authority over them. In exceptional cases, he even had the power, all other means failing, to expel the insubordinate offender.[28]

By these means, namely, the acknowledgment of a supreme moderator who had the right of visitation and the regular holding of general chapters, the Pachomian cenobites eliminated the existence of separate and independent monasteries, and consequently identified themselves with one great organization whose head resided at Tabennis. In view of this situation, they even adopted a common name, since they were known as the "monks of Tabennis" regardless of their residence elsewhere.[29] Such a complete hierarchical arrangement approaches closely the concept of a true Order and is not to be found in the West until the imperfect attempts at centralization originating at Cluny and the successful organization of the Mendicant Orders in the thirteenth century.

Pachomius likewise adumbrated future developments in the history of the Church by building a monastic organization parallel to that of the episcopate of the Church, and yet completely separate from it. This was the beginning of the history of exemption. St. Basil (329–379) in his Rule made the bishop his monastic superintendent and amalgamated the regular and secular life of the Church. For him monasteries were to be as much a part of the external organization of Christianity as the parish churches them-

---

[26] *Epistola Patris Nostri Pachomii*, c. vii—*MPL*, XXIII, 96.

[27] *S. Pachomii Abbatis Tabennensis Regula ad Monachos*, cc. 8, 31, 49, 151, 161, and 163—*Codex Regularum*, I, 26–35.

[28] Cassianus, *De Coenobiorum Institutis*, IV, c. 16—*MPL*, XLIX, 159; *Epistola Ammonis*, c. xii and xvi—Bollandus, *Acta Sanctorum*, III, 14 maii, 351, 352–353.

[29] Cassianus, *op. cit.*, IV, c. 1—*MPL*, XLIX, 151–152; *Vita S. Pachomii*, cc. 57 and 86—Bollandus, *Acta Sanctorum*, III, 14 maii, 316 and 328.

selves. The legislation of St. Pachomius for his cenobites was the first step in this direction.

3. Basilian Monasticism

St. Basil of Caesarea (329–379) is the chief exponent of the third and last system of monasticism which has its origin in the Oriental Church. Its distinctive characteristic is the introduction of the completely common life into monasticism. St. Basil was acquainted with Pachomian cenobitism,[30] but he conceived a monastic life that was essentially original and departed considerably from the monastic ideals of St. Pachomius. Despite the fact that he wrote two Rules, the so-called *Regulae fusius tractatae* and the *Regulae brevius tractatae*,[31] St. Basil did not found an Order in the true juridic sense of the word. These rules, however, did become guides for the Oriental monks during his lifetime and have remained the principal legislation for all Oriental monastic organizations to the present day. His primary concern as a lawgiver was not to stress exterior laws, ceremonies and rites, but rather to give practical precepts for the interior reformation of the monks and the regulation of the spiritual life of the individual rather than the minute control over his exterior ascetical practices.

The Rules of St. Basil reveal an almost complete absence of instruction or legislation concerning the office of a supreme moderator outside of several passing remarks about the spiritual qualities necessary in a superior, and even these are but verbatim passages quoted from the Sacred Scriptures.[32] If he does mention specific

---

[30] Clarke, *St. Basil the Great. A Study in Monasticism* (Cambridge, 1913), p. 34.

[31] Mazon, *Las Reglas,* pp. 37–39; Clarke, *op. cit.,* pp. 69–74.

[32] *S. Basilii Caesareae Cappadociae Episcopi Regula ad Monachos,* Interrogatio XV—*Codex Regularum,* I, 79. "Quid sentire de se debet is qui praeest, in quibus praecipit, vel imperat? Apud Deum, quidem, sicut minister Christi et dispensator mysteriorum Dei; timens ne praeter voluntatem Dei, vel praeter quod in sacris scripturis evidenter praecipitur, vel dicat aliquid, vel imperet, et inveniatur tamquam falsus testis Dei, et sacrilegus, vel introducens aliquid alienum a doctrina Domini, vel certe subrelinquens et praeteriens aliquid eorum, quae Deo placita sunt. Ad fratres autem esse debet, tamquam si nutrix foveat parvulos suos: paratus autem, secundum voluntatem Domini, et secundum quod unicuique expedit, communicare cum eis non solum Evangelium Dei, sed etiam animam suam; memor praecepti Dei ac

powers of the superior he prefers to set down general principles rather than precise rules, and occasionally even allows superiors to decide matters in accordance with local needs instead of rigorously applying a coldly formulated principle.[33]

The election of the general superior is restricted to the heads of the neighboring monasteries,[34] and the chosen one is confirmed in his office only after undergoing a period of probation before the acceptance by the brotherhood.[35]

St. Basil shows reluctance to accept any of the democratic arrangement of previous monastic founders by eliminating the notion of a general chapter which would impose a limitation on the exercise of power on the part of the general superior. The supreme moderator in his system has an almost absolute power and must be obeyed even unto death.[36]   Only one exception to this blind obedience is foreseen, namely, in the case of a superior issuing an order which is clearly contrary to the word of God.[37]

The superior, however, is not left without a council.   The best educated monks form a privileged class and from among these the superior himself appoints a council with the express duty of admonishing the superior himself, if in their opinion he is committing a serious mistake.[38]   Any subordinate with a grievance is at liberty to appeal to this body for satisfaction.   Even in the absence of the superior this council does not take upon itself

---

Domini nostri dicentis: Mandatum novum do vobis, ut diligatis vos invicem, sicut ego dilexi vos. Majorem hac charitatem nemo habet, quam ut ponat animam suam pro amicis suis." Cf. also Morison, *St. Basil and His Rule* (Oxford, 1912), pp. 50–57, for a brief résumé of the qualities expected in a superior according to the teaching and practice of St. Basil.

[33] *Regulae fusius tractatae*, c. xxxii—*MPG*, XXXI, 994–995; *Regulae brevius tractatae*, cc. cv-cvi—*MPG*, XXXI, 1155.

[34] *Regulae fusius tractatae*, c. xliii—*MPG*, XXXI, 1030.

[35] *Loc. cit.* and the *Regulae brevius tractatae*, c. ccciii—*MPG*, XXXI, 1298.

[36] This is the customary attitude of all founders of religious orders and congregations. Once a Rule is officially adopted, however, it usually becomes the supreme ruler of the brethren because it represents the voice of the founder and then binds the superiors just as much as the subordinates. Cf. Clarke, *op. cit.*, p. 92.

[37] *Regulae brevius tractatae*, cc. cxiv and ccciii—*MPG*, XXXI, 1159 and 1298.

[38] *Regulae fusius tractatae*, c. xxvii—*MPG*, XXXI, 987.

supreme authority, but one of its members is chosen to take his place "lest a democratic state of things may arise."[39]   At times also the entire brotherhood may be assembled together, particularly in the matter of receiving or expelling members, but even this general assembly was never entrusted with any considerable power.

Among other duties of the general superior St. Basil lists the obligation that he rule by example rather than by word, that he be merciful and compassionate, and that he lead his monks to the perfect imitation of Christ.[40]   He should remember that he is entrusted with the special watch over the souls of his subordinates, for which he will be called to render an account by God.[41]   If he suspects a brother of sin, then a special degree of watchfulness is required and a proportionate punishment must be meted out.[42]   He has complete control of the daily routine within the community and it is his duty to assign work whether it be manual labor or literary activities.[43]   Of course, the great numerical growth of the community rendered impossible the personal performance of many of these duties and accordingly resulted in the appointment of various aides and vicars, to whom the supreme moderator delegated much of his power.

C. The Abbot in the Monastic Orders in the West to the X Century

1. Pre-Benedictine Rules

a. Italian Monasticism

Western Europe received its monasticism directly from Egypt into Italy as early as 339, when two Antonian monks accompanied St. Athanasius (✠373) on his visit to Rome.[44]   The monastic movement spread throughout Italy, so that by the middle of the fourth century monasteries of men and women appeared in all the principal cities of the country.   Nothing, however, of importance

---

[39] *Ibid.,* c. xlv—*MPG,* XXXI, 1031.

[40] *Ibid.,* c. xliii—*MPG,* XXXI, 1027.

[41] *Ibid.,* c. xxv—*MPG,* XXXI, 986.

[42] *Regulae brevius tractatae,* cc. xix and cvi—*MPG,* XXXI, 1095 and 1155.

[43] *Ibid.,* cc. xcvi, cv—*MPG,* XXXI, 1150 and 1155.

[44] Butler, *Benedictine Monachism* (London, 1919), p. 17; Spreitzenhofer, *Die Entwicklung des alten Mönchtums in Italien von seinen ersten Anfängen bis zum Auftreten des h. Benedikt* (Wien, 1894), p. 5.

in the line of legislation concerning their general superiors was introduced, since the Antonian system was adopted *in toto*, particularly after a Latin translation was made of the *Vita S. Antonii* about the year 380. There immediately followed an extensive distribution of the *Lives of the Fathers of the Desert.*[45]

Eusebius (✠371), the bishop of Vercelli, is worthy of mention, since he was the first to combine the monastic and clerical states by introducing the common life among the clergy of his cathedral.[46] As bishop, he exercised universal authority over all the clergy of his diocese including those who in a special way led the common life at the cathedral church. These "choir-monks" served as a type for the Augustinian canons of the following century, who in their turn became the prototypes of all future congregations of Canons Regular in the West, particularly in the eleventh and twelfth centuries.[47]

b. French Monasticism

Southern France was the scene of the earliest and widest spread of European monasticism. About the year 360 St. Martin of Tours (c. 316–397) founded an eremitical monastery near Poitiers, life at which was an accurate reproduction of the life of the Antonian monks.[48] St. Honoratus (✠429) founded a monastery at Lerins in 410, and Cassian (c. 360–430/35) established two monasteries near Marseilles in 413–416.[49] These two founders adopted the characteristic features of Pachomian monachism, and the writings of Cassian, particularly his *Institutes*[50] and his *Collations,*[51] reflect this ideal.

The first monastic rule of Western monasticism which departed from the traditions of the Oriental monks was composed by Caesarius of Arles (470–542).[52] It has a close similarity to the

---

[45] Heimbucher, I, 213.

[46] Spreitzenhofer, *op. cit.*, pp. 13–17.

[47] Mazon, *Las Reglas*, pp. 42–43.

[48] Butler, *Lausiac History*, I, 128–129.

[49] Heimbucher, I, 130.

[50] *Joannis Cassiani Abbatis Massiliensis de Coenobiorum Institutis—MPL*, XLIX, 53–476.

[51] *Joannis Cassiani Abbatis Massiliensis Collationum XXIV Collectio—MPL*, XLIX, 477–1328.

[52] *S. Caesarii Regula ad Monachos—MPL*, XCVII, 1099–1104.

Augustinian writings, especially the *Epistola 211* and the *Sermones 355* and *356*.[53]   None of these Rules, nor the Rules of St. Aurelian (✠ c. 550),[54] of St. Ferreolus (✠581) [55] and of St. Donatus (✠ c. 660),[56] give us any explicit legislation on the supreme moderator. Since none of these organizations was an Order in the strict juridic sense, even though at times several monasteries embraced the observance of the same Rule, the supreme jurisdiction remained in the hands of the founder of the society or of some local superior appointed by him or elected by the subordinates.

c. Spanish Monasticism

Of early Spanish monasticism very little is known prior to the eighth century.   Iberian monks, however, are mentioned by Euric (464–484) in his legislation as already existing in the fifth century [57] but nothing is known about their hierarchical organization.

In 636 St. Isidore (560–636), Bishop of Seville, formulated a Rule for monks under his jurisdiction.[58]   Its eclectic nature manifests a decided tendency to amalgamate Pachomian and Benedictine legislation.[59]   In this Rule, St. Isidore stressed the peculiar virtues necessary in an abbot and the manner of procedure to be adopted with his subordinates.[60]   Several chapters dealt exclusively with delinquent brethren and the punishment for their crimes, such as their excommunication by the superior, who was either the *"pater monasterii"* or the abbot.[61]

Other Spanish Rules, as for example the Rules of St. Fructuosus (✠ c. 665),[62] contain no legislation bearing on our study.   One

---

[53] Mazon, *Las Reglas*, p. 79.

[54] *S. Aureliani Regula ad Monachos—MPL*, LXVIII, 385–394.

[55] *S. Ferreoli Ucetiensis Episcopi Regula ad Monachos—MPL*, LXVI, 959–976.

[56] *Sancti Donati Vesontionensis Episcopi Regula ad Virgines—MPL*, LXXXVII, 273–298.

[57] *Codex Euricianus*, CCCXXXV—*Fontes Iuris Germanici Antiqui* (Hanover, 1894), p. 19; Mazon, *Las Reglas*, pp. 62–63.

[58] *Sancti Isidori Hispalensis Episcopi Regula Monachorum—MPL*, LXXXIII, 867–894.

[59] Mazon, *Las Reglas*, pp. 66–70.

[60] *MPL*, LXXXIII, 870.

[61] *MPL*, LXXXIII, 884–887.

[62] *Sancti Fructuosi Bracarensis Episcopi Regula Monachorum—MPL*, LXXXVII, 1099–1110 and 1111–1127; Mazon, *Las Reglas*, pp. 70–74.

feature, however, of his *Regula Monastica Communis*, namely the appended *Pactum*, provides something new in monastic legislation. According to this remarkable document a pact existed between the abbot and the monk of his monastery. In accordance with this pact the latter bound himself to the performance of all the duties of the monastic life under the guidance of the abbot, whom he empowered to inflict specific punishments for certain infringements of the Rule. The monks, however, reserved for themselves the right to appeal to other abbots or to their bishop, if the abbot dealt with them in an arbitrary or tyrannical manner.[63] In this extraordinary document is found the earliest and clearest statement in Western monastic legislation of the concept of a complete subordination of the monk to the will and jurisdiction of the general superior.

d. Celtic Monasticism

Very little is known of the cenobitic life which flourished in Ireland and Wales, where great monasteries numbering several hundred monks each were very numerous.[64] St. Patrick (✠461), the Apostle of Ireland, is likewise the founder of its monasticism.[65] His practice of founding monasteries and encouraging regular ascetical exercises bears a close resemblance to the practice of St. Martin of Tours in his diocese.[66] He retained supreme authority over the entire church in Ireland, including the monastic establishments to such an extent that he even appointed their abbots.[67]

In the sixth, seventh and eighth centuries there was introduced in Ireland the practice whereby the abbot became a bishop of the territory under the monastic control. Thus originated and spread in the monasteries a tradition of government which rested in the hands of abbots as endowed with episcopal powers.[68] There was, however, also an exercise of jurisdiction on the part of abbots who

---

[63] *MPL*, LXXXVII, 1127–1130.

[64] Butler, *Benedictine Monachism* (London, 1919), p. 19.

[65] Ryan, *Irish Monasticism: Origins and Early Development* (Dublin, 1931), pp. 59–96.

[66] *Ibid.*, p. 94.

[67] *Ibid.*, p. 92.

[68] *Ibid.*, p. 172.

were not bishops, particularly in the smaller monastic establishments.[69]

The most famous of the Irish monastic legislators is St. Columban (543–615), who wrote a Rule that bears his name, but it was more properly a collection of ascetical exhortations than legislation in the true canonical sense of the word.[70] The second part of this Rule is really a penal code. Exterior life in his monastic communities was governed more by custom, established during the lifetime of the founder, than by legislation. Unquestioning obedience was demanded of the monks as the virtue without which cenobitical life could not be conceived.[71] As would be expected, the founder was naturally the first supreme moderator of the community. Among his privileges was that of selecting his own successor. This practice continued until the middle of the seventh century, when the new abbot was elected through the vote of the brethren.[72] It was also customary for the early abbots to belong to the same family or hereditary line to which the founder belonged, or to that of the donor of the land upon which the monastery was erected.[73]

e. African Monasticism

African monasticism is very closely identified with the life and teaching of St. Augustine (354–430), the Bishop of Hippo, who organized community life with some of his closest friends at Tagaste soon after his baptism.[74] Upon settling down in Hippo after his ordination to the priesthood, St. Augustine formed a second community, of which he was the supreme moderator even after his consecration as bishop.[75] Eventually he also directed a group of devout women, whom he addressed as the "handmaids of

---

[69] *Ibid.,* pp. 175–179.

[70] Mazon, *Las Reglas,* pp. 86–87.

[71] Ryan, *op. cit.,* pp. 250–255.

[72] *Ibid.,* pp. 264–265.

[73] Heimbucher, I, 140.

[74] Possidius, *Vita Sancti Aurelii Augustini Hipponensis Episcopi,* cc. iii–v —*MPL,* XXXII, 36–38. Zumkeller gives an excellent account of the nature of the daily life at this primitive monastery. Cf. *Das Mönchtum des heiligen Augustinus* (Würzburg, 1950), pp. 46–57.

[75] Leclerq, *L'Afrique Chrétienne* (2 vols., Paris, 1904), II, 70–77; Zumkeller, *op. cit.,* pp. 70–78.

God" and for whom he prescribed a Rule of ascetical life in the form of a letter.[76]   Undoubtedly, the voluminous writings of St. Augustine formed a rich source of primitive legislation for monastic life in Western Europe [77] and exerted also a considerable influence upon the Benedictine Rule.[78]

In none of his monastic writings did St. Augustine touch upon the rôle of a general superior of an organized Order of religious. During his lifetime he governed all religious communities within his diocese by virtue of his rôle as founder and episcopal superior. In common with that of all his predecessors in Western monasticism, his treatment of the superior was decidedly from the viewpoint of ascetical theology rather than from that of canonical legislation.   The superior was to seek rather to be loved than to be feared, to give good example, to provide for the sick, to correct and punish the erring, and to be mindful at all times that he would be called to render an account to God alone for his stewardship.

2. The Rule of St. Benedict

St. Benedict (481–553) never intended or founded an Order in the proper canonical sense of the word.   His primary purpose was rather the reform of the entire monastic system than the institution of another Order among many rival Orders.   To achieve this end St. Benedict composed a Rule,[79] which was the first of its kind and which, in one form or another, governed most monks for nearly six hundred years, and which serves as a guide for numerous Orders and Congregations even to our day.[80]

---

[76] *Epistola CCXI—MPL,* XXXIII, 960–965; Mazon, *Las Reglas,* p. 55.

[77] St. Augustine never wrote a monastic Rule *ex professo.* The historical and doctrinal determination of the so-called *Regula S. Augustini* has intrigued many able historians. For a precise presentation of this involved question confer the able study of Mandonnet, *St. Dominic and His Work* (Herder, St. Louis, 1944), pp. 195–253; Gwynn, *The English Austin Friars* (Oxford, 1940), pp. 1–7; Heimbucher, I, 125–126; Mazon, *Las Reglas,* pp. 54–62.

[78] Lambot, "L'Influence de Saint Augustin sur le Règle de Saint Bénoît," *Revue liturgique et monastique,* XIV (1929), 320–337.

[79] Linderbauer, *S. Benedicti Regula Monasteriorum.* Florilegium Patristicum, Fasc. XVII (Bonn, 1928) (hereafter cited as *Regula*); Heimbucher, I, 154–177; Mazon, *Las Reglas,* pp. 44–53; Ferroglio, *La Condizione Giuridica degli Ordini Religiosi* (Torino, 1931), pp. 19–51.

[80] Bastien, "Conspectus Historico-Iuridicus de Regimine Monasterii in

All the so-called monastic Rules prior to St. Benedict's time were merely collections of scriptural passages, pious counsels and fervent exhortations by saintly men whose holiness attracted disciples desirous of imitating their religious life. The Rule of St. Benedict departed from this practice inasmuch as it contained true laws obliging the monks on the strength of their religious profession.[81] From that time forward one can speak of a religious state in the strict juridic sense, a state which thenceforth was perfected through the addition of more accurate and precise laws in the course of the centuries.

In accordance with the provisions of the Rule, St. Benedict succeeded in regulating the internal and external monastic life of the monks. The internal religious life of the monks was subjected to the dictates of an abbot whose powers were absolute; the external monastic life was regulated by these absolute powers of the abbot over the individual monastery, which, however, remained completely autonomous [82] until the advent of the Congregations whereby the autonomy was in a certain measure restricted.[83]

Even though St. Benedict himself founded at least twelve monasteries during his lifetime and exercised a general control over all of them, he nevertheless conceived of each of these houses as completely autonomous. The idea of a superior general, a grand abbot or an abbot primate was completely foreign to his monastic constitution; it is an outgrowth of subsequent legislation on the

---

Ordine Sancti Benedicti," *Ius Pontificium*, IX (1929), 296–305; X (1930), 44–55.

[81] Mayer, *Benediktinisches Ordensrecht in der Beuroner Kongregation* (3 vols., Beuron, 1929–1936), I, 64, 67, n. 8.

[82] This is an important fact to be kept in mind, i.e., that St. Benedict's Rule was composed exclusively for the individual monasteries, and not for an Order.

[83] Ever since the eleventh century, and particularly after the Fourth Lateran Council (1215), many distinct Benedictine congregations were formed by means of federation. In our day, fourteen such Congregations exist, namely, the Cassinese or Old Italian (1421), the English (1215; 1336; 1619), the Swiss (1602), the Bavarian (1684), the Hungarian (1500; 1802), the Brazilian (1828), the French (1837), the American-Cassinese (1855), the Beuron (1868), the Subiaco or Cassinese of the primitive observance (1872), the Swiss-American (1881), the Austrian of the Immaculate Conception (1889), the St. Ottilien (1904) and the Belgian (1920). Concerning these Congregations cf. Heimbucher, I, 267–271; Mazon, *Las Reglas,* p. 51.

part of the Holy See.[84]   Even when the number of daughter-houses grew and a wider authority was logically needed, so that the patriarchal framework of necessity developed into a more democratic type, the paternal rights of the monastic abbot were respected.   With the rise of the monastic Congregations into which the Benedictine were grouped, there arose also the office of the abbot-general; with the perfection of the concept of a monastic Order in modern times, there arose in turn the office of the abbot-primate.[85]

In practice the commentators on the Rule of St. Benedict apply, *mutatis mutandis,* the precepts and legislation concerning the monastic abbot to the widened office of the supreme moderator. Of particular importance in this regard is the specific legislation by various branches of the Benedictine Order, e.g., the Cluniacs and Cistercians, which will be given separate consideration in the following chapter.

In the second chapter of the Rule, entitled *"Qualis esse debeat Abbas,"* St. Benedict set down his concept of a true superior, the qualities he should possess and the manner of his governance of the brethren.   His position in the community was summed up in the expression: the abbot is the vicegerent of Christ.[86]   His deeds were to correspond to his name of superior and he was to be mindful of the judgment of God in all his decisions.   In no way was he to show partiality, for he was to keep in mind the apostolic rule of mingling gentleness with severity in his every act of reproving, entreating or rebuking his subordinates.[87]   In the very concept of

---

[84] Williams, *Monastic Studies* (Manchester: University Studies, 1938), pp. 77–78.

[85] Leo XIII, brief *Summum semper,* 12 iulii, 1893 : "Omnes congregationes benedictinorum, quos nigros vocant, veram fraternam confoederationem ineunt, quae tamen confoederatio nullam congregationem alteri subjicit. Ut autem confoederatio haec unitatem aliquam habeat, firmis manentibus omnium benedictinorum quos diximus, congregationibus, eorumque constitutionibus vel declarationibus ; propriisque unicuique eorum archiabbate vel abbate generali vel abbate praeside nec non et procuratore generali ac visitatoribus servatis ; item firmis manentibus iuribus atque privilegiis uniuscujusque monasterii, abbas primas omnium congregationum creabitur, qui Romae degat pro negotiis totius ordinis bonum directe respicientibus."—*Acta Sanctae Sedis,* XXVI (1893), 372.

[86] This same idea is reiterated in chapter XLIV of the *Regula.*

[87] *Regula, c.* II, pp. 20–22.

his title the abbot was to find not only the source but also the character and extent of his power and the measure of his responsibility.[88] In all places and at all times external honor was to be shown to him. Of particular interest was the position of pre-eminence reserved to him in all liturgical functions.[89]

Following the long-established tradition of monasticism, St. Benedict laid down the rule that the abbot was to be elected by the monks from among their own number.[90] His tenure of office was for life unless, in very rare instances, he was deposed after being declared unworthy of holding the office.[91] Despite his supreme jurisdiction, upon which no formal limitation was placed save that of the Rule itself and his accountability to God, the abbot was nevertheless advised to seek the counsel of the brethren.[92] This practice resulted eventually in the institution of the general chapter, which curtailed the power of the abbot, at first in liturgical and disciplinary matters and, later, in the broadly legislative sphere within the community.[93]

The Rule of St. Benedict served, despite the fact that it did not treat of the supreme moderator *ex professo*, to lay down the immediate principles for this office and its logical juridico-historical development. His abbatial system recognized in the superior practically unlimited discretionary powers and rights, but equally imposed upon him the unlimited and undivided responsibility for all things. Subsequent legislation in the various Orders simply clarified this position by way of positive laws.

---

[88] Delatte, *The Rule of St. Benedict.* Translated by Dom Justin McCann (London, 1921), p. 35.

[89] *Regula*, cc. XII, XIII and XLVII. This aspect of the Abbot's rôle is capably summarized by Gasquet, *English Monastic Life* (London, 1922), pp. 50-52, and is given a more detailed treatment by Butler, *op. cit.*, pp. 184-199.

[90] *Regula*, c. LXIV; Schmitz, *Histoire de l'Ordre de Saint Bénoît* (8 vols., Maredsous, 1942), I, 19. For a brief history of the vicissitudes of the elective system in monasticism, cf. Knowles, *The Monastic Order in England* (Cambridge, 1941), pp. 395-403; Delatte, *op. cit.*, pp. 441-455.

[91] Knowles, *op. cit.*, pp. 403-404.

[92] *Regula*, c. III, *De adhibendis ad consilium fratribus.*

[93] Knowles, *op. cit.*, pp. 411-417; Butler, *op. cit.*, pp. 224-225.

CHAPTER II

THE OFFICE OF THE SUPREME MODERATOR
FROM THE X TO THE XII CENTURY

A. The X and XI Century

From the time St. Benedict wrote his Rule for the governance of
the monks in the West until the tenth century no new monastic
Order made its appearance. Benedictine monasticism continued to
spread throughout the countries of Europe, and the Canons Regular, following the Augustinian Rule, were introduced by numerous
bishops into their cathedral churches. Pristine fervor in the
monasteries was slowly being diminished and a restoration of
discipline was apparently needed at the time of the establishment
of the Carolingian Empire in the beginning of the ninth century.

During the following three centuries the whole social and political fabric of Europe was being gradually reorganized on a broader
scale with the establishment of great estates and kingdoms. The
sorely needed monastic reforms reflected the concepts of feudal
integration evolved in the progress of European civilization, and
the tendency to centralization became the ideal of all monastic
reformers.[1]

In the light of this historical setting the present chapter will be
devoted to the critical examination and appraisal of the office of
the supreme moderator in the Cluniac reform and to the particular
legislation of the Camaldolese and Carthusian Orders.

1. The Congregation of Cluny

The Congregation of Cluny dates its origin to the foundation of
the monastery at Cluny in Burgundy in 910. In that monastery
began the earliest reform of the Benedictine Order.[2] Some of the

---

[1] Evans, *Monastic Life at Cluny, 910–1157* (London, 1931), pp. 18–19.

[2] Heimbucher, I, 183–188; Helyot, *Dictionnaire des Ordres Religieux ou*

reforms introduced at Cluny are traceable to the suggestions offered by St. Benedict of Aniane (✠821), who at the great chapter held at Aix-la-Chapelle in 817 foreshadowed the question of establishing a centralized government which was not part of the original Benedictine monachism.[3] The realization, however, of these reforms did not take place until the remarkable succession of great abbots at Cluny in the eleventh and twelfth centuries,[4] and particularly during the long regime (1049–1109) of Abbot Hugh of Semur, when these reforms were crystallized and Cluny reached the zenith of its influence and prosperity.[5]

Though the Cluniac monks were always recognized as members of the Benedictine family, their spirit and organization is a distinct departure from the Benedictine tradition. Whereas all Benedictine abbeys up to that time had remained independent and autonomous with only the universal acceptance of a common rule serving as a loose bond of union among them, the reform at Cluny tended to eliminate the independence of the daughter-abbeys by retaining absolute control over the newly-founded houses, thus introducing the concept of the civil feudal hierarchy into monastic organization and legislation. By multiplying the number of new foundations and by incorporating the ones already existing, the Congregation of Cluny came into being almost automatically, and the principle of submission to Cluny as a means of reform became firmly and definitely established.[6]

During the Cluniac reform the tendency was to increase the power and prestige of the abbot of Cluny, who became eventually

---

Histoire des Ordres Monastiques, Religieux et Militaires, et des Congregations Séculières de l'un et de l'autre Sexe, qui ont été establies jusqu'a Présent (4 vols., Paris, 1847), I, 1002–1044, s. v. *Cluny* (hereafter cited as *Dictionnaire*) ; Evans, *op. cit.,* pp. 1–9.

[3] Smith, *The Early History of the Monastery of Cluny* (London, 1920), pp. 5–8.

[4] The probable succession of the first seven abbots of Cluny is as follows: St. Berno (910–927), St. Odo (927–948), St. Aymar (948–954), St. Maiolus (954–994), St. Odilo (994–1048), St. Hugh (1049–1109), Ponce (1109–1122). Cf. Schmitz, *Histoire de l'Ordre de Saint Bénoît,* I, 132, footnote 2; Evans, *op. cit.,* p. xix.

[5] Schmitz, *op. cit.,* I, 133.

[6] Smith, *Cluny in the Eleventh and Twelfth Centuries* (London, 1930), pp. xxvi–xxvii.

the head of an Order in the juridic sense.[7]   The first indication of his supreme authority came with the modification of his daily routine, which placed him above monastic discipline and the *consuetudines* of the abbey.   In view of the increasing part the abbots began to play in public life, they were gradually freed from the bonds of communal life, especially with regard to the spiritual exercises, the common table and the common dormitory.   The next step was to extend the legislative, judicial and administrative powers of the Cluniac abbot to embrace the government of the filial abbeys.   This was achieved by way of papal sanction and confirmation.[8]   The best example of the exercise of this power lies in the fact that the superior of every abbey, however great, was the nominee of the Abbot of Cluny.[9]

The monks of all the subordinate daughter-abbeys were ranked as monks of Cluny and were considered as children of the mother-house.   Novices of these dependent abbeys were authorized to receive the habit with the permission of the abbot of Cluny, and could be admitted to profession by him alone.[10]   In theory, at least the supreme, plenary and immediate power over all the houses belonging to the Congregation was exercised by the abbot of Cluny, who in consequence became constantly occupied in journeys and visitations.   In practice, however, a great measure of independence remained with the local abbots, for the laws were not infrequently subject to such transgressions as the unauthorized reception of novices or undue procrastination in proceeding to Cluny for the profession of the monks.[11]

---

[7] Molitor, *Aus der Rechtsgeschichte benediktinischer Verbände* (3 vols., Münster, 1928), I, 124–125: "Sein Abt war *Dominus et Pater, Prior Abbas, Pater principalis et Caput Ordinis, Pater et iudex totius Ordinis, Pater et Principium Ordinis.* Er hatte das *regimen* 'seines Klosters und des Gesamtordens.'"

[8] Evans, *op. cit.*, p. 25.

[9] Gasquet, *Monastic Life in the Middle Ages* (London, 1922), p. 220.

[10] *S. Petri Mauritii, dicto Venerabilis Abbatis Cluniacensis IX, Statuta Congregationis Cluniacensis,* c. XXXIV: "Statutum est, ut nullus in Monachum Cluniacensem recipiatur absque Cluniacensis Abbatis praecepto et permissione, sicut mos est, nisi ad succurendum: exceptis magnis et utilibus personis, quae si differentur, levitate fortassis animi retrocederent, nec in incepto conversionis proposito permanerent."—*Codex Regularum,* II, 184.

[11] Knowles, *The Monastic Order in England* (Cambridge, 1941), p. 147.

For the first time in monastic legislation one encounters in the Cluniac statutes express laws governing the economic transactions of the daughter-abbeys.   No monk in the Congregation could donate, sell or exchange any of the land or treasures belonging to the abbey churches without the permission of the abbot of Cluny.[12] Slowly there grew up the custom of exacting from all subordinate houses a yearly tribute to be paid to the mother-abbey at Cluny in imitation of the yearly census paid to the Holy See by the churches throughout Europe.[13]   With this economic subjection the extension of the supreme moderator's authority reached the ultimate peak of its development in the Cluniac reform.

The Abbot of Cluny remained up to the thirteenth century the absolute head of his Order, which he governed without the aid of general chapters or visitors.[14]   His prestige in the Church was enormous.[15]   The needed monastic reforms were obtained through the sole application of the principle of submission of the filial abbeys to the mother-abbey, for the latter remained the guardian of the purity of monastic observance.   With the operation of this new principle there was evolved, in place of an autonomous monastery under its abbot, an independent Order under a monarchical head.[16]   Cluny, as the mother-abbey and head of hundreds of filial abbeys, owed much of its importance to its gradual evolution into an Order.   It was this development which necessarily and inherently made the abbey of Cluny greater and more powerful than any other single autonomous abbey.

---

[12] *S. Petri Mauritii, dicto Venerabilis Abbatis Cluniacensis IX, Statuta Congregationis Cluniacensis,* c. XLIV: "Statutum est, ne quis terras, vel thesauros ecclesiarum dare, vendere, commutare, pro vadimonio alicubi, vel apud aliquem sine domini Abbatis praecepto vel consilio deponere vel impignorare audeat; quod si fecerit, a Fratrum suorum et totius Ecclesiae communione alienum se esse cognoscat."

[13] Knowles, *op. cit.,* p. 148.

[14] Schmitz, *op. cit.,* I, 138.

[15] E.g., whenever the Abbot of Cluny made his appearance at Rome he enjoyed the privileges and dignity of a Cardinal. Cf. Tamburini, *De Iure Abbatum et Aliorum Praelatorum* (3 vols., Lugduni, 1650), I, 21: "Abbas Cluniacensis ex privilegio Calixti Papae II, quotiescumque Roman accedebat, Cardinalitia dignitate potiebatur."

[16] Evans, *op. cit.,* p. 26.

2. The Camaldolese

St. Romuald of Ravenna (ca. 952–1027) founded the Camaldolese Order in 1012 as a reformed branch of the Benedictine congregation.[17] For the first time in the West the eremitical life of the East was successfully combined with the cenobitical life of the West. Having founded several monasteries, St. Romuald exercised supreme authority over the brethren until his death. The example of his life, the encouragement of his teaching, and the living oral tradition served as a substitute for a written Rule.[18] In this respect St. Romuald belonged with others in the eleventh century to the class of reformers who, after finding a life of solitude and austerity and attracting many disciples to it, died among them without leaving any permanent institute to survive them.[19] Not until the generalate of Blessed Rudolph (1074–1087), who was the fourth abbot-general of Camaldoli, was an attempt made to stabilize the practices of Camaldoli and to draw up constitutions binding the entire Order.[20] These, however, are now lost. Holstenius (1596–1661) in his collection of monastic Rules reprinted the approved general constitutions of 1572, but these reflected the constitutional development of the sixteenth century rather than the primitive doctrine of the founder.[21]

The rôle of the abbot-general in the Camaldolese Order was a throw-back to the early centuries of monasticism as it was practiced in Syria and Egypt. St. Romuald, the founder, remained the supreme head of the Order until his death. Subsequently the abbots of Camaldoli, who held their position for life, exercised a limited jurisdiction over the rest of the monasteries.[22] The pristine ideal of the supreme abbot of the Benedictine Rule was preserved until perceptible changes were wrought through the influence of legislation within monastic groups outside of the

---

[17] Grandi, *Dissertationes Camaldulenses* (Lucca, 1707), p. 6; Heimbucher, I, 315.

[18] Helyot, *Dictionnaire*, I, 585.

[19] Knowles, *op. cit.*, p. 193.

[20] Heimbucher, I, 316; Helyot, *Dictionnaire*, I, 589.

[21] *In Regulam d. Patris Benedicti Declarationes et Constitutiones Patrum Ordinis Camaldulensis—Codex Regularum*, II, 192.

[22] Grandi, *op. cit.*, pp. 22–24.

Order.[23] No significant change was introduced in the concept of the supreme moderator by the Camaldolese themselves, but they did preserve and propagate the injunctions of the Benedictine Rule concerning the paternal exercise of the office of the abbot in contradistinction to the reforms introduced by the contemporary Cluniac movement, which departed from the Benedictine ideal.

3. The Carthusians

The Carthusians, like the Camaldolese monks who preceded them, reflect an example of the periodic efforts made by religious men, living in the great monasteries as monks or in the cathedral churches as canons, to return to the stricter and more observant monachism as exemplified by the eremitico-cenobitical life of the Eastern monks. This tendency pointed not so much to a reform of the existing Orders but rather to a search for a more perfect religious life. St. Bruno (1030–1101), the founder of the Carthusians, typifies the kind of men who left the security of monastic life to embrace the austerity of the eremitical life. In 1084 St. Bruno and his companions were given a site for their hermitage by Hugh, Bishop of Grenoble (1080–1132), who likewise acted as their abbot and provisor. This location became known as the Grande Chartreuse and is considered the mother-house of the Order.[24] After spending some years in the service of the Apostolic See, Bruno established several other colonies of hermits in Calabria, placing them loosely under the governance of the Grande Chartreuse.

Although Bruno was the founder of the community of Chartreuse, he was not the legislator of the Carthusians.[25] The hermitages which he established did not differ from the hundreds of similar groups scattered through the length and breadth of Italy and France in imitation of the Oriental solitaries. He left no Rule, no Statutes nor any Book of Customs for the hermits to follow. Even their lack of a definite name is in keeping with their

---

[23] This is apparent in the detailed Constitutions approved in 1572, which devote several chapters to the various aspects of the General Abbot's office, e.g., Book I, c. 2, 3, 56, 63, 64; Book II, cc. 13 and 14. Cf. *Codex Regularum,* II, 204–299.

[24] *Heimbucher,* I, 376–391.

[25] Knowles, *The Monastic Order in England* (Cambridge, 1941), p. 376.

lack of a definite Rule. They merely called themselves "Christ's poor men."[26]

Before leaving for Rome, however, Bruno appointed Landuin (✠1120) as prior of the Grande Chartreuse and acting head of the entire community. During his own lifetime Bruno guided the monks by means of his personal example and the faithful observance of the Evangelical counsels. When absent, Bruno continued his connections with the Grande Chartreuse by means of an occasional correspondence, giving the monks many salutary instructions, but refraining from setting down precepts and laws obliging them in conscience.[27] For many years only general directives relating to silence and diet were given by the priors in conjunction with the customs established by oral tradition, which later was strengthened by a vow of stability and obedience thus insuring and maintaining a settled, uniform custom within the community.[28] This state of affairs continued until the time of Guigo (✠1137), the fifth prior of the Grande Chartreuse, who perceived the need, in consequence of the numerical increase of vocations, of some written legislation and accordingly proceeded to record the usages of the mother-house together with some additions born of experience, thus saving the Order for the Church.[29] Guigo's *Consuetudines* were approved by Pope Innocent II in 1133 and served as the basis for all future Carthusian legislation, especially the *Statuta Antiqua* of 1258, the *Statuta Nova* of 1368, and the *Tertia Compilatio* of 1509, all of which combined were printed for the first time in 1510 as the Carthusian Rule.[30] Of the three compilations, the *Statuta Antiqua* were the most important, for therein the constitution of the Order was determined. Thus in the 175 years since its origin, the Order, while increasing numerically, was also developing organically.

Other specific legislation being lacking, the Grande Chartreuse retained a pre-eminence of origin and veneration even during the

---

[26] Thompson, *The Carthusian Order in England* (London, 1930), p. 12.

[27] Currier, *History of Religious Orders* (New York, 1914), p. 154.

[28] Thompson, *op. cit.*, p. 20.

[29] Knowles, *op. cit.*, p. 376.

[30] Heimbucher, I, 382.

lifetime of St. Bruno.[31]   The prior of the Grande Chartreuse community, duly elected by the professed members residing there, was always considered to be the supreme moderator of the Order. From the earliest extant documents it is apparent that he bore the title of the "Great Dom" and was usually addressed as the "Reverend Father," never as "abbot."[32]   Notwithstanding this privilege he was not placed above the rest of the priors, since his position always remained equivalent to that of a *primus inter pares.*[33]   In the first general chapter held in 1142 he was officially constituted the general prior and was given the power of retaining in or dismissing from office any recalcitrant and incorrigible prior of another house after securing the advice of the general chapter.[34]   By 1256, together with the five definitors elected by the priors of the elder houses (primarum domorum), he was granted the full power to enact or define ordinances for common observance.[35]   His authority was strengthened upon the omission of the words *"secundum regulam"* originally in the Benedictine form of the formula for profession, with the implication that the monks vowed obedience not only to the Rule but to the general prior and his commands.[36]

The real governing power within the Order, however, was vested in the general chapter, which was composed of all the priors and visitors assembling annually to discuss the welfare of the Order.   All superiors, including the prior of the Grande Chartreuse, put their resignations into the hands of this chapter, which could remove or reinstate them at will.   The Great Dom, as head of the Order, administered the laws passed at the general chapter,

---

[31] Baumann, *Les Chartreux.* Collection "Les Grands Ordres Monastiques" (chez Bernard Grasset, 1928), p. 159.

[32] (Boutrais), *The History of the Great Chartreuse* (London, 1934), p. 209.

[33] Le Masson, *Commentarium in Guigonis Carthusiae Maioris Prioris Quinti Consuetudines:* "Unde semper in ordine nomen prioris usurpatum est ad designandum eum qui aliis praepositus est, ut indicaretur, eum qui aliis praeest inter nos, esse tantum primum inter pares, et aequalium directorem ac ministrum, non dominum."—*MPL,* CLIII, 662–663.

[34] Le Couteulx, *Annales Ordinis Cartusiensis ab anno 1084 ad annum 1429* (8 vols., Monstrolii, 1887–1891), I, 375.

[35] *Ibid.,* IV, 158.

[36] Thompson, *op. cit.,* p. 32.

but these ordinances did not become permanent unless they were renewed at two successive chapters. This legislative and administrative arrangement was the basis of the internal Carthusian organization since the first general chapter held by St. Anthelm in 1142.[37]

Outside the sessions of the general chapter the prior of the Grande Chartreuse wielded a truly supreme power, which, however, was not to be considered as despotic or absolute. He could by personal precept override the provisions of the statutes, especially by the exercise of his very extensive rights of dispensation, which were equal to those of the general chapter itself.[38] The statutes of the general chapters frequently singled him out as possessing certain powers not given to the priors of other monasteries, as for example the changing of visitors for a just cause.[39] Nevertheless he was held responsible for his actions before the general definitory, which could censure, condemn and even depose him. As general superior, however, he had the privilege of being excluded from the annual visitation to which all other houses had to submit. Instead, a visitation every six years by two priors designated by the general chapter was instituted at the Grande Chartreuse, and a report embodying the necessary recommendations was made to the following chapter.[40]

In fine, since the definite establishment of the polity of the Carthusian Order, the general prior of the Grande Chartreuse always held a primacy of honor and a relative authority as perpetual president of the general chapter. At the same time, however, except in his own monastery, he had no greater power than the other priors, since decisions made by him in the interim between general chapters were subject to being vetoed by the subsequent general chapter. The Carthusians preferred to limit the authority of the supreme moderator in order to prevent the corruption of the Rule and its observance at the hands of an incompetent individual.

---

[37] *Acta Primi Capituli Ordinis Carthusiensis—MPL*, CLIII, 1125–1128; Knowles, *op. cit.*, p. 379.

[38] Thompson, *op. cit.*, pp. 99–100.

[39] *Statuta Nova Capituli Generalis—MPL*, CLIII, 1144.

[40] Boutrais, *op. cit.*, pp. 210–211.

B. The XII Century

In the twelfth century, monasticism reached the culmination of its constitutional development and at the same time found itself at the threshold of being superseded by the Mendicant Orders. The principles and practices of the Benedictine and Augustinian Rules were being re-examined and tested under the critical eye of a religious revival which tempered the wisdom of the old legislation with provisions for the exigencies of current religious, social, economic and historical conditions. This work was done not by rabid fanatics and innovators but by holy men of the caliber of Peter the Venerable (✠1156), St. Stephen Harding (✠1137) and St. Bernard (✠1153).

The first quarter of the twelfth century witnessed, on the one hand, a conscious break with the traditional regulations and monastic usages and, on the other hand, the formulation of new statutes and constitutions which acquired a more legal and formal shape in keeping with the revived interest in law. Dom Knowles sees in this increased activity of framing new systems of religious life a parallel to the impetus given to the framing of civil constitutions by the outbreak of the American and French Revolutions at the close of the eighteenth century.[41]

The constitutional framework of the religious community founded by St. Benedict and St. Augustine embraced a group of men living together in one monastery or abbey. No provision was made in their simple legislation for the amazing multiplication of filial monasteries which sprang up in the course of the twelfth century and brought with themselves many problems of government and organization resulting in the need of a supervisory and directive power vested in a supreme moderator or a governing board. Thus, twelfth century legislation saw the modest beginnings of two religious institutes, namely, the offices of the general superior and of the general chapter, which in the next century played a very significant part in the constitutional development of the Mendicant Orders.

In this section of the chapter the legislative development of the office of the supreme moderator will be considered according to the constitutional framework of representative Orders of the twelfth

---

[41] *The Monastic Order in England* (Cambridge, 1941), p. 207.

century, namely, the Cistercian Order, the Premonstratensian Order, the Gilbertine Order and the Military Orders. Particular attention will be paid to the changing concept of the position enjoyed by the supreme moderator in the respective communities and in their relation to one another.

1. The Cistercian Order

The Cistercian Order was confirmed by Pope Calixtus II in 1119 and by Eugene III in 1152.[42] Stephen Harding (✠1137), the co-founder and third abbot of Citeaux, is credited with the crystallization of the official legislation of the new foundation in the remarkable *Carta Caritatis* which he promulgated in 1119.[43] This epoch-making document manifests a compromise between the Benedictine and Cluniac systems of government by avoiding the complete isolation of the individual monastery of the former and the total centralization or dependence of the daughter-foundations of the latter. This happy medium was achieved through a system of reciprocal visitations between Citeaux and the other abbeys of the Order, which resulted in an intimate relationship between the monasteries without disturbing their autonomy.

In the *Carta Caritatis* the title of *"maior abbas"* was granted to the abbot of Citeaux as well as to the abbots of all other mother-houses,[44] and hence the case was clearly not one of an absolute monarchical arrangement.[45] The abbot of Citeaux, however, did enjoy certain prerogatives not granted to the other major superiors. For example, on the occasion of his visiting an abbey of the Order, he was accorded the privilege of preeminence in dignity and authority over the local abbot, even though he was expressly forbidden "to presume to deal with, order, or touch upon any affair of that house against the will of the abbot or of

---

[42] Heimbucher, I, 338.

[43] Mahn, *L'Ordre Cistercien et son Gouvernement des Origines au Milieu du XIII Siècle* (1098–1265) (Paris, 1945), p. 69; Heimbucher, I, 332.

[44] *Carta Caritatis*, IV, 18 and V, 23—*MPL*, XLXVI, 1381–1382.

[45] In place of a reference to the "Abbot-General," it was a common practice to use the title of "Abbot of the Mother House for all Cistercian Abbeys." In 1178 the title of *Pater Universalis Totius Ordinis* was already applied to the Abbot of Citeaux by Herbert of Torres in his work *De Miraculis S. Bernardi Libri Tres*. Cf. Williams, *Monastic Studies* (Manchester: University Press, 1938), p. 80.

the brethren." [46]   He was also freed from the then prevalent custom, i.e., prior to the *Carta Caritatis*, that required the Abbot of Citeaux to pay a tax to all the houses of the Order for the right of leadership over them, although other abbeys could exact a contribution from their respective filiations.[47]

A successful curtailment of the autocratic power of the *"Maior Abbas"* of Citeaux was assured by the introduction of the system of mutual visitation.[48]   While the abbot of Citeaux could visit all abbeys once or more frequently during the year, the abbots of the four major monasteries (La Ferté, Pontigny, Clairvaux, Morimond) had once a year on a day of their own choosing to make an official visitation of Citeaux.[49]   If any laxity in the observance of the Rule was found during any of these visitations, the Abbot was to be warned not more than four times.   If he proved himself incorrigible, he was to be deposed by the General Chapter or, if the deposition was urgent, by an assembly of the abbots of the filiation of Citeaux and some other Cistercian houses, who then had the right to appoint another to the office of the *"maior Abbas."* [50]

It is to be noted that with the introduction of a supreme moderator within the Cistercian Order came the simultaneous institution of the General Chapter.   According to the *Carta Caritatis*, the annual attendance of all the abbots at the general chapter of Citeaux was obligatory.   While in session, the chapter had the full power to consult, legislate and correct throughout the extent of the Order.   To it also belonged the power of electing and deposing all abbots, including the abbot of Citeaux.[51]

---

[46] *Carta Caritatis,* II, 6—*MPL,* CLXVI, 1379.

[47] *Carta Caritatis,* Prologue—*MPL,* XLXVI, 1378.

[48] This system of regular visitation was not novel in itself, for it had appeared even among the cenobites of Egypt under Pachomius. It had also been prescribed for all bishops in the I Council of Orange (441). The novelty here, however, consisted in the fact that major monastic superiors were burdened with the duty of visitation and were furnished with a minute code on which to base their visitation. Cf. Knowles, *The Monastic Order in England,* p. 213.

[49] *Carta Caritatis,* II, 9—*MPL,* XLXVI, 1380.

[50] *Carta Caritatis,* V, 27—*MPL,* CLXVI, 1383.

[51] *Carta Caritatis,* III, 12-17—*MPL,* CLXVI, 1380-1381. Cf. also Janaus-

Thus the *Carta Caritatis* claimed no autocracy for the supreme abbot, nor did it conversely inaugurate a democratic form of government among the religious.[52]   The family spirit and responsibility of the patriarchical form of Benedictine monasticism was preserved, but with modifications.   Unlike the Cluniac reform, which united all abbeys into one vast scattered family with a mother-house and hundreds of daughter-monasteries, the Cistercian system united all the scattered families into one Order, i.e., the union was achieved not among daughter-monasteries alone but among the mother-houses as well.   For the first time in history one can speak of an order in the strict sense of the word, and consequently, for the first time, is it permissible to refer to a true supreme moderator of an Order.   Centralization in the monastic life was coming into its own, and in the *Carta Caritatis* was reflected a working compromise between the Benedictine and Cluniac systems.   With the insistence on mutual visitation and the annual general chapter, the Cistercians established procedures that were to be incorporated, in one form or another, in all subsequent monastic legislation.

2. The Premonstratensian Order

The Premonstratensian Order, or the Norbertines, as they are often called after their founder, St. Norbert (✠1134), were founded in 1120 at Prémontré.[53]   They constituted the first true order of Canons Regular [54] with the established purpose of stabilizing a community of priests who united the contemplative life

---

chek, *Originum Cisterciensium Tomus I* (Vindobonae, 1878), p. vi; Mahn, *op. cit.*, pp. 197–216.

[52] Mahn, *op. cit.*, pp. 187–190.

[53] Heimbucher, I, 434.

[54] The clerics living in common under the direction of St. Augustine and those who embraced the Rule of St. Chrodegang (✠766) were not strictly canons regular, for though leading a common life, they did not profess religious vows. On the other hand, the Congregation founded in Avignon at the Church of Sts. Justus and Rufus in 806 and those which were established in the eleventh century by St. Ivo (✠1117) never achieved a union under one supreme moderator. Cf. *Codex Regularum*, V, 162. The Congregation of the Canons Regular of the Lateran achieved a definitive organization in the fifteenth century under Pope Eugene IV, and hence postdate the present proposed study.

with the active exercise of the sacred ministry. At first the Rule of St. Augustine was adopted, since it was written for a group of clerics under similar circumstances.[55] A modification, however, was soon obtained through the addition of various statutes, based principally on the legislation prevalent at Cluny and on the newer developments of the Cistercian Order, imparting to the new community a distinctive monastic character.[56]

All power in the Order was vested in the hands of the Abbot of Prémontré, whose position gave him the right to exercise supreme authority over all the houses of the Order.[57] From the very beginning he was chosen for life and was entitled to visit all the subordinate abbeys in order to supervise the untarnished observance of the Rule and constitutions and to eradicate by means of paternal admonition, correction and punishment any abuses which perhaps had crept in.[58] Similarly as in the Cistercian Order, his power was considerably circumscribed by the fact that the abbots of the most prominent subordinate abbeys (Laon, Floreffe and Cuissy) were privileged to exercise the right of a supervisory visitation of Prémontré and its abbot.[59]

A check and balance system further curtailed the absolute power of the general abbot. Regular attendance on the part of the abbots at the annual general chapter to be held at the mother-abbey of Prémontré served to limit the exercise of power of the general abbot by reserving certain functions exclusively to the chapter itself.[60] In addition, the appointment of visitors who upon exami-

---

[55] Helyot, *Dictionnaire*, III, 266–273, s. v. *Prémontré*.

[56] Knowles, *op. cit.*, p. 205.

[57] The Abbot of Prémontré was known as "abbot-general," the *"dominus Praemonstratensis"* and the *"primus pater ordinis."*—Heimbucher, I, 442.

[58] Innocentius IV, bull *In eminenti:* "Abbas autem Praemonstratensis Ecclesiae, quae Mater esse dignoscitur aliarum, non solum in iis Ecclesiis, quas instituit, sed etiam in omnibus tam Abbatibus quam Fratribus debita Patri obedientia impendatur."—*Codex Regularum,* V, 167.

[59] Heimbucher, I, 442. Mahn shows a detailed influence of previous Cistercian legislation upon this institute. Cf. especially Mahn, *op. cit.*, pp. 243–244.

[60] *Codex Regularum,* V, 293 : "Communi quippe assensu Patrum statutum est ut semel in anno, sese visitandi gratia, Ordinis reparandi, confirmandae pacis, et conservandae charitatis, omnes Abbates nostri Ordinis pariter ad Capitulum Generale nostri Ordinis conveniant, in Ecclesia Praemonstratensi, et non alibi, in Solemnitate B. Dionysii."

nation were to report to the Abbot General regarding the state of the abbeys not only facilitated his surveillance over the Order, but at the same time deprived him of the right to make his personal visitation the sole measure of monastic observance and discipline.[61]

In the Premonstratensian Order there appeared for the first time the specific privilege of the supreme moderator to tax all the affiliated houses for the benefit of the Order in general, and of the abbey of Prémontré in particular.[62] Besides being an indication of submission to the abbot general, as superior, the practice provided likewise for the efficient exercise of the functions associated with the office of the supreme moderator.

The institution of a supreme moderator for congregations that transcended national boundaries tended to introduce problems theretofore not experienced in monastic government. Apart from the psychological and social difficulties experienced by the supreme moderator in understanding the temperament and peculiar needs of his diversified subjects, national complications arose with far-flung implications when a subordinate religious was forced to choose between obedience to the laws of his own country and the religious obligations he owed to the foreign supreme moderator of his own Order. This was of paramount importance in the payment of the yearly tax to be sent to the monastery or abbey housing the generalate.

3. The Gilbertine Order

The Gilbertine Order was founded by St. Gilbert of Sempringham (1083–1189) in England in 1141 and was confirmed by Pope Eugene III.[63] It is the only Order founded in England. Being based on the practical needs of the country, it never gained a foothold on the continent. Originally founded as a community of nuns, the Order soon developed into four distinct groups, one of nuns, one of canons, one of lay-brothers and one of lay-sisters. The statutes were based on the Rule of St. Benedict for the nuns, and on the Rule of St. Augustine for the canons, with modifica-

---

[61] *Statuta Ordinis Praemonstratensis—Codex Regularum*, V, 312–314.
[62] Gasquet, *Monastic Life in the Middle Ages* (London, 1922), p. 252.
[63] Heimbucher, I, 417.

tions introduced by St. Gilbert and St. Bernard which approached the ordinances found in the Cisterican Rule.[64]

All groups of the Order were ruled by the master or prior general, who had the official title of "Prior of All." [65] The rights and obligations of his office were signalized in a most detailed account in the chapters of the Rule drawn up by St. Gilbert. Not only were the spiritual and moral qualities of the supreme moderator stressed,[66] but also the administrative and economic rôle of the "prior of all" received exhaustive treatment.[67]

The authority of the "prior of all" was absolute in regard to all four groups of religious constituting the Gilbertine Order. His daily life was completely devoted to an almost continual visitation of the various convents under his care. If it became impossible for him to visit a particular house, he was empowered to appoint two canons and a lay-brother to substitute for him, with certain reservations as to the extent of their power.[68] He filled by appointment all the chief offices of the community, received the profession of the novices, affixed his seal to all charters, gave or withheld his consent regarding all contracts of the purchase, the sale, or the transfer of property. No transaction involving the legal or economic status of the Order was permitted without his direct participation as a guiding and controlling factor.[69]

In the approved Rule were set down the details of the process regulating the election of the "prior of all" together with a minute

---

[64] The *Institutiones Beati Gilberti* are printed as an intercalation between pp. 946 and 947 in Dugdale's *Monasticon Anglicanum* (6 vols., London, 1817–1830), VI, xxix-lviii (hereafter cited as *Monasticon*). They are also to be found in *Codex Regularum*, II, 466–487, under the title: *Regulae Ordinis Sempringensis sive Gilbertinorum Canonicorum.*

[65] *Institutiones Beati Gilberti*, VII—*Monasticon*, xxxiii.

[66] *Institutiones Beati Gilberti*, III: "In cuius electione, non tantum quaeratur profunditas scientiae litterarum, vel generis nobilitas, quantum cultus religionis et morum disciplina, discretionisque subtilitas. Quia si non sit affabilis et institutionum ordinis diligens executor et virtutum amator, non est admittendus, sed omnino reprobandus. Similiter quicumque prece vel precio, arte vel studio magisterii praelationem arripere contenderit, reprobetur."—*Monasticon*, xxx.

[67] *Institutiones Beati Gilberti*, V–VI—*Monasticon*, xxxii-xxxiii.

[68] *Capitula de Summis Scrutatoribus*, I—*Monasticon*, xxxiv.

[69] *Institutiones Beati Gilberti*, IV—*Monasticon*, xxxi-xxxii.

description of the liturgical functions accompanying the election.[70] He was to be chosen by the general chapter at which the priors of all the religious houses convened upon the notification of the death of the supreme moderator as announced by the prior of the house in which he died.[71] This same general chapter had likewise to assemble once a year at Sempringham during the Rogation Days. The prior, the cellarer, and the prioress of each house were to be in attendance.[72]

Notwithstanding his absolute power, the "prior of all" could be deposed by the general chapter if it was deemed necessary. The reasons, however, for his deposition had to be set down and he had to be admonished three times by four priors of the Order before his official deposition at the next general chapter held at Sempringham.[73]

The importance of the Gilbertine legislation concerning the office of the supreme moderator consisted in its providing the connecting link between the Augustinian and the Benedictine Rules by the adaptation of the constitutional legislation of the Cistercians and the incorporation of the practices of Grandmont and Fontevrault.[74] Furthermore, the successful regime of the double monastery of canons and nuns, prepared the way for the subsequent affiliation of the Second Orders with the great Mendicant Orders of the thirteenth century.

4. The Military Orders

During the time of the Crusades the great Military Orders such as the Knights Templars and the Hospitallers of St. John of Jerusalem were founded for the protection of pilgrims against the persecution of the Mohammedans at the Holy Places. This unique institute of a regular Order of knighthood consisted in a brotherhood or confraternity which combined the essential obligations of a religious life with the solemn dedication of the knighthood to defend the cause of Christ and the Church by force of arms. The close analogy between the order of priesthood and the order of

---

[70] *Op. cit.*, III—*Monasticon*, xxx.

[71] *Loc. cit.*

[72] *Institutiones de Magno Capitulo*, I—*Monasticon*, xcv–xcvi.

[73] *Institutiones Beati Gilberti*, IV—*Monasticon*, xxxii.

[74] Heimbucher, I, 326–329.

chivalry resulted in a working union of monasticism with chivalry. The rites in the conferment of knighthood followed in close parallel the rites in the conferring of priestly orders.

Many such Military Orders arose during the twelfth century.[75] Their similarity of purpose was reflected in a like similarity of constitution, even though basically they differed in the original acceptance of one or the other of the monastic Rules prevalent during their time. The military organization of these Orders was uniform, though their monastic organization varied slightly according to the peculiar constitutions of each Order. Notwithstanding their acceptance of the monastic vows, these military Orders were primarily interested in warfare, and hence their preceptories or commanderies which were dispersed throughout Europe and the East bore a closer resemblance to a feudal castle or manor-house than to a monastery. Their canonical legislation, however, did contribute several new facets to the concept of a general superior.

Though founded in 1118, the Knights Templars were first confirmed by Honorius II at the Council of Tryes in 1128, when they received their official Rule, in whose composition St. Bernard of Clairvaux (1091–1153) collaborated with their founder, Hugh des Payens (1070–1136).[76] In this *Regula Pauperum Commilitonum Christi, sanctae Civitatis et Templi Salomonis* one finds

---

[75] E.g., the Order of the Holy Sepulchre was founded in 1099, the Order of St. Lazarus in 1112, the Knights Hospitallers of St. John of Jerusalem in 1113, the Knights Templars in 1118, the Teutonic Knights in 1190. It is interesting to note that the Knights Hospitallers of St. John were the forerunners of the Knights of Malta, who currently are in the process of having their constitutions examined by a board of six Cardinals appointed by Pope Pius XII. Since the death of Prince Chigi Albani della Rovere no new Grand Master has been appointed, pending the approval of the new Constitutions. Incidentally, the prerequisites are rather demanding, for he will have to be of noble lineage, a celibate, and a professed knight of the Order in solemn vows. Upon election he will hold office for life. Cf. *Civiltà Cattolica,* 1952, I, 218; 1953, II, 210, IV, 715 and the *Osservatore Romano,* 14–15 febbraio, 1955.

[76] Thompson, "The Monastic Orders"—*The Cambridge Medieval History,* edited by J. R. Tanner, C. W. Previté-Orton and Z. N. Brooke (8 vols., Cambridge, 1929–1943), V, 682.

the basic exposition of the rôle played by the Grand Master in the governance of the Military Order.[77]

Theoretically, the government of the Order was vested in a council, but in practice the Grand Master exercised considerable authority. He was elected for life and could be chosen from any of the various eight tongues which constituted the official territorial divisions of the Order. Despite his supreme authority, he could exercise it only under the direct control of a grand chapter and of the aid of several councils appointed by himself. Since the Grand Master was not compelled to admit all the Knights to the council, but only those whom he knew "to be worthy and profitable to give advice" [78] he succeeded in assuring himself of an almost completely independent internal administration of the Order. In consequence also of the constant state of warfare that existed in the twelfth century, the general councils could not be held frequently, and accordingly some momentous decisions were made on his own responsibility. Even at a general chapter his own opinion prevailed through the simple expedient of his packing the chapter with ordinary knights whom he chose to regard as worthy of giving advice for the reason simply that their opinions coincided with his own. In important matters, however, such as the granting of lands, the declaration of war, the conclusion of a peace treaty, the suppression of a quarrel within the Order, the Rule insisted that it was fitting for all the brethren to be called together to arrive at a satisfactory decision.[79]

Besides exercising the supreme authority within the Order, the Grand Master was a temporal sovereign and ranked as a prince at the royal courts. Even in the councils of the Church he took precedence over the ambassadors and peers and sat with the bishops. Despite this high political rank, he could command the brethren only in the name of the Temple or of the Pope, never as the representative of any secular power.[80]

The most important contribution to the working concept of the

---

[77] *Codex Regularum,* II, 431–440.

[78] *Ibid.,* p. 439: "Ut omnes Fratres ad secretum consilium non vocentur sed quos idoneos et consilio providos Magister cognoverit."

[79] *Loc. cit.*

[80] Campbell, *The Knights Templars: Their Rise and Fall* (New York, n.d.), p. 72.

supreme moderator in the military orders was the practical achievement of an economic centralization. Up to that time, within the other religious congregations, every abbey was autonomous despite the occasional imposition of a levied tax in support of the mother-house. In the Military Orders, all the houses were bound to contribute their revenues, after deducting running expenses, to a central treasury whose outlays were controlled by the Grand Master and his council.[81] With this innovation the general superior of an Order widened his authority to include not only the spiritual and socio-domestic welfare of his subjects but also the protection of the economic status of the entire Order.

---

[81] *Regula Militum Hospitalis Sancti Joannis Hierosolymitanis sive Institutum Equitum de Malta—Codex Regularum,* II, 446.

CHAPTER III

THE SUPREME MODERATOR IN THE
MENDICANT ORDERS OF THE XIII CENTURY

The end of the twelfth century and the beginning of the thirteenth inaugurated a new economic and political order in the life of Western Europe and the Church. The center of gravity shifted from the large rural estates to the towns and cities, which grew and multiplied with amazing rapidity. The economic advance was accompanied with luxurious living and the cultivation of the arts and sciences; the political advance resulted in movements for freedom and independence and the rise of the bourgeois class. Repercussions of both these aspects of civil life are found in the history of the Church which at that time suffered from a dissolute and apathetic clergy and from a laity which was succumbing to the heretical teachings of the Cathari, the Albigenses and the Waldenses. At that point it was necessary for the Church to provide for the world virtuous and zealous priests and religious, detached from worldly goods and pursuing the evangelical ideals and counsels. The providential rise of the Mendicant Orders offered an effective solution for the socio-religious difficulties of the day.[1]

Of the many Mendicant Orders which sprang up in the thirteenth century,[2] four received official approbation from the Church and have survived to our day, namely, the Friars Minor or Franciscans, the Friars Preachers or Dominicans, the White Friars or the Order of the Brothers of the Blessed Virgin of

---

[1] A good summary of the status of Church and State at the close of the twelfth century is found in the excellent work of Bennet, *The Early Dominicans* (Cambridge, 1937), pp. 1–17.

[2] E.g., Beguines, Begards, Humiliati, Poor Men of Lyons, etc., all of which were suppressed by the second Council of Lyons in 1274. Concerning these mendicant movements one may profitably consult the authoritative work of Grundmann, *Religiöse Bewegungen im Mittelalter* (Berlin, 1935).

Mount Carmel, popularly called the Carmelites, and the Austin Friars or the Order of the Friars Hermits of St. Augustine.[3] Though each of these had a separate origin and distinct characteristics, each nevertheless promoted the practice of voluntary poverty not only individually but also in common, and effected a reconciliation between the contemplative and active religious life independently of the local parochial and diocesan organization in the Church.

The period of great abbeys and monasteries, as the fountainheads of the religious, social, political and economic life of Europe, came to an end. In its stead a new era of "Orders" arose with its perfected system of organization, administration and unity of action. No longer was the sole sanctification of the hermit or of the monk the primary purpose of religious life, but an apostolic ministry culminating in the evangelization of the masses was introduced as another inseparable element of the monastic life. In realizing these new concepts of monasticism, the Mendicant Orders succeeded also in reforming the inner and external life of the Church.

In this chapter the writer proposes to investigate the Mendicant constitutions of the thirteenth century with a view to establishing their contribution to the development of the concept of the supreme moderator. The self-imposed limitation of investigating solely the thirteenth century legislation is not completely arbitrary, for the constitutional development of the Mendicant Orders was substantially completed within that span of years, so that only a very few incidental changes were to be made in the course of the centuries until the advent of the new Code of Canon Law in 1918. Attention, therefore, will first be given to an analysis of the office of the Minister General according to the Franciscan Rule and Constitutions and, secondly, to an appraisal of the constitutional development of the office of the Master General in the Order of Friars Preachers. Only these two Orders, to the exclusion of the Carmelites and the Augustinians, are treated as completely exemplifying the juridic determination of the supreme moderator's

---

[3] *Secundum Concilium Lugdunense (1274)*, sess. 23—Mansi, *Sacrorum Conciliorum Nova et Amplissima Collectio* (53 vols. in 60, Parisiis, 1901–1927), XXIV, 96 (hereafter cited as Mansi).

office and position in the hierarchical organization of the Mendicant Orders during that period of the Church's history.

A. The Franciscans

St. Francis (1182–1226), the Poverello of Assisi, founded the Order of Friars Minor, or the Franciscans as they are universally called, in April, 1208, when he vested his first two disciples in the crude garb of the Mendicants.[4]   Their life and rule consisted in the literal adoption of three scriptural texts chosen at random from the *Liber Evangeliorum*.[5]   When the number of disciples increased, St. Francis gave them his primitive Rule, which was nothing more than a simple commentary on these scriptural passages, and proceeded to Rome, where Pope Innocent III gave it his approval *viva voce* on April 16, 1209.[6]   The original text of this Rule has perished, although attempts at reconstruction have been made from quotations and references made to it by the early Franciscan writers.[7]   This Rule represents the stage in the history of the Order at which St. Francis governed it absolutely with his personal authority and example.   St. Francis, however, did not, even during his lifetime, remain the sole general superior of the friars, for he had elected or personally appointed superiors or vicars over himself and the brethren.[8]

At the yearly chapters that were held at the Portiuncula in Assisi, corrections and additions were made to this primitive Rule to meet the problems and difficulties that arose.   During those years the juridical development of the Order took place without being incorporated into the Rule or codified in a set of Constitu-

---

[4] Huber, *A Documented History of the Franciscan Order, 1182–1517* (Milwaukee and Washington, D.C., 1944), p. 8.

[5] Holzapfel, *Manuale Historiae Ordinis Fratrum Minorum* (Friburgi, 1909), p. 5. The texts were: Matt., XIX, 21; Luke, IX, 2–3; Matt., XVI, 24.

[6] *Ibid.*, pp. 5–6.

[7] Müller, *Die Anfänge des Minoritenordens und der Bussbrudenschaften* (Freiburg, 1885), pp. 185–188; Boehmer, *Analekten zur Geschichte des Franciscus von Assisi* (Tübingen und Leipzig, 1904), pp. 88–89; Mandić, *De Legislatione Antiqua Ordinis Fratrum Minorum* (Mostar, 1924), pp. 122–125; Cuthbert, *Life of St. Francis of Assisi* (London, 1927), pp. 465–476.

[8] Bernard of Quintavalle (✠1245) was chosen superior and leader of the journey St. Francis and his first disciples made to Rome. At the chapter of May 17, 1220, St. Francis appointed Peter Cataneo (✠1220) as Vicar and, shortly before his death, Brother Elias (✠1253).

tions. The patriarchal form of government ceded to the representative, and a firmer organization, unity and uniformity within the Order were obtained. With the assistance of Caesarius of Spires (✠1238), St. Francis revised his Rule in a longer form (23 chapters) and then promulgated it at the general chapter of 1221.[9] This Rule is often called the *Regula Prima* or *Regula non bullata,* for it never received any sanction through a papal bull.

Finally, under the storm and stress of historical events, St. Francis had a vision which induced him to reduce the Rule to a more compendious form (12 chapters). He assimilated the suggestions of the brethren and Cardinal Ugolino (the later Pope Gregory IX), and for these he secured papal approval on November 29, 1223, from Pope Honorius III in the Bull *Solet annuere*.[10] In addition to this Rule of life, the statutes and constitutions promulgated at general chapters held regularly from the very foundations of the Order served for the government of the Franciscan Order.[11] In these legislative documents was established the governing principle of all Mendicant Orders, i.e., an active life coupled with the observance of poverty not only for the individual members but for the Order as a whole.

The concept of the supreme moderator in the Franciscan Order is portrayed in more or less general terms in the Franciscan Rule because of the necessarily generic nature of a Rule of life as a piece of legislation. Specific aspects of his office must be sought in the practical exercise of his jurisdiction as recorded in history or as incorporated in the more precise enactments of the general chapters and codified in the approved Constitutions which are periodically brought up to date during the historical and juridical evolution of the Order. The generic legislation on this point in

----

[9] Holzapfel, *op. cit.,* p. 8.

[10] *Bullarium Franciscanum* (Prima series, Tom. I–III, ed. J. Sbaralea, Romae, 1759–1764; Tom. IV, ed. A. Rossi, Romae, 1768; Secunda series, Tom. V–VIII, ed. C. Eubel, Romae, 1897–1904; Nova series, Tom. I (1431–1455), ed. U. Hüntemann; Tom. II–III (1455–1484), ed. J. M. Pou y Marti, Quaracchi, 1929–1949), Prima series, I, 15–19.

[11] A syllabus of the printed Constitutions indicating their provenance and date of origin is compiled by Marinus a Neuchirchen, "Constitutionum Generalium Primi Ordinis Seraphici Series Chronologica"—*Collectanea Franciscana,* XII (1942), 377–396; Bertinato, *De Religiosa Iuventutis Institutione in Ordine Fratrum Minorum* (Romae, 1954), pp. 157–161.

the Rule remains constant; its specific interpretation and application vary in the course of centuries. Our analysis of the ruling head of the Franciscan Order is limited to the broad outlines of the Rule and the particular legislation of the Friars during the thirteenth century.[12]

In the first few years of its existence the Franciscan organiza-

---

[12] Shortly before his death St. Francis was asked directly by the brethren to describe the qualifications of the ideal Minister General. He answered: "Tam magni, et multimodi exercitus ducem, tam ampli, et dilatati gregis Pastorem, nullum, fili, sufficientem intueor. Sed volo vobis unum depingere, in quo reluceat, qualis esse debeat huiusmodi familiae pater. Homo, inquit, debet esse vitae gravissimae, discretionis magnae, famae laudabilis. Homo, qui privatis amoribus careat, ne, si in parte plus diligit, in toto scàndalum generet. Homo, qui sanctae orationis studii sit amicus, qui certas horas animae suae; certas gregi sibi commisso distribuat. Nam primo mane Missarum sancta debet praemittere, et longa devotione seipsum, et gregem divino tutamini commendare. Post orationem vero seipsum in publico statuat ab omnibus disputandum, omnibus responsurum. Homo, qui personarum sordidum non faciat angulum, apud quem tam minorum, et simplicium cura vigeat, quam Sapientum, et Maiorum. Homo, cui si concessum est literatura a Domino praecellere, plus tamen in moribus piae simplicitatis imaginem ferat, faveatque veritati. Homo, qui execretur pecuniam, nostrae professionis, et perfectionis praecipuam corruptelam. Homo, qui nostrae Religionis caput imitandum se caeteris praebeat, nullis unquam loculis abutatur: sufficere debeat huic pro se habitus, et libellus, pro Fratribus vero scriptorium, et sigillum. Non sit aggregator librorum, nec lectioni multum intentus, ne detrahat officio, quod erogat studio. Homo, qui consoletur afflictos, cum sit refugium, vel bonum tribulatis; ne, si apud eum remedia defecerint sanitatum, desperationis morbus in infirmis praevaleat. Protervos ut ad mansuetudinem alliciat, seipsum prosternat, et aliquid sui iuris delaxet, ut animas lucrifaciat Christo. Ad refugium Ordinis reducat oves, quae perierunt. Viscera pietatis non claudat; sciens tentationes esse praevalidas, quae ad tantum possunt impellere casum. Non oportet eum arridere honoribus, nec favoribus, plusquam iniuriis delectari. Promptiorem cibum, si quo indiget, non in abditis, sed in publicis locis sumat, ut aliis tollatur verecundia, debilibus providendi corporibus. Ad eum maxime pertinet, latentes distinguere conscientias, et ex occultis venis eruere veritatem: auresque non afferre multiloquiis. Talis denique debet esse, qui retinendorum honorum cupiditate universalem formam iustitiae nullatenus labefaciat. Non tamen, ut ex superflua mansuetudine torpor nascatur, nec ex lassa indulgentia, dissolutio disciplinae. Sicque ab omnibus timeatur, ut ab ipsis timentibus diligatur."—*Chronologia historico-legalis Seraphici Ordinis Fratrum Minorum Sancti Patris Francisci* (4 vols., Neapoli, Venetiis, Romae, 1650–1796), I, 19–20 (hereafter cited as *Chronologia*).

tion was already developed along the lines of a predominantly representative form of government in both its administrative and legislative spheres.[13]   At the head of the whole Order stood the Minister General, since the eighth chapter of the Rule charges all the brethren "always to have one of the brothers of this religion as Minister general and servant of the whole brotherhood."[14]   This was the first instance in monastic and ecclesiastical legislation of a supreme moderator in the full canonical sense.   Here also was contained the explicit statement of the hierarchical arrangement within the Order, in vogue since 1217, according to which there was a juridic subordination of convents and their guardians to the provinces and their provincials, and of both to the supreme and universal jurisdiction of the Minister General, the head and ruler of the whole Order.[15]

According to the *Regula bullata* of 1223, the Minister General was elected by the Provincial ministers and *Custodes* at the Pentecost chapter.   His tenure of office was for life, since the Rule envisaged an election of a successor only upon his death or deposition for incompetency.[16]   Since the competency clause was worded

---

[13] Kybal, *Die Ordensregeln des heiligen Franz von Assisi.* Beiträge zur Kulturgeschichte des Mittelalters und der Renaissance, Band 20 (Leipzig und Berlin, 1915), pp. 106–112.

[14] *Rule of the Friars Minor,* chapter VIII—Robinson, *The Writings of Saint Francis of Assisi* (Philadelphia, 1906), p. 70 (hereafter cited as *Rule*).

[15] Waddingus, *Annales Minorum seu Trium Ordinum S. Francisci.* Editio tertia auctior et emendatior ab an. 1208–1622 (25 vols., Quaracchi, 1931–1934). *Continuatio eorumdem Annalium* exarata a P. Aniceto Chiappini, vols. 26–30 (1623–1660) (Quaracchi, 1933–1951), I, 273–274.

[16] *Rule,* chapter VIII, pp. 70–71. "All the brothers are bound always to have one of the brothers of this religion as minister general and servant of the whole brotherhood, and they are strictly bound to obey him. At his death the election of a successor must be made by the provincial ministers and *custodes* in the Whitsun Chapter, in which the provincial ministers are always bound to convene at the same time, wheresoever it may be appointed by the minister general, and that once in three years or at a longer or shorter interval as may be ordained by the said minister. And if at any time it should be apparent to the whole of the provincial ministers that the aforesaid minister general is not sufficient for the service and the common welfare of the brothers, let the aforesaid ministers, to whom the election has been committed, be bound to elect for themselves another as *custos* in the name of the Lord. But after the Whitsun Chapter the ministers and custodes

in broad terms, it received a historical interpretation embracing many possibilities, e.g., resignation, elevation to ecclesiastical dignities, whether cardinalitial or episcopal, heresy or suspicion of heresy, lack of administrative ability, or scandal, whether real or construed.[17]

The Minister General exercised supreme jurisdiction over the entire Order.[18] In fact, he was the first in the history of the Church to be a general superior of three Orders, the first of the Friars, the second of the Poor Clares, and the third of religious men and women living in the world.[19] He wielded his authority over the individual friars mediately, i.e., through their respective provincial ministers; over the provinces, his authority was direct and immediate, circumscribed only by limitations found in the constitutions, which at times prescribed that he act only in conjunction with the general chapter or at least upon consultation with it. His power of dispensation extended only to personal precepts and to constitutional legislation in individual cases and for a limited time only. He was not permitted to dispense from the entire Constitutions nor for the whole Order; this right was reserved exclusively to the General Chapter acting with the approval of the Holy See. From 1239, the power of the Minister General was furthermore limited, not only by the precept of St. Francis that he was not to command anything against the Rule and consciences of the brethren, but also by the Constitutions. Since the chapter held at Assisi in 1236, the Minister General's power over the superiors was confirmed. He then received absolute authority to remove from office any provincial superior and to institute Visitors who were legally authorized to correct abuses not only in the ranks of the subordinates but also among the Superiors themselves.[20] However, by a precept of the general

---

may each, if they wish and it seem expedient to them, convoke their brothers to a chapter in their custodies once in the same year."

[17] Huber, *op. cit.*, p. 634.

[18] *Rule*, chapter I, p. 64.

[19] Holzapfel, *op. cit.*, pp. 156–157.

[20] *Chronologia*, I, 22: "Eo tempore licebat Ministro Generali quoscumque ex inferioribus, seu Provincialibus Ministris, sua absoluta authoritate, ab officio dimovere, et alios quoscumque subrogare . . ipse enim Generalis Minister Visitatores instituit, quos ad omnes Provincias destinavit, quibus

chapter of 1239, he was deprived of the power of nominating and appointing provincials and guardians, so that he retained only the faculty of confirming the elections held in the respective provinces.[21]   Finally, the chapter in Milan, in 1285, imposed the obligation upon the general superior to resign from office whenever he was promoted to an ecclesiastical dignity.[22]

The list of rights and privileges of the Minister General grew to vast proportions in the course of time.   Among the more distinctive of these was his right of examining and approving preachers,[23] and the custom of extending to individuals, and even to entire communities, the *suffragia* (prayers and good works) of the Friars in gratitude for favors bestowed on behalf of the Order.[24]

Since the Order of the Friars Minor evolved slowly its machinery of government, it is only at the great legislative chapter of Narbonne in 1260, held during the generalate of St. Bonaventure, that the experience and decrees of its predecessors were codified into a framework of constitutional law which was to serve as a guide throughout the centuries to our own day.   In these *Constitutiones Narbonnenses,* as they are called, the foregoing description of the extent of the Minister General's office was crystallized in its final form.[25]

St. Francis was not simply an inheritor and interpreter of the old monastic tradition.   His concept of a religious Order and its supreme moderator stemmed from the successful blend of the temper of his age with his personality.   He gave a new vigor to the life of the Church, not with the outer measures of discipline introduced by the reforming legislators of his day, but with inner

---

praecepit, ut mores restituerent, rigorose visitarent, corrigerentque abusus, tam in capite, quam in membris."

[21] *Ibid.,* I, 24–25; De Gubernatis, *Orbis Seraphicus* (4 vols., Romae, 1682), I, 71–72.

[22] *Chronologia,* I, 33; De Gubernatis, *op. cit.,* I, 59–64.

[23] *Rule,* chapter IX, p. 71: "And let no one of the brothers dare to preach in any way to the people, unless he has been examined and approved by the minister general of this brotherhood, and the office of preaching conceded to him by the latter."

[24] Huber, *op. cit.,* p. 636.

[25] Ehrle, "Die ältesten Redactionen der Generalconstitutionen des Franziskanerordens," *Archiv für Litteratur- und Kirchengeschichte des Mittelalters,* VI, 87–138 (hereafter cited as *ALKM*).

sanctification and the re-introduction of the life of the Gospels into everyday life. The Minister General became a new type of general superior, for the Friars formed one great body with a unity of purpose, and not simply an aggregate of communities unified only by a common rule as in past monastic organizations. By removing the principle of stability, St. Francis introduced a more discernible dominion over the religious whom the general superior could move at will. Furthermore, the mode of election, the division of the Order into guardianates and provinces, the method of representation at general chapters and the regular appointment of visitors, introduced the democratic form of government into religious life and offered constitutional safeguards for the effective exercise of the supreme moderator's duties as well as a reliable system of control over his office.

B. The Dominicans

The Order of Friars Preachers, or the Dominican Order as it is universally known, was founded by St. Dominic (1170–1221) about 1206 and officially confirmed on December 22, 1216, by Pope Innocent III.[26] Under the influence of the Canons Regular of Prémontré, with whom Dominic was originally associated, the Augustinian Rule was adopted with an addition of original *Consuetudines* which regulated the ascetical and canonical life of the newly-formed Order.[27] These *Consuetudines* formed the first part (*prima distinctio*) of the primitive Constitutions of the Dominicans which, being entirely disciplinary, regulated the inner life of the Friars. In 1220 St. Dominic convoked the first general chapter at Bologna, at which another set of *Consuetudines* duly drawn up formed the second part (*secunda distinctio*) of the Dominican Constitutions. Therein was contained the core of the governmental machinery and the basis for all future Dominican legislation. In this section the Dominicans relinquished certain aspects of the life of canons to which they had hitherto been bound, adopted the practice of strict poverty as St. Francis had done, and established the institute of general chapters as the

---

[26] Heimbucher, I, 469–523; Walz, *Compendium Historiae Ordinis Praedicatorum* (Romae, 1930), pp. 1–10.

[27] Mandonnet, *St. Dominic and His Work* (St. Louis, 1944), pp. 195–352.

supreme legislative body of the Order.[28]   At the succeeding general chapters new statutes were added and codified in a new text, first by Jordan of Saxony (✠1237) in 1228, and then by the great canonist Raymond of Peñafort (✠1275) in 1239. These new Constitutions, with a few modifications introduced by subsequent general chapters or the new Code of Canon Law, are still in force today.[29]

From the very foundations of the Order of Preachers, St. Dominic acted as the supreme moderator of the brethren.[30]   Tradition holds that he desired to resign from this office at the general chapter held in 1220, but that he was not released from his office.[31] At the second general chapter, held at Pentecost time in 1221, the Order was divided into eight provinces with their own respective

---

[28] Walz, *op. cit.*, pp. 28–31.

[29] The first Constitutions, promulgated in 1228 by Jordan of Saxony (which will henceforth be called *Constitutiones Jordanianae*), were edited by Denifle in "Die Constitutionen des Prediger-Ordens von Jahre 1228," *ALKM*, I (1885), 165–227. A more recent edition of the same was undertaken by Heribert Scheeben in "Die Konstitutionen des Predigerordens unter Jordan von Sachsen," which were printed in the collection *Quellen und Forschungen zur Geschichte des Dominikanerordens in Deutschland*, Heft 38, (Köln, 1939). The second codification of the Constitutions, promulgated by Raymond of Peñafort in 1239 (which will henceforth be called *Constitutiones Raymondianae*), were also edited by Denifle in "Die Constitutionen des Predigerordens in der Redaction Raimunds von Peñafort," *ALKM*, V (1889), 530–564.

[30] Ventura of Verona summarized very succinctly the extent of St. Dominic's jurisdiction and the self-imposed limitation of his power through the introduction of the definitors at a general chapter. He testified: "Tunc temporis ipse b. frater Dominicus habebat plenam potestatem et dispositionem et ordinationem et correctionem totius ordinis fratrum Praedicatorum post dominum papam. Et eodem anno fuit celebratum primum generale capitulum ordinis, ipso teste presente, apud Bononiam. Et tunc placuit ipsi fratri b. Dominico, quod diffinitores constituerentur in capitulo, qui haberent plenam potestatem super totum ordinem et super magistro et ipsis diffinitoribus, scilicet diffiniendi, ordinandi, statuendi et puniendi, salva reverentia magistrali."—*Acta Canonizationis S. Dominici*, n. 2 (edited by Walz) in *Monumenta Ordinis Fratrum Praedicatorum Historica*, XVI (1935), 123–167 (hereafter cited as *MOPH*).

[31] Mortier, *Histoire des Maîtres Généraux de l'Ordre des Frères Prêcheurs* (8 vols.. Paris, 1903–1920), I, 123–124.

provincials and thus there was completed the theoretical organization of the Dominican hierarchy.[32]

To place the office of the supreme moderator of the Dominican Order in its proper perspective, one must realize that from the very beginning the Order of Preachers was governed by a series of chapters, conventual, provincial, general and most general (*generalissimum*). The first ruled the convent, the second the province, and the last two the entire Order. In the conventual and provincial chapters only statutes having limited authority could be passed; in the general chapter, an alteration of the Constitutions could be achieved through an ordinance that became approved in three successive annual chapters; the *generalissimum* chapter, however, could by one legislative act give any precept the full force of immediately being a part of the official constitutions. Not all authority was delegated from the greater to the lesser chapters, but conversely the greater chapters derived it from the lesser. Accordingly, the legislative power of the general chapters of the Order became absolutely autocratic, universal and without appeal.[33]

The supreme moderator of the Order of Preachers bore the title of Master General[34] and had full and general power within the Order.[35] He was duly elected by the electoral general chapter, which consisted of all the provincial priors and of two representatives from each of the Provinces elected at the provincial chapter.[36] Upon election he needed no confirmation, since no higher authority than the general chapter existed. Immediately upon his election the Master General was privileged to choose two or three companions, one of whom was to be a lay brother, the other a competent notary, and the third, if desired, a man of learning, who

---

[32] *Ibid.,* I, 129.

[33] Galbraith, *The Constitution of the Dominican Order, 1216 to 1360* (Manchester, 1925), pp. 37–38.

[34] Walz, *op. cit.,* p. 73. The title of "Master General" was adopted from the usage of the military Orders. Originally the supreme moderator in the Dominican Order bore the designation of *"prior ordinis"* or *"magister ordinis."* Pope Gregory IX used the title of *"Magister Generalis"* for the first time in 1233.

[35] Humbertus de Romanis, *Opera de Vita Regulari* (2 vols., Romae, 1888–1889), II, 192 (hereafter cited as Humbertus): ". . habeat plenam et generalem potestatem in ordine."

[36] *Constitutiones Jordanianae,* d. II, n. 10—*ALKM,* I, 215.

could aid in the solution of difficult problems.[37]   His tenure of office was for life, unless he resigned or was deposed.[38]   Existing as the permanent principle of unity in the Order, he had the right to visit, supervise and correct the entire Order, the duty to undertake, suggest or approve useful projects, to give dispensations, to fulfill the mandates of the general chapters, and to confer personally with the Holy Father to receive instructions concerning the Order's welfare and activity.[39]

The supreme power of the master general was limited in two ways.   The first limitation consisted in his responsibility to the general chapter, over which he presided and the agenda of which he thereby controlled.[40]   Nevertheless, since the definitors composing the general chapter were subject to change yearly, each of the assemblies viewed the problems under discussion from a fresh angle, and therefore the opportunities for collusion were minimized.   Whenever a vote was taken, the master general's counted for one, thus giving the delegates an opportunity to outvote him.[41] Further control of the master general by the general chapter obtained when he rendered an account of the economic status of the Order and indicated his disposal of the money matters entrusted to him.[42]   Above all, the general chapter sat in judgment over the master general, having the power to punish and even depose him in order to correct any excesses, heresy or criminal act on the part of the supreme moderator.[43]

The second limitation was subjective in nature, being of his own making, since prudence demanded at times that he limit the exercise of his prerogatives.   Humbert of Romans (✠1277) furnished a classical example of this curtailment in the granting of permis-

---

[37] Humbertus, II, 193–194.

[38] Walz, *op. cit.,* p. 73.

[39] Mandonnet, *op. cit.,* p. 67.

[40] Humbertus, II, 182–183.

[41] *Constitutiones Jordanianae,* d. II, n. 7—*ALKM*, I, 214.

[42] Galbraith, *op. cit.,* p. 134.

[43] Gerardus de Fracheto, *Vitae Fratrum Ordinis Praedicatorum,* ed. by B. Reichert—*MOPH*, I, 103. It is recorded concerning Jordan of Saxony, the second Master General, that the Friars "accusaverunt eum in capitulo generali." Cf. also *Constitutiones Jordanianae—ALKM*, I, 214; *Constitutiones Raymundianae—ALKM*, V, 556; *Acta Capitulorum Generalium ab Anno 1220 usque ad Annum 1303—MOPH*, III, 22.

sions. The master general was to refrain from granting concessions to Friars who could easily procure the same from their conventual or provincial superiors, or, if he had granted the permission, he was to notify the subordinate's superior of the concession.[44]

In spite of these limitations the master general remained the most powerful individual in the Order. Every novice made his vows according to the formula of profession in which obedience was promised to the Master General personally.[45] Besides having all the right of the provincial superior, the master general was endowed with an authority which was peculiarly his own. Whereas a provincial could receive an illegitimate person into the Order, it was only with the Master General's permission that the latter could be elected as a conventual prior.[46] Only the Master General could grant permission to an apostate from one province to be received into another.[47] Only he, with the approval of the provincial and general chapters, could re-invest delinquent preachers-general, conspirators and apostates with the right of eligibility to office in the Order.[48] It was his exclusive privilege to convoke a *generalissimum* chapter,[49] to confirm the election of a provincial prior,[50] and to appoint a Procurator General.[51] No professed friar could leave the Order without the license of the *"prior ordinis."* [52] Finally, he functioned as the executor of the

---

[44] Humbertus, II, 192.

[45] *Constitutiones Jordanianae*, d. II, n. 16—*ALKM*, I, 202–203.

[46] Galbraith, *op. cit.*, p. 135.

[47] *Acta Capitulorum Generalium ab Anno 1220 usque ad Annum 1303*—*MOPH*, III, 221.

[48] *Ibid., MOPH*, III, 144.

[49] *Constitutiones Raymundianae*—*ALKM*, V, 559; *Acta Capitulorum Generalium ab Anno 1220 usque ad Annum 1303*—*MOPH*, III, 7. *De facto* the *generalissimum* chapter has been convened only twice since the foundation of the Order, namely in 1228 and 1236. In 1262 this power of the Master General was circumscribed in consequence of the provision that a request by half of the provinces sufficed for its convocation. Cf. Galbraith, *op. cit.*, pp. 109–110, and *Acta Capitulorum*—*MOPH*, III, 113.

[50] *Constitutiones Jordanianae*, d. II, n. 15—*ALKM*, I, 217.

[51] Walz, *op. cit.*, p. 78.

[52] *Bullarium Ordinis FF. Praedicatorum*, ed. T. Ripoll and A. Bremond (8 vols., Romae, 1729–1740), I, 12.

enactments of the general chapter concerning the recitation of the divine office, the regulation of studies and the declaration and interpretation of constitutional legislation.[53]

In the constitutional framework of the Dominican Order the office of the supreme moderator was distinguished through the importance given to the elective process in the setting up of all authority, and to the singular form of election of the supreme moderator by electors expressly chosen for this function rather than by the body of provincial superiors alone. Consequently, the form of government of the Dominican Order was in the extreme of an elective and representative character, combining in itself the absolute authority of the monarchy with the proportional representation of the democracy. The concept of the office of the supreme moderator thus reached the peak of its development in the constitutional organization of religious Orders. With only minor variations it persists to our own day.

[53] *Acta Capitulorum Generalium ab Anno 1220 usque ad Annum 1303—MOPH*, III, 68, 126, 173, 204.

PART TWO

A CANONICAL COMMENTARY

CHAPTER IV

THE AUTHORITY OF THE SUPREME MODERATOR

A. The Power of Jurisdiction

1. The Concept of Jurisdiction

It is inconceivable to speak of a society without at once admitting the existence of some regulating authority within it. The Church as established by Christ for the salvation of mankind was not deprived of this regulating power, for the Apostles were commissioned to exercise this authority.[1] Customarily a threefold office of the Church is recognized, namely, the teaching office, the priestly office and the pastoral office, which entail correspondingly the teaching authority, the ministerial authority and the ruling authority. Since, however, the teaching authority is traditionally absorbed in the ministerial, only the ministerial and the ruling authorities are considered. The first, which is conferred through an act of consecration, consists in the universal and permanent capacity to perform acts by which divine grace is transmitted (*potestas ordinis*); the latter, which is conferred by the Church in its canonical mission, is the broad authority to guide and rule the Church (*potestas iurisdictionis seu regiminis*).

The concept of jurisdiction as equivalent to the authority comprising the essential characteristic of a perfect juridical society has undergone a slow process of historical evolution. Its present signification has a Roman law background wherein its etymological meaning of *ius dicere* was restricted to the judicial forum.[2] Under the influence of ecclesiastical legislation, Emperor Justinian (527–565) in his *Novellae* used the term in its wider signification of the public power to rule a community, thus extending it to

---

[1] Matt., XXVIII, 18.

[2] Kerckhove, "De notione iurisdictionis in Iure Romano," *Jus Pontificium,* XVI (1936), 49; Victor a Iesu Maria, *De Iurisdictionis Acceptione in Iure Ecclesiastico* (Romae, 1940), pp. 4–5.

include the notion of authority in general.[3] Ecclesiastical legislation from the time of St. Gregory the Great (590–604) adopted this more general concept of jurisdiction to include the power of general administration, both spiritual and temporal.[4] In subsequent centuries, however, especially the ninth and eleventh, jurisdiction still remained a loose term in canonical literature. Pope Nicholas I (858–867), defending the rights of the Church against Emperor Michael III (842–867), preferred to speak simply of episcopal powers,[5] while the fourth canon of the Council of Clermont (1095) [6] and the twenty-second canon of the Council of Bourges (1031) [7] favored the term "care of souls" (*cura animarum*) as corresponding to the sum-total of ecclesiastical powers enjoyed by the bishops.

At the time of Gratian (✠ ca. 1157), under the influence of the revival of interest in Roman law studies at the University of Bologne, the classical definition of jurisdiction was formulated and then perpetuated for many centuries thereafter.[8] Jurisdiction thus was considered as a generic term, embracing all judicial powers to which were annexed sundry other powers.[9] The IV general Council of the Lateran (1215) broadened the scope of the signification of ecclesiastical jurisdiction by including in its concept not only the judicial powers exercised in matrimonial causes, but also the powers of inflicting public penances and of granting indul-

---

[3] N. (131.3); N. (120.6).

[4] Hilling, "Über den Gebrauch des Ausdrucks *iurisdictio* im kanonischen Recht während der ersten Hälfte des Mittelalters," *Archiv für katholisches Kirchenrecht*, CXVIII (1938), 165–170; Wernz-Vidal, *Ius Canonicum* (7 vols. in 9, Romae; Tom. II, *De Personis*, 2 ed., 1928), II, 49 (hereafter this volume will be cited as *De Personis*); Lega, *Praelectiones in Textum Iuris Canonici* (4 vols., Romae, 1896–1901), Tom. I, *De Iudiciis Ecclesiasticis*, Lib. I, n. 42; Victor a Iesu Maria, *op. cit.*, pp. 29–31.

[5] C. 6, D. XCVI.

[6] C. 6, C. XVI, q. 2.

[7] Hefele-Leclercq, *Histoire des Conciles* (11 vols. in 21, Paris: Letouzey et Ané, 1907–1952), IV, 691 (hereafter cited simply as Hefele).

[8] "Iurisdictio autem est . . . potestas de publico introducta cum necessitate iuris dicendi et aequitatis statuendae."—D. II, 1, 3.

[9] This is apparent from the axiom "Iudex, iudicium, clerus, connubia, crimen," which was applied to the collection of Bernardus Papiensis (✠1213), entitled the *Breviarium Extravagantium* (c. 1187), and all subsequent five-part collections.

gences.[10] At the same Council mention was made of the duty of bishops to minister to the spiritual and temporal welfare of their sees, and thus again there was indicated the extension of their jurisdictional powers to both forums.[11] Pope Gregory IX (1227–1241) further contributed to the elaboration of the concept of jurisdiction by distinguishing between the ordinary and delegated episcopal powers.[12] By the middle of the thirteenth century, the term "jurisdiction" was crystallized in its technical meaning to designate simply the "public power of ruling a juridically perfected community." Distinguished from it was the power of orders, and excluded from it was the administration of temporalities.[13]

A further development in the extent of the concept of ecclesiastical jurisdiction occurred in the writings of Joannes Teutonicus (✠1245), who in his *Summa ad Decretum*, written around 1210, was the first to include in the notion of jurisdiction the power to be exercised in the internal as well as the external forum. In other words, he identified the *"potestas clavium"* with the *"potestas iurisdictionis."* [14] This position was adopted by St. Raymond of Peñafort (1175–1275), who explicitly stated: "Alii autem dicunt, et credo verius, quod non nisi una sit clavis, quae quidem est potestas seu iurisdictio." [15]

2. Commentary on Canons 196 and 197, § 1.

Canon 196 begins with the dogmatic statement that the power of jurisdiction or of government exists in the Church by divine ordinance. This thesis is sufficiently proved in fundamental

---

[10] It firmly prohibited the abbots "manum extendere ad ea quae sunt episcopalis dignitatis, de causis matrimonialibus cognoscendo, iniungendo publicas poenitentias, concedendo indulgentiarum litteras."—C. 12, X, *de excessibus praelatorum et subditorum*, V, 31.

[11] "Ut propter necessitates ecclesiarum et utilitates, in spiritualibus et temporalibus administrent."—C. 44, X, *de electione et electi potestate*, I, 6.

[12] ". . . quum in ecclesiam (i.e. monachorum) nullam iurisdictionem habeas ordinariam aut etiam delegatam."—C. 19, X, *de officio iudicis ordinarii*, I, 31.

[13] Kerckhove, "De Notione Iurisdictionis apud Decretistas et Priores Decretalistas, (1140–1250)," *Jus Pontificium*, XVIII (1938), 12–13.

[14] *Ibid.*, pp. 13–14; Victor a Iesu Maria, *op. cit.*, p. 86.

[15] *Summa de Poenitentia* (Veronae, 1744), Lib. III, tit. xxiv, pp. 451–452.

theology and public ecclesiastical law with arguments based upon the premise that Christ in establishing His Church made it a public and perfect society.[16]   As a perfected society, whose purpose is the sanctification of its members, the Church must contain within itself all the means necessary to achieve its end without dependence upon the will of others. Since this power of government belongs to a supreme and independent society, it is likewise a public power that differs from the private authority one may exercise over a single person or over an imperfectly constituted society, e.g., a father over his family, or a religious superior of a non-exempt community over his subjects.

No philosophical definition of jurisdiction is attempted in the Code, but the description of jurisdiction from the aspect of its extending to the external and internal forums, together with the explicative words *seu regiminis,* enable one to arrive at its extensive definition, namely, jurisdiction is the power proper to a juridically perfect society and therefore embraces legislative, judicial and executive authority. This division of ecclesiastical jurisdiction is in keeping with the enumeration found in the legislation of canon 335, § 1.[17]   Obviously, then, in identifying *iurisdictio* with *regimen,* the Code is implying a distinction from the power of orders which flows not from the Church's essential nature as from a juridically perfect society, but from the fact of consecration, whereby is given the permanent capacity to perform acts by which divine grace is transmitted. Jurisdiction is con-

---

[16] The theological aspect of jurisdiction within the Church is well treated in Tanquerey, *Synopsis Theologiae Dogmaticae* (3 vols., 23 ed., Paris-Tournay-Rome, 1930), I, 560–569; Billot, *Tractatus de Ecclesia Christi* (4 ed., Romae, 1921), pp. 324–334; Herrmann, *Institutiones Theologiae Dogmaticae* (7 ed., 2 vols., Lyons, 1937), I, 347–370. The following treatises on public ecclesiastical law present a competent treatment of jurisdiction in its philosophico-juridical aspects: Ottaviani, *Institutiones Iuris Publici Ecclesiastici* (2 ed., 2 vols., Romae: Typis Polyglottis Vaticanis, 1935), I, 215–219 (hereafter cited as *Institutiones*); Marchesi, *Summula Iuris Publici Ecclesiastici* (Neapoli: M. D'Auria, 1948), pp. 61–64; Coronata, *Ius Publicum Ecclesiasticum* (3 ed., Taurini-Romae: Marietti, 1948), pp. 65–73.

[17] "Ius ipsis [episcopis] et officium est gubernandi dioecesim tum in spiritualibus tum in temporalibus cum potestate legislativa, iudiciaria, coactiva ad normam sacrorum canonum exercenda."

ferred by way of a canonical mission; the power of orders, by means of an act of ordination.

Furthermore, canon 196 recognizes the necessity of a twofold species of jurisdiction within the Church, since the sanctification of its members involves their guidance in the internal as well as the external forums. Jurisdiction, in so far as it seeks primarily the private welfare of the faithful by way of confidential direction and guidance (*per se* and ordinarily) in their moral relations with God, is called jurisdiction of the internal forum, i.e., the forum of conscience.[18] The immediate effect of the exercise of this authority is the precise determination of the status of the faithful in the eyes of God.[19] Jurisdiction, when its exercise provides primarily and directly for the common good of the Church as for a juridically perfect society, and regulates the external ecclesiastical relations of the faithful with accompanying public juridical consequences, is called jurisdiction of the external forum. It must be noted, however, that both species of jurisdiction are public in nature, and the Church, as a juridically perfect society which possesses this power, may impart it to its ministers who constitute the governing body within the constitutional framework of the ecclesiastical hierarchy.[20] Despite the substantial difference between the power of the external and internal forum inasmuch as one is related to the common good of the ecclesiastical society and the other to the individual good of a specific member of this community, the latter is also called the power of jurisdiction for it comes within the province of the external forum and is acquired by a canonical mission which is an act of the external forum.[21]

---

[18] Ojetti, *Commentarium in Codicem Iuris Canonici* (4 vols., Romae, 1927–1931), IV, 156–157 (hereafter cited *Commentarium*).

[19] Vermeersch-Creusen, *Epitome Iuris Canonici* (4 ed., 3 vols., Mechliniae-Romae, 1929–1931), I, n. 276 (hereafter cited as *Epitome*).

[20] Ottaviani, *Institutiones*, I, n. 120; O'Brien, *The Provincial Superior*, p. 13.

[21] Jone, *Commentarium in Codicem Iuris Canonici* (3 vols., Paderborn: Schöningh, 1950–1954), I, 197; Van Hove, *Prolegomena* (Mechliniae-Romae, 1928), p. 27. More elaborate treatment of the distinction and relations between the external and internal forums may be found in Ciprotti, "Il fine della Chiesa e il diritto," *Archivio di Diritto Ecclesiastico*, IV (1942), 36–40; Oesterle, "De relatione inter forum externum et internum," *Apollinaris*, XIX (1946), 73–86.

In canon 197 another fundamental division of jurisdiction is made on the basis of its immediate source. Ordinary power of jurisdiction is that which the law itself attaches to an office; delegated power of jurisdiction, on the other hand, is not attached to an office but is committed to a person.[22] As Beste points out, this division is exhaustive and, therefore, all power of jurisdiction within the Church, regardless of the one by whom it is possessed, is reducible to one of these two categories.[23]

The permanent bond between the ordinary jurisdiction and the permanent ecclesiastical office may have its origin in either divine or human law, be it universal or particular law, written law or custom. Thus, by divine law the pope has such ordinary jurisdiction for the universal church and a bishop for his diocese. By human law this ordinary jurisdiction is possessed by cardinals, patriarchs, archbishops, heads of orders, and cathedral chapters, and, in the internal forum, by parish priests.[24] It must be remembered that the office to which ordinary jurisdiction is attached must be taken in its strict signification,[25] for otherwise the shared power is simply a delegated power, as for example the power to dispense from matrimonial impediments, or to absolve from censures, when it is by law conferred upon a confessor.[26]

A further important distinction in ordinary jurisdiction must likewise be kept in mind, for it can be either proper or vicarious.[27] If the lawfully appointed incumbent exercises in his own name the power that is inherent in his office, his is a proper ordinary jurisdiction. If, however, his power is still ordinary inasmuch as it is attached by law to his office, but is exercised not in his own name but in that of another, his is a vicarious ordinary jurisdiction.

Opposed to these two categories of ordinary jurisdiction is that which is delegated. It derives its power either from a special

---

[22] Can. 197, § 1. "Potestas iurisdictionis ordinaria ea est quae ipso iure adnexa est officio; delegata, quae commissa est personae."

[23] Beste, *Introductio in Codicem* (3 ed., Collegeville, Minnesota: St. John's Abbey Press, 1946), p. 216 (hereafter cited as *Introductio*).

[24] Cf. Abbo-Hannan, *The Sacred Canons* (2 vols., St. Louis: Herder, 1952), I, 253, footnote 9, for a list of examples.

[25] Can. 145, § 2.

[26] Canons 990, § 2; 1044; 1045, § 3; 2254; 2290.

[27] Can. 197, § 2.

authorization of one enjoying ordinary jurisdiction (*delegatio ab homine*) or through some provision made in the law (*delegatio a iure*).[28] In other words, whenever jurisdiction is not obtained automatically in virtue of the law by the incumbent of an ecclesiastical office, but arises from an act subsequent to the acquisition of the office, it becomes delegated jurisdiction. It is thus committed, not to an office, but to a person, and is exercised, not in virtue of a law and an office, but in virtue of a right vested in another.[29]

B. The Dominative Power

1. The Nature of Dominative Power

Since authority is characteristic of all societies, one must find in imperfectly constituted societies a power analogous to the power of jurisdiction that exists in perfectly constituted societies. Such authority in the imperfectly constituted society may arise naturally, as for example the father's power as the head of a family, or it may arise through an agreement by which one person subjects himself to the rule of another, as for example in a religious community. In either case the subordinate is obliged to be guided by the will of the superior in the selection of the means wherewith to obtain the end of the society. By natural and positive law this authority must correspond to the nature and characteristics of the society in which it is found.[30] Consequently, in so far as the society is public or private, in the same degree the accompanying dominative power must be considered public or private, as for

---

[28] E.g., the Council of Trent transferred some papal rights to bishops "tamquam Apostolicae Sedis delegati." Cf. Sessio VI, *de ref.,* cc. 2, 3. For a detailed study of the *"delegatio a iure"* confer the articles written by Crisci, "Evolutio historica delegationis a iure," *Apollinaris,* IX (1936), 270–299, and "De delegatione a iure in iure canonico vigenti," *Apollinaris,* X (1937), 513–535.

[29] Chelodi-Ciprotti, *Ius Canonicum de Personis* (3 ed., Vicenza-Trento, 1942), p. 207 (hereafter cited *De personis*).

[30] Larraona, "De potestate dominativa publica in Iure Canonico," *Acta Congressus Iuridici Internationalis* (5 vols., Romae, 1935–1937), IV, 148–149: "Potestas respondet adaequate ex iure naturali, et respondere debet ac respondere praesumitur ex iure positivo, naturae ac characteribus societatis ad quam regendam ordinatur."

example in a family, in a non-exempt institute, or in an exempt religious Order.[31]

In the course of a long historical development of monastic Rules and Constitutions, the nature and extent of dominative authority was clarified and circumscribed with the result that the present Code admits the existence of a dominative power possessed by superiors and chapters of religious Orders and exercised by them over their subjects according to the norms of their particular constitutions and the common law.[32] Authors agree in tracing the development of dominative power from an original condition of master and slave to the *societas herilis* in which servants freely contracted to give their services to a master.[33] From this institution the authority which the superior of an imperfectly constituted society exercises over his subjects received its name dominative power, inasmuch as the master was regarded as having dominion over his servant.

In keeping with the old Roman law abhorrence for the multiplying of definitions, the Code refrains from giving a philosophical definition of dominative power. In fact, there is a striking absence of any formal treatment of dominative power as such. This can be explained if one realizes that jurisdiction is essentially an attribute of the juridically perfect society with which the Code is primarily concerned, while dominative power is an attribute of an imperfectly constituted society, the legislation for which the Code leaves in great measure to the particular enactments of individual Rules and Constitutions. Nonetheless, mention is made

---

[31] Larraona, "Commentarium Codicis," *Commentarium pro Religiosis,* VII (1926), 32–33 (hereafter cited *CpR*) ; Kindt, *De Potestate Dominativa in Religione* (Parisiis : Desclée, 1945), pp. 229–236 (hereafter cited as *De potestate dominativa*) gives an analysis of the argumentation of Larraona and also an extensive list of authors maintaining the same opinion. Some canonists are wont to restrict dominative power to a simple domestic authority and, therefore, consider it to be private in nature in contradistinction to the power of jurisdiction, which is essentially a public power. Among the chief exponents of this view are Michiels, *Normae Generales Iuris Canonici* (2 vols., Lublin, 1929), I, 134–135, and Toso, "De Conceptu Legis iuxta Aquinatis Doctrinam," *Jus Pontificium,* IV (1924), 34–35.

[32] Can. 501, § 1. "Superiores et Capitula, ad normam constitutionum et iuris communis, potestatem habent dominativam in subditos."

[33] Kindt, *De potestate dominativa,* pp. 35–46.

throughout the Code of authoritative acts of superiors which are certainly acts of dominative power, even though they are not expressly referred to as such in common law. Explicit reference to dominative power is found only in canons 501, § 1, and in 1312, § 1 and § 2. These canons will now be examined for any further light they may throw upon the nature of dominative power.

2. Commentary on Canons 501, § 1, and 1312, § 1 and § 2

The basic doctrine in canon 501, § 1, which recognizes the existence of dominative power in religious superiors has been the constant teaching of the Church. Pope Gregory I (✠604) maintained that the monks had always to remain under the authority of their abbots.[34] Innocent III (1198–1216) treated of this power as residing in abbots and claustral priors. Its purpose was that of directing the religious in their quest for perfection.[35] The Council of Trent (1545–1563) reaffirmed the possession of this power on the part of superiors as enabling them to demand the observance of all means in the attainment of their goal.[36]

The first part of canon 501, § 1, which is of interest here reads as follows: "Superiores et Capitula, ad normam constitutionum et iuris communis, potestatem habent dominativam in subditos. . . ." Although this canon does not describe explicitly the nature of dominative power, but limits itself to a simple affirmation of its existence, one may, nevertheless, discover in it several important aspects of dominative authority. In a general way the active and passive subjects of this authority are indicated together with a general principle of its extent and limitation.

The active subjects are designated with the words *"Superiores et Capitula."* One may deduce from this that dominative power is, therefore, an authority proper to the religious state. Furthermore, since the Code invokes no distinction, neither should we, and in consequence this power must be acknowledged in *all* superiors, though not necessarily in the same degree, in accord-

---

[34] C. 6, C. XVIII, q. 2.

[35] C. 6, X, *de statu monachorum et canonicorum regularium*, III, 35.

[36] Sess. XXV, *de regularibus*, c. 1—Schroeder, *Canons and Decrees of the Council of Trent* (St. Louis, 1941), pp. 217–218; 485–486.

ance with the hierarchical division of superiorships within religious communities.[37]

The passive subjects of this dominative authority are determined by means of the phrase *"in subditos."* One becomes a subject in a religious community by way of a religious profession which is at least temporary. Obviously, then, non-subjects in the juridic sense are excluded in such a way that Superiors and Chapters have no dominative power over them. This same phrase seems to insinuate the nature of the extent of the superior's dominative authority which may be exercised, directly or indirectly, solely over the *person* of the subject. The power which directly affects the common good, e.g., the administration of temporal goods, even though it promotes indirectly the particular good of the religious subject, nevertheless is not exercised *in subditum* and consequently does not fall within the sphere of dominative power. It must be noted that even in such an act the superior may include an act of dominative power which directly affects the subject.[38]

The scope of dominative authority is limited with the phrase *"ad normam constitutionum et iuris communis."* In these words one finds a restatement of the ancient rule, commonly admitted by authors, that superiors may command only according to the Rule and the common law. St. Francis expressed this very forcibly and classically in his *Rule:* "The Friars who are Ministers and servants of the other Friars shall visit and admonish their Friars, and shall humbly and charitably correct them, not commanding them anything against their conscience and our Rule." [39]

Dominative power acquires a further elucidation and a division in canon 1312, § 1 and § 2. In the first paragraph of this canon the Code ordains that one who legitimately exercises dominative power over the will of the person who made a vow may validly and also, for a justifying reason, lawfully annul it in such a way that its obligation never subsequently revives.[40] It is apparent

------

[37] Kindt, *De potestate dominativa,* p. 259; Heston, "Some Aspects of Government in Religious Communities," *The Jurist,* X (1950), 37 (hereafter cited as "Aspects of Government").

[38] Kindt, *De potestate dominativa,* p. 260.

[39] C. X. "Unde firmiter praecipio eis, ut obediant suis Ministris in omnibus quae promiserunt Domino observare et non sunt contraria animae et Regulae nostrae."

[40] Can. 1312, § 1. "Qui potestatem dominativam in voluntatem voventis

immediately that reference is here made to a general dominative power which is not exclusively reserved to religious superiors, for commentators agree that the canon under consideration refers to the power of a father over his children and of the husband over his wife. Traditional canonical and moral teaching attaches to their legitimate superiors this same authority over the will of religious subjects making vows.

In the second paragraph of canon 1312 the Code introduces a new formula in connection with dominative power, for it ordains that one who has power, not precisely over the will of the person making a vow, but rather over the object matter of the vow, may suspend the obligation of the vow for such time as its fulfillment is prejudicial to him.[41] Consequently, an explicit distinction in dominative power is introduced. One is exercised *in voluntatem voventis*, the other, *in voti materiam*. By virtue of the first, a more intimate relation between the superior and the subject is indicated, while the second presupposes a direct dependence of the matter and only an indirect dependence of the person. The dominative power *in voluntatem* signifies the dependence of will upon will, person upon person; the dominative power *in voti materiam* indicates only the dependence of the matter upon the person of the superior and mediately, through the matter, the subjection of the will of the subordinate to the will of the superior. It is also clear that the Code presupposes the possibility that the power *in voti materiam* can exist apart from the dominative power *in voluntatem voventis*.

In view of these remarks concerning the historical evolution of the concept of dominative power and the sparse references to it in the Code, the following conclusions are in order:

1. Dominative power is the authority possessed by all the heads of imperfectly constituted societies, whatever be their nature, to insure the attainment of the private good of individuals and the established ends of the society.

2. Religious, in virtue of their vow of obedience, subject them-

---

legitime exercet, potest eius vota valide et, ex iusta causa, etiam licite irrita reddere, ita ut nullo in casu obligatio postea reviviscat."

[41] Can. 1312, § 2. "Qui potestatem non quidem in voluntatem voventis, sed in voti materiam habet, potest voti obligationem tandiu suspendere, quandiu voti adimplementum sibi praeiudicium afferat."

selves to the dominative power of their proper superiors in accordance with the Constitutions of the institute and the provisions of the common law. To insure the fulfillment of the Constitutions and to safeguard the order of the house or institute, the superiors may perform acts which will include injunctions and precepts, the administration of temporalities, the employment of coercive measures, and the occasional relaxation of the Constitutions.[42]

3. Acts of government resulting from the exercise of dominative power are of a private nature in contradistinction to acts of government performed in the exercise of jurisdiction which are of a public nature. Hence, exempt religious superiors share in a more intimate manner in the direct government of the Church by virtue of their power of jurisdiction; superiors of non-exempt communities are limited to acts within the scope of dominative power exclusively. However, certain acts of dominative power, such as the admission of members and the superior's prohibition of the reception or the exercise of an Order, are considered to exhibit a social and juridical character, and, therefore, assume a public nature. It is, therefore, expedient to divide dominative authority into *potestas privata* and *potestas publica,* the latter being properly distinguished from the public power of jurisdiction.

4. Dominative power as exercised in religious communities, be they exempt or non-exempt, may be defined as that authority which the superiors possess over their professed subjects and by reason of which they govern their personal actions within the limits defined by the common law and particular Constitutions, for the attainment of the established end or purpose of the society.[43]

---

[42] Kindt, *De potestate dominativa,* pp. 57–64.

[43] This definition is in keeping with the standard definitions offered by modern canonists. Some representative definitions of the dominative power of religious superiors are the following: Kindt, *De potestate dominativa,* p. 322: "Potestas ecclesiastica ordinis privati, quam Ecclesia, ob personalem religiosorum in voto obedientiae peractam mancipationem, Superioribus Religionis legitimis concedit in personam subditorum, ad normam Constitutionum et iuris communis, quaeque obligat ex virtute religionis et quandoque specialis obedientiae" and De Carlo, *Ius Religiosorum* (Parisiis, 1950), p. 49: "Potestas dominativa est religionis potestas regendi fideles, qui ex con-

5. Jurisdiction in an exempt religious Order may be defined as that authority which the Church grants to the superiors over their subjects and which includes the legislative, judicial executive and coercive powers, in the external and internal forums, to promote the sanctification of their subjects.[44]

C. The Authority of the Supreme Moderator

1. The Nature of the Supreme Moderator's Authority

In establishing His Church upon earth, Christ willed to embrace three distinct classes of persons, namely, the clerics, the faithful or the laity, and the religious.[45] In view of this divine institution, the religious state is necessarily a public state within the Church. Since the Church retains its supreme and exclusive right over all its members whatever be the ramifications of their Christian life, including also those who seek higher perfection, it determines the concrete form in which this religious state is to exist. In the course of many centuries, the religious state underwent a slow process of juridical evolution, reaching its final form in the almost two hundred canons of the Code devoted exclusively to the class of persons within the Church known as religious.[46]

A life in common among the members of a society is a normal

tractu admissionis vel vi voti obedientiae eidem sese gubernandos committunt."

[44] Authors vary considerably in their terminology when defining ecclesiastical jurisdiction. Biederlack (*Ius Ecclesiasticum Privatum* [Romae, 1909], p. 34) defines it as "potestas publica regendi subditos in ordine ad vitam aeternam consequendam tum quoad intellectum tum quoad voluntatem per verum et proprie dictum imperium." De Carlo (*loc. cit.*) gives a brief and simple definition: "Potestas iuridictionis seu regiminis est publica religionis potestas fideles regendi ad finem supernaturalem."

[45] Can. 107. "Ex divina institutione sunt in Ecclesia clerici a laicis distincti, licet non omnes clerici sunt divinae institutionis; utrique autem possunt esse religiosi."

[46] The canonical legislation embraces the complete organization of religious life. Canons 501-517 determine the government of the religious in the external forum; canons 518-530 do the same for the internal forum; the right of religious to possess and administer temporal goods is dealt with in canons 531-537. Finally, the entire internal regimen of religious, from their acceptance and probation in the society to their later possible dismissal or departure from it, is governed by the legislation contained in Canons 538-672.

form of the religious state recognized by the Church.[47]   This communal life, as does every form of society, presupposes the existence of a director or a superior endowed with an authority that enables him to direct his subjects to the attainment of the aims of the society.   From what has been said in the previous pages concerning the nature of dominative authority, and from the explicit statement of canon 501, § 1, the supreme moderator exercises dominative power over all his subjects within the bounds of the common law and particular Constitutions.[48]

Concomitant with the granting of the privilege of exemption to regulars the Church also recognized the possession by their superiors of ordinary jurisdiction.[49]   This was a logical step, since the exempt religious no longer remained within the jurisdictional competence of the local ordinary, and such jurisdiction had to be supplied by their major superiors on the universal and provincial levels.   The present Code formally grants the power of jurisdiction to superiors of clerical exempt religious, extending it to the internal as well as the external forum.[50]

In accordance with this concession, the supreme moderator of exempt religious Orders possesses authority or power in the internal forum as it is exercised in the moral domain of conscience.   Its sole and immediate purpose is the private good of his

---

[47] Can. 487. "Status religiosus seu stabilis in communi vivendi modus, quo fideles, praeter communia praecepta, evangelica quoque consilia servanda per vota obedientiae, castitatis et paupertatis suscipiunt, ab omnibus in honore habendus est."

[48] Kindt (*De potestate dominativa*, pp. 268–269; 273–274) enumerates many of the faculties possessed by the general superior as the result of his dominative power. Cf. also Schaefer, *De Religiosis ad Normam Codicis Iuris Canonici* (3 ed., Romae, 1940), pp. 228–231 (hereafter cited as *De religiosis*).

[49] C. 17, X, *de excessibus praelatorum et subditorum*, V, 31; c. 30, X, *de privilegiis et excessibus privilegiatorum*, V, 33; c. 3, *de privilegiis*, V, 7, in VI°; c. 24, de electione et electi potestate, I, 6, in VI°; Wernz, *Ius Decretalium ad usum praelectionum in scholis textus canonici sive iuris decretalium* (6 vols. in 10, Romae-Prati, 1898–1914), III, 763 (hereafter this work will be cited as *Ius Decretalium*); Bouix, *Tractatus de Iure Regularium* (3 ed., 2 vols., Parisiis, 1883), II, 378 (hereafter this work will be cited *De Iure Regularium*).

[50] Can. 501, § 1. Cf. Molitor, *Religiosi Iuris Capita Selecta* (Ratisbonae, 1909), p. 250.

subjects secured by ordering their internal relations with God. If it is exercised solely in the sacrament of penance, it is sacramental, as for example the absolution from reserved censures in urgent cases; [51] otherwise, if exercised outside of confession, it is extra-sacramental, as for instance the dispensation from a vow.

In virtue of his jurisdiction in the external forum, the supreme moderator exercises an immediate authority in the public government of his subjects, by regulating their external social relations with the Church.[52] Because of this grant of ordinary powers in the external forum, he enjoys the status of a prelate in keeping with the proper meaning of the term adopted in church legislation.[53] Furthermore, being a major superior of a clerical exempt religious community, he is likewise included in the class of ordinaries.[54]

Some difficulty is encountered in the interpretation of the phrase "ad normam constitutionum et iuris communis," as inserted in the first part of the first paragraph of canon 501. This qualification undeniably limits the extent of the superior's dominative power. Authors are agreed that this phrase applies equally to the second half of the paragraph which deals with the power of jurisdiction enjoyed by superiors of clerical exempt communities.[55] In the course of this dissertation historical and *de facto* implemented limitations of jurisdictional competence by the common law and particular Constitutions will be indicated. An example of restriction by the common law is immediately noted in the second paragraph of canon 501 [56] and in the reservation of

---

[51] Can. 2254.

[52] Schaefer (*De religiosis*, pp. 227–228) lists the faculties possessed by religious superiors in virtue of their jurisdictional powers.

[53] Can. 110. "Quamvis Praelati titulo, honoris causa, a Sede Apostolica etiam nonnulli clerici donentur sine ulla iurisdictione, proprio tamen nomine Praelati in iure dicuntur clerici sive saeculares sive religiosi qui iurisdictionem ordinariam in foro externo obtinent."

[54] Can. 198, § 1. Cf. also Coronata, *Institutiones*, I, 604; Larraona, "Commentarium Codicis," *CpR*, IV (1923), 76, footnotes 335 and 337.

[55] Coronata, *Institutiones*, I, 635; Schaefer, *De religiosis*, p. 229; Larraona, "Commentarium Codicis," *CpR*, III (1922), 135, footnote 203; Clancy, *The Local Superior*, pp. 28–29; O'Brien, *The Provincial Superior*, pp. 16–17.

[56] "Superioribus quibuslibet districte prohibetur quominus in causis ad S. Officium spectantibus se intromittant."

particular rights to certain major superiors;[57] the Franciscan Constitutions offer an instance of limitation by the particular law by their reserving to the general superior the power of dispensing from an impediment of illegitimacy in a postulant about to enter the novitiate.[58]

2. The Extent of the Supreme Moderator's Authority

The Code offers in canon 502 a succinct statement of the extent of the supreme moderator's authority.[59]   His authority extends over all the provinces, the houses and the members of the institute, but must be exercised according to the Constitutions. The seemingly obvious simplicity and clarity of this canon explains the almost complete lack of commentary upon it in canonical literature.   A closer examination, however, reveals a considerable number of implications.

The initial analysis of the terminology employed in this canon indicates that the concept of the authority acknowledged to the general superior includes the jurisdictional and dominative powers of a superior in a clerical exempt community, as mentioned in the preceding canon.[60]   This authority is general, in view of the explicit and unqualified use of *"omnes;"* it is immediate, in the light of the limiting clause *"exercendam secundum constitutiones,"* which is also indicative of possible exceptions.[61]

In the last mentioned clause one may find two other important implications.   First, even though the authority of the general superior is supreme, it is not absolute, since provision is made for possible limitations furnished by the particular Constitutions.[62]

---

[57] Examples of such restrictions placed upon minor superiors to the benefit of the major superiors may be found in canons 1156, 1163, 1176, § 2, 1192, 1402, 1579, § 1.

[58] *Regula et Constitutiones Generales Ordinis Fratrum Minorum* (Romae, 1953, art. 20.

[59] "Supremus religionis Moderator potestatem obtinet in omnes provincias, domos, sodales religionis, exercendam secundum constitutiones; alii Superiores ea gaudent intra fines sui muneris."

[60] Can. 501, § 1; cf. Schaefer, *De religiosis*, p. 225, footnote 54.

[61] Chelodi-Ciprotti, *De personis*, p. 397; Wernz-Vidal, *Ius Canonicum*, III, 89.

[62] Pejška, *Ius Sacrum Congregationis SS. Redemptoris* (Hranice, Moravia, 1923), p. 302.

Secondly, one may suspect that a more precise determination of the extent of the supreme moderator's authority is to be found in particular legislation than in the legislation of the Code, since canon 502 provides for possible variations according to the needs of different religious institutes. Very often the Constitutions of the Order intend to exercise some control over the supreme authority of the general superiors. Their purpose is accomplished in several ways. They may either require their supreme moderator to consult or seek the consent of his Council before exercising his authority, or some matters of grave importance may be totally removed from his competence and placed in the hands of the general chapter. In matters of lesser importance he may even be required, for the sake of expediency, to leave their execution to the lesser superiors.[63]

That canon 502 legislates for the general superior's jurisdiction over all provinces, houses and religious subjects taken in their strict canonical signification is certain, but one must also include in this extension the non-canonical usage of these terms. In support of this contention three arguments may be adduced. The first is based on a classic rule of interpretation which states that *"verba generalia generaliter sunt intelligenda"* or *"ubi lex non distinguit, neque nos distinguere debemus."* [64] Accordingly no canonical restrictions should be placed upon the comprehension and extension of the terms *"provincia," "domus"* or *"sodales,"* since no qualifying words are added to these nouns. The second argument rests upon the untoward consequences which would result from the strict interpretation of the extension of these words to the exclusion of their non-technical meanings. One would have the anomaly of the subjects of a lesser superior being free from the jurisdiction of a higher superior to the detriment of the hierarchical arrangement of authority within the Church. Finally, the third argument is founded upon the actual *praxis* of general superiors, who in keeping with the provisions of the common law and the particular Constitutions *de facto* exercise

---

[63] Jone, *Commentarium,* I, 409–410.

[64] Reiffenstuel, *Jus Canonicum Universum* (3 ed., 4 vols., Ingolstadii, 1739), Lib. I, tit. 2, § xvi, (I, 159); Schmalzgrueber, *Ius Ecclesiasticum Universum* (5 vols. in 12, Romae, 1843–1845, Lib. V, tit. 40, reg. 19, p. 550.

their authority over provinces, houses and religious subjects, though all of these be understood in their widest signification.

In view of this interpretation the word "province," which is strictly defined in the Code as "the union of several religious houses under one and the same superior, and constituting part of the same institute," [65] embraces similar divisions within the institute, though the divisions reflect specific differences as found in the particular legislation. Examples of such divisions are Custodies,[66] Commissariats (provincial or independent) [67] and Congregations.[68]

The term *"domus"* likewise must be taken in its widest signification, since no limitation is placed by the Code. It embraces definitely the strict concept of a religious house, be it a *domus formata* or a *domus non-formata* (a house fully organized or a house only partially evolved).[69] Since, however, not all houses of religious are religious houses in the canonical sense, these others must also be included within the jurisdictional sphere of the supreme moderator. In this sense would be included filial houses,[70] hospices and hospitals, schools, summer houses and the like.[71]

Two pertinent observations concerning the supreme moderator's authority *"in omnes domos"* of his Institute must be made. On the basis of this power the general superior may exempt a specific religious house from the authority of the provincial superior by subjecting it immediately to his own jurisdiction.[72]

---

[65] Can. 488, n. 6: ". . . plurium religiosarum domorum inter se coniunctio sub eodem Superiore, partem eiusdem religionis constituens."

[66] *Regula et Constitutiones Generales Ordinis Fratrum Minorum,* art. 337; Larraona, "Commentarium Codicis," *CpR,* IV (1923), 45–46, especially footnote 305; Coronata, *Institutiones,* I, 602.

[67] *Regula et Constitutiones Generales Ordinis Fratrum Minorum,* art. 338 and 347; Coronata, *Institutiones,* I, 602.

[68] Can. 488, n. 2: "   . plurium monasteriorum sui iuris inter se coniunctio sub eodem Superiore."

[69] Can. 488, n. 5.

[70] Responsum S. C. de Religiosis, 1 febr., 1924—*Acta Apostolicae Sedis,* XVI (1924), 95–96 (cited hereafter *AAS*).

[71] De Carlo, *Ius Religiosorum,* p. 26.

[72] Wernz-Vidal, *Ius Canonicum,* I, 89. This is a common practice among religious Orders with reference to their International Universities, special

Secondly, despite this power in all the religious houses of his Institute; the supreme moderator is deprived of its exercise when, by special privilege, the Holy See exempts a particular religious house from the direct obedience to a general superior by placing it under the immediate jurisdiction of a Roman Congregation.[73]

In accordance with canonical definition, the *"sodales religionis"* or members of the religious community are those who have made profession of vows in any Institute, be they simple or solemn, temporary or perpetual.[74] This restricted meaning of the term, however, cannot obtain in our canon. The jurisdiction of the supreme moderator extends to all those who live in religious houses, even though they are not religious. As domicile is the most common determinant of the subjection to a local ordinary, so likewise a relationship of dependence upon the general superior arises from inhabitance in a religious house. Candidates, oblates and postulants,[75] tertiaries and novices,[76] although not united to the Institute by any strict bond of profession, may be counted among the members of the Institute, and fall under the jurisdiction of the general superior, especially since he very often decides their fate in religion.

From the legislation found in other canons one may also include under this concept of *"sodales"* all persons dwelling day and night in a religious house by reason of hospitality or sickness, also the retreatants, workmen, servants, and the like.[77] These persons are not *"sodales"* who constitute part of the community, but they are placed in certain determined instances under the jurisdictional and dominative powers of the religious superior. In these instances, a contract or any association sufficient to subject them under the common discipline is sufficient for the general superior to assume authority over them.

---

research Institutes, and monasteries pursuing extraordinary, supra-provincial interests.

[73] S. C. de Propaganda Fide, 28 maii 1926—*AAS*, XVIII (1926), 491–492.

[74] Can. 488, n. 7.

[75] Can. 540, § 1.

[76] Can. 562.

[77] Canons 514, § 1; 567, § 1; 875; 1245; 1313; 1320; Creusen, *Religieux et Religieuses d'après le Droit Ecclésiastique* (4 ed., Louvain, 1930), p. 43.

3. The Determination of Competency of Superiors

A logical corollary to the question of the extent of the supreme moderator's jurisdiction is the establishment of the competency of various superiors according to some general norms. The Code is not always specific in its terminology. This results in some confusion, particularly with regard to matters which seem to fall under the jurisdictional competency of both major superiors, the supreme moderator and the provincial. Lest the enforcement of the law suffer, or a superior be hindered in the lawful exercise of his legal right, the following rules are suggested.

If the Code simply extends general faculties to superiors (*superiores*) without any further explicit or implicit restrictions as to the rank of the superior involved, no distinction is to be invoked as to which superior has the right to exercise authority. Legally all the superiors, the lesser and the major, share this right. At times, however, the Code provides for a limitation that may be imposed by the particular Constitutions. Usually the tendency in such cases is to deprive lesser superiors of jurisdiction in favor of the major superiors. The abuses, however, of such practice must be avoided. The particular law should never reduce the office of a lesser superior to a mere honorary title without any authority.[78]

For the effective government of a religious community it is expedient that authority be de-centralized wherever that is possible, so that lesser superiors may share in the actual government of the subjects immediately under their control. As O'Brien points out, a universal restriction of the power of these lesser superiors would make the privilege of the exemption of religious very burdensome.[79] The easy accessibility of the lesser superior is an important factor in the allocation of some jurisdictional rights in the hands of these superiors. Such rights should not be reserved to the more distant major superior, particularly the supreme moderator.

Since the first rule relates to the cases wherein the mutual competence of superiors is involved, the general rules of precedence

---

[78] Larraona, "Commentarium Codicis," *CpR,* III (1922), 135, footnote 203; VII (1926), 240–241; Schaefer, *De religiosis,* p. 225.

[79] *The Provincial Superior,* p. 20.

must likewise be observed. If the matter is of local interest, the local superior is the immediate authority competent to exercise jurisdiction; if it is of more than local interest, so that it involves the common good of a province, then the provincial obtains competency; if the matter transcends the provincial limits, then jurisdiction is reserved to the supreme moderator. Two general rules, however, are applicable in these cases, namely, the right of a higher superior to supervise the acts of the lesser, and the rule of law in cases of mutual competence whereby jurisdictional power belongs to him who first acts in the case and thus renders the other superior's power inoperative.[80]

Secondly, whenever the Code speaks of the major superior (*superior maior*) or of the ordinary (*ordinarius*) without any additional indication of the person, or without recognition of the power of specification to be made by the Constitutions, then the supreme moderator and the provincial superior are equally competent.[81] According to this principle only the limitations as delineated in canon 502 are admitted, and no provision is made for the enactment of a particular law for the curtailment of the jurisdiction of either superior. Consequently, this has a practical import upon the power of the supreme moderator, for the general superior cannot deprive the provincial of his authority by reserving jurisdiction to himself. To deny the rights granted by the common law to one of the major superiors would under these circumstances be tantamount to the unlawful enactment of a particular law.

The general superior, however, in view of his supreme jurisdiction over all the provinces, houses and members of his Order, may restrict temporarily the authority granted to the provincial superior in a particular case, because of his duty to seek the common good of the entire Order. If the circumstances warrant

---

[80] Can. 1568; Schaefer, *De religiosis,* p. 241; Goyeneche, "Consultationes," *CpR,* III (1922), 217; XII (1931), 131–133.

[81] E.g., can. 503, which empowers major superiors to constitute notaries for the ecclesiastical offices within their jurisdiction; can. 990, § 1, which grants ordinaries the power to dispense their subjects from irregularities arising from an occult crime; can. 2237, which deals with the remission of penalties established by the common law.

it, he may even suspend that right entirely, particularly if extant abuses demand such disciplinary action.[82]

Thirdly, if the Code uses the phrase "major superior designated by the Constitutions" (*super maior secundum constitutiones*) or some similar expression, then only one of the major superiors is competent, namely, the one indicated in the particular legislation of the Order.[83]   Whenever one superior is so determined, the other's jurisdiction is restricted, and he has no right to interfere. This denial of competence precludes the interference of one of the major superiors in matters belonging to the other as well as the nullification of the act of a lesser superior should he presume to exercise authority in matters restricted to one of the major superiors.   Here again the possibility of the general superior's intervention is based upon the introduction of the common-good element, which he is duty bound to obtain and preserve.

Fourthly, whenever the Code commits a function to the immediate major superior (*superior maior immediatus*) then the provincial superior is meant.   The particular law is then incapable of ruling otherwise.   This is especially the case when admonitions must be made before the dismissal of religious in solemn vows.[84]

The practical application of these norms will be demonstrated in the examination of the legislative, judicial and executive powers of the supreme moderator.

---

[82] E.g., can. 2389; cf. Goyeneche, "Consultationes," *CpR*, III (1922), 218; Schaefer, *De religiosis*, p. 241.

[83] Canons 511 and 543.

[84] Canons 659, 661 and 663.

CHAPTER V

THE PERSON OF THE SUPREME MODERATOR OF CLERICAL EXEMPT RELIGIOUS INSTITUTES

A. Canonical Qualifications of the Candidate

The Code and the particular Constitutions of a religious institute determine the necessary qualifications of a candidate for the office of supreme moderator. To be validly chosen as a superior, the candidate must under pain of nullity possess all the qualities required by the common law and the Constitutions; all other requisite qualifications for the candidate relate simply to the factor of lawfulness. Prescinding from the conditions laid down in the respective Constitutions of religious institutes (their consideration is outside the scope of the present dissertation), the basic requirements laid down in the Code are reducible to one fundamental rule along with the three requisites delineated in canon 504.

No one may become the supreme moderator of a clerical exempt religious Order if he is not a priest, in keeping with the general rule that all superiors of a clerical institute, whether exempt or not, must be priests, in order to fulfill their duties in the care of souls in the external and internal forum.[1] In some of the older Rules and Constitutions provision was made for the possibility of actually having a lay-brother serve as a major superior with a priest of the Order detailed for the performance of the functions demanded by the pastoral care.[2]

---

[1] Canons 154; 501, § 1; 514, § 1.

[2] Principally because of the shortage of priests in the early days of the Franciscan Order, a lay brother frequently served as the superior of a community. The Rule envisages such a state of affairs when it prescribes the following: "Si qui fratrum, instigante inimico, mortaliter peccaverint, pro illis peccatis, de quibus ordinatum fuerit inter fratres ut recurratur ad solos Ministros provinciales, teneantur praedicti fratres ad eos recurrere, quam citius poterint, sine mora. Ipsi vero Ministri si presbyteri sunt, cum misericordia iniungant illis poenitentiam; si vero presbyteri non sunt, iniungi

The three qualities required by the common law in the candidate for the office of supreme moderator are stated in canon 504. The candidate must be professed in religion for at least ten years, born of lawful wedlock, and more than forty years of age. Even though the Code allows particular Constitutions to make more stringent and extensive requirements, those enumerated in the canon are the minimum expressly set down for validity.[3] Any particular legislation to the contrary is therefore abrogated. In the event of the election of a candidate lacking one or more of these qualities, recourse may be interposed with the Holy See for a dispensation; in the case of a postulation, confirmation must be obtained.[4]

As the first qualification for a valid candidacy canon 504 requires that the candidate be a member of the same institute for at least ten years from the date of his first profession.[5] This requirement had its origin at the time of the rise of the Mendicant Orders in the thirteenth century. Pope Boniface VIII (1294–1303) legislated that solemn profession in the respective Orders was required of all candidates for the office of general superior. He did not, however, set any definite length of time for the duration of which the profession had to obtain.[6]

The computation of the years of profession begins with the date of simple, not solemn, profession and must be made according to the rule stated in canon 34, § 3, n. 1 and 3, i.e., one computes the years in calendar fashion, not counting the first day, but including the entire last day. A religious who has availed himself of an indult of exclaustration could include in this computation the

---

faciant per alios sacerdotes Ordinis, sicut eis secundum Deum melius videbitur expedire."—*Regula et Constitutiones Generales Ordinis Fratrum Minorum* (Romae, 1953), c. vii.

[3] E.g., some Rules and Constitutions demand of their candidates for the office of superior general such further requirements as perfect health, an age of 45 or 50 years, a religious profession of twenty years' duration, a degree in theology or canon law, etc.

[4] Coronata, *Institutiones,* I, 640, footnote 6; Abbo-Hannan, *The Sacred Canons,* I, 513.

[5] ". . . ad munus Superioris maioris inhabiles sunt qui eandem religionem professi non sunt a decem saltem annis a prima professione computandis . . ."

[6] C. 28, *de electione et electi potestate,* I, 6 in VI⁰; c. 1, *de electione et electi potestate,* I, 3, in Clem.

time of the exclaustration.[7] If, however, one rejoins his community after a period of secularization, then the computation of the time of his eligibility for the office of general superior begins with the date of his new profession.[8] The same rule applies to readmitted dismissed religious.[9] Likewise the time a solemnly professed religious has spent in military service is computed, for the religious has remained a subject of his superiors. Coronata adduces this same argumentation in favor of the eligibility of a religious who, the while his vows were suspended, spent some time in the military service.[10]

The phrase "professed in the same institute" (*eandem religionem professi*) must be attended to if the question ever arises of naming a general superior who has made his religious profession in another institute. The duration of profession in another institute may not be computed for the purpose of his valid qualification.[11] Since the noun *"religio"* is used, and not *"congregatio"* or *"provincia,"* it is permissible for a member of any congregation or province to be validly elected as the general superior. A Cistercian, however, could not be legally elected to serve as the supreme moderator of the Benedictines, for, in spite of the identity of their Rules, they constitute different Institutes or Orders.[12] Neither could a religious of one of the Franciscan Families (O.F.M., O.F.M.Conv. or O.F.M.Cap.) serve as the general superior of another.[13]

The second qualification refers to the candidate's being born of lawful wedlock, since canon 504 invalidates the candidacy of one who is of illegitimate birth.[14] Ordinarily the particular Constitutions reject any subsequent legitimation as qualifying a candidate

---

[7] S. C. de Religiosis, *Cum in Codice*, 19 iul. 1919—*AAS*, X (1919), 321; Larraona, "Commentarium Codicis," *CpR*, VII (1926), 247.

[8] Vermeersch-Creusen, *Epitome*, I, n. 734.

[9] Can. 640, § 2; Abbo-Hannan, *The Sacred Canons*, I, 513–514.

[10] *Institutiones*, I, 640.

[11] C. 1, *de electione et electi potestate*, I, 3, in Clem.; Abbo-Hannan, *The Sacred Canons*, I, 513.

[12] Augustine, *A Commentary on the New Code of Canon Law* (8 vol., Vol. III, 3 ed., St. Louis: Herder, 1922; vol. VIII, 3 ed., St. Louis: Herder, 1931), III, 117 (hereafter cited as *Commentary*).

[13] Schaefer, *De religiosis*, p. 936.

[14] "... qui non sunt ex legitimo matrimonio nati."

for the office of supreme moderator.[15]   Unless the Code expressly states otherwise, legitimation by subsequent marriage suffices to obtain canonical effects equal to those enjoyed by legitimate offspring.[16]   Legitimation is insufficient only in the case of candidates for the cardinalate, the office of a *praelatus nullius* and the episcopate.[17]

Legitimation granted by way of a general indult in the dispensation from a diriment impediment is equivalent to legitimation by subsequent marriage.[18]   Legitimation, however, resulting from solemn profession [19] or from a general dispensation,[20] even though it is sufficient for the reception of major orders and the acquisition of non-consistorial benefices, does not suffice for eligibility for the office of supreme moderator in an exempt religious Order. Solemn profession is not strictly a legitimation, but is equivalent to it in the removal of an irregularity arising *ex defectu*.[21]   The validation of a marriage by way of a radical sanation (*sanatio in radice*) renders a candidate eligible if his birth was subsequent to the time in which the retroactive juridical effects of the sanation became valid.[22]   Those who were born prior to the time when the sanation became operative may gain legitimation according to the norms set down in canon 1051.[23]

The last qualification required for a valid candidacy is the requirement of canonical age. Canon 504 specifies that the candidate for the office of general superior must have completed his fortieth year of age. In this respect the Code extends the age limit beyond the requirements found in the *Decretals*, being moti-

---

[15] *Regula et Constitutiones Ordinis Fratrum Minorum*, art. 376.

[16] Can. 1117.

[17] Canons 232, § 2, n. 1; 320, § 2; 331, § 1, n. 1. In all of these canons the prohibitive clause *"arcentur illegitimi, etiamsi per subsequens matrimonium fuerint legitimati"* or its equivalent is found.

[18] Can. 1051; Schaefer, *De religiosis*, p. 243.

[19] Can. 984, n. 1.

[20] Can. 991, § 3.

[21] Larraona, "Commentarium Codicis," *CpR*, VII (1926), 196, footnote 249.

[22] Can. 1138, 1; Vermeersch-Creusen, *Epitome*, I, n. 576.

[23] Ledwolorz, "Illegitimität und Irregularität als Hindernisse für Bestellung zu bestimmten Ordensämtern in klösterlichen Genossenschaften," *Ephemerides Iuris Canonici*, II (1946), 255–257.

vated by the practical considerations of vaster experience, both in theological and economic spheres, needed to cope with modern conditions.[24]

In addition to these three requirements for a valid candidacy relative to the office of general superior, the penal section of the Code contains further legislation whereby a religious becomes incapable of holding ecclesiastical or religious offices. As a rule this punishment takes the form of depriving the religious of eligibility for office, thus preventing him from being elected to an office in the community.[25] The lack, however, of eligibility is not always a form of penalty, as for example in the case of retired religious who are cardinals or bishops.[26]

Outstanding among the qualities necessary for a licit promotion to the office of superior general are the personal virtues of the candidate. The classical enumeration of these by St. Francis has been listed elsewhere in this dissertation.[27] Besides being endowed with the necessary theological and canonical knowledge for fulfilling his obligations according to the mind of God and the Church, the supreme moderator should be possessed of great humility and piety, charity and justice, patience and fortitude, and love of religious discipline. Above all, he should be the leader of his brethren through his good example in the observance of the Rule and the Constitutions.[28] This personal worthiness of the candidate must be determined by the electors of major superiors, for they bind themselves under oath to choose the candidates possessed of the best qualities.[29]

---

[24] Augustine, *Commentary*, III, 118.

[25] Canons 2294, § 1; 2345; 2346; 2368, § 1; 2394, n. 1; 2395; Schönsteiner, *Grundriss des Ordensrechtes* (Wien, 1930), p. 120; Biederlack, *De Religiosis* (Oeniponte, 1919), p. 40.

[26] Can. 629, § 2.

[27] Cf. pp. 67–68.

[28] Cf. Valuy, *Le Gouvernement des Communautés Religieuses* (8 ed., Paris, 1925) and Micheletti, *De Superiore Communitatum Religiosarum, Manuale Asceticum, Canonicum ac Regiminis* (Romae, 1911), who furnish an exhaustive treatment of all the personal qualities expected in a good religious superior.

[29] Can. 506, § 1; O'Brien, *The Provincial Superior*, pp. 27–28.

B. The Appointment of the Supreme Moderator

Since the Code does not specify the manner of the appointment of general superiors, but leaves it to the particular Constitutions of the respective Orders to determine the procedure, the treatment of the appointment of general superiors is outside the scope of the present dissertation. Any of the three canonical procedures in the selection of superiors, namely, appointment, election or postulation, are admitted, provided that the general norms enacted by the Code are followed.

Appointment of the general superior can be made only by a higher superior, namely, by the Supreme Pontiff. Election must take the form specified in the Constitutions; if it be held in chapter, the legislation in canons 160–182 of the Code must be observed.[30]   Postulation can be admitted only in an extraordinary case, provided that the Constitutions do not prohibit it.[31]   If the Constitutions are simply silent concerning postulation, even though they do not expressly approve of it, it is allowed, for commentators are in accord that silence in this connection is not equivalent to a prohibition.[32]

C. The Term of Office

It is not within the scope of this dissertation to concern itself with the question whether it is more expedient to have temporary or permanent general superiors.[33]   The common law does not determine the length of the supreme moderator's term of office, nor does it prohibit repeated re-elections. The Code shows its preference for a limited duration of office for major superiors, but allows particular Constitutions to rule otherwise.[34]   It was customary for the founders of religious Orders to retain their superiorship for the duration of their life, even though the Constitutions of their Institute provided for a temporary tenure of

---

[30] Can. 507, § 1.

[31] Can. 507, § 3.

[32] Beste, *Introductio,* p. 338; Abbo-Hannan, *The Sacred Canons,* I, 517–518; Coronata, *Institutiones,* I, 645.

[33] Augustine (*Commentary,* III, 119–120) presents a practical analysis of the *pro* and *con* arguments relative to a temporary or permanent tenure of office. Cf. also Beste, *Introductio,* pp. 336–337.

[34] Can. 505.

office.[35] The Sacred Congregation for Religious, however, has decreed that even the founders of Orders are subject to this general legislation, unless an indult has been obtained from the Holy See[36] or unless the Constitutions provide for their permanent tenure. In practice, a six- or twelve-year term for the supreme moderator of exempt religious is a common arrangement. The Jesuits and the Redemptorists, however, elect their general superiors for life.[37]

D. Obligation to Accept the Office

The legislation of the Code is very specific about the acquisition of the powers of government and their acceptance by the newly appointed or elected candidate. If no confirmation is required, the newly-elected general superior immediately acquires full powers of government; whenever the election requires a subsequent confirmation, the newly-elected superior acquires only the *ius ad rem* without being able validly to exercise immediately the powers of his office.[38] Upon notification of his election or nomination, every appointee to a superiorship is granted the right to renounce his office.[39] Among the pre-Code authorities, however, opinions differed concerning the refusal of a valid nomination or election to an office. According to some, the candidate could withhold his acceptance only before confirmation was obtained, for the election became consummated through the confirmation, and a spiritual bond came into existence which was not soluble through any act of the appointee alone.[40] To support their position, they adduced the rule of law, *"beneficium invito non datur,"* with the proviso that in cases of necessity or of great

---

[35] Chelodi-Ciprotti, *De personis,* p. 398.

[36] S. C. de Religiosis, 6 martii, 1922—*AAS,* XIV (1922), 163.

[37] Abbo-Hannan, *The Sacred Canons,* I, 514.

[38] Can. 176, § 3.

[39] Can. 175.

[40] Reiffenstuel, *Jus Canonicum Universum,* Lib. I, tit. 6, n. 34, p. 275; Schmalzgrueber, *Ius Ecclesiasticum Universum,* Lib. I, tit. 6, n. 70, p. 356; Donatus, *Rerum Regularium Quadripartita Praxis Resolutoria* (4 vols., Neapoli, 1652-1661), II, tract. I, q. iv, p. 125 (hereafter cited *Rerum Regularium Praxis*); Piatus, *Praelectiones Iuris Regularis* (3 ed., 2 vols., Parisiis, 1906), I, 582-583 (hereafter cited *Praelectiones*).

utility for the Church the superiors could command acceptance of the office. According to others, the candidate was free to advance his reasons for refusing the office to which he was duly elected, but was obliged to accept it if his superior insisted in virtue of obedience.[41]

Under the present law concerning elections the general provisions of the Code must be followed unless the particular Constitutions determine otherwise.[42] Since the Code grants the candidate the right to renounce his election to an office, the one newly-elected as general superior has the privilege of accepting or refusing the burdens of the office.[43] If, however, the supreme moderator was appointed by a higher superior, i.e., the Pope, the general rules of the Code concerning elections would not hold, and the appointed religious would not be free to renounce his office.[44] Acceptance in this case would be a matter not of choice but of obedience. Nevertheless, even in this case the candidate has the right to explain his reasons for declining the office before acceding to the wishes of his superior.[45]

A purely moral problem may arise when the newly elected general superior knows himself to be unfit for the office, or if he foresees that the office would be an occasion of sin. If the lack of fitness arises from a publicly known impediment, then recourse is open for a dispensation; if the lack of fitness is a hidden fault, the candidate may accept the office without disclosing his lack of qualification, since no one is obliged to defame himself.[46] Whenever the candidate knows that the office to which he has been appointed or elected is an occasion of sin for himself, he may accept the office and take positive measures to remove the proximate occasion. The common good of the community which justified his election takes precedence over the private good of the religious himself.

---

[41] Appeltern, *Compendium Praelectionum Iuris Regularis* (2 ed., Parisiis, 1913), p. 370 (hereafter cited *Compendium*).

[42] Can. 507, § 1.

[43] Canons 175 and 184.

[44] Larraona, "Consultationes," *CpR*, II (1921), 341.

[45] Wernz-Vidal, *Ius Canonicum*, III, 108.

[46] Piatus, *Praelectiones*, I, 553; Goyeneche, "Consultationes," *CpR*, VI (1925), 207.

CHAPTER VI

THE LEGISLATIVE POWER OF
THE SUPREME MODERATOR

Having considered the preliminary notions of the jurisdictional and dominative power exercised by the supreme moderator, and having examined the legislation of the Code concerning his qualifications for the office of general superior, the writer will attempt to present a detailed treatment of his powers, obligations and privileges according to the legislative, judicial and executive functions he performs. By analyzing the supreme moderator's rights and duties in the next three chapters, the writer proposes to draw a composite picture of the supreme moderator's office as determined in the common law of the Church.

A. Possession of Legislative Power by Supreme Moderator

A legislator is one who is able to command and enjoin efficaciously for the common good. Consequently, this legislative power is not the possession of a private person, but resides in a public official within a juridically perfect society. Possession of legislative authority or of the power to enact laws is one of the principal functions of public jurisdictional power, which has for its purpose the direction of the subjects to their ultimate end.[1] The legislative function, however, is separable from jurisdictional power and is not necessarily connected with it, so that a superior who possesses jurisdiction may nevertheless be lacking in the authority to enact laws.

Since the supreme moderator of an exempt religious Order

---

[1] Michiels, *Normae Generales,* I, 135: "Iamvero, potestas leges ferendi est attributio hujus auctoritatis publicae seu jurisdictionis in foro externo specialis et exclusiva, et indubitanter quidem, praecipua, (cui per modum necessariae consequentiae adduntur: potestas leges latas exequendi, de earum observatione iudicandi, et transgressionem coercendi)."

possesses ecclesiastical jurisdiction in the internal and external forum,[2] it follows that there is inherent in his office the power to enact true ecclesiastical law. Moreover, the analogy between the relationship of the general superior to his subjects and the relationship of the local ordinary to his subjects [3] argues in favor of his possession of the legislative power which is specifically granted by the Code to the local ordinary.[4] To ignore this analogy would be completely unwarranted.[5] Nowhere, however, in the Code is it stated explicitly that the Supreme Moderator has or does not have legislative power. Though the Code does not grant this power to the general superior specifically as it does in the case of the local ordinary, it likewise does not deny the absolute capacity of the general superior to possess the right to enact laws. Since this is the case, the principle of canon 501, § 1, must be applied, and the actual existence of legislative authority must be sought in the constitutions of the respective Orders.

In practice the Constitutions of the various exempt Orders restrict the exercise of legislative authority to the general chapters.[6] In only two instances have particular Constitutions granted legislative power to their general superiors, namely, those of the Carmelites and those of the Jesuits.[7] In consequence of this restriction true legislation in religious communities, understood in the strict sense of the enacting of laws properly so-called, emanates from the Holy See or from the general chapters. It is found in the Code, in the decrees of the Sacred Congregations, and in the canonically approved Rules and Constitutions.

B. The Power of Issuing Precepts

The power of imposing a precept is closely allied to the power of enacting a law. A precept may be defined as a command given

---

[2] Can. 501, 1.

[3] Can. 198, 1.

[4] Can. 335, 1.

[5] Can. 20.

[6] Fanfani, *De iure religiosorum,* 67; Vermeersch, *De Religiosis,* I, 252; Wernz-Vidal, *Ius Canonicum,* III, 109; Piatus, *Praelectiones,* I, 614.

[7] Schaefer, *De religiosis,* p. 227; Vermeersch-Creusen, *Epitome,* I, n. 574; Piatus, *Praelectiones,* I, 604.

to his subjects by a competent superior.[8] It is usually an order which is lacking in some quality essential to a law.[9] It is not, however, to be confused with a counsel, exhortation, admonition or suggestion, since it must necessarily possess the quality of an order or command, which is lacking in these.

To distinguish clearly between a law and a precept it is necessary to keep in mind the points of similarity and difference existing between them. A precept, like a law, must always be given by a legitimate superior, i.e., by one having the title by reason of office, and not by reason of dignity stemming from orders, age or education. A juridical relationship between the superior and subject created by law, not by emergency or moral consideration, is the basis for a law and a precept.[10]

Unlike the power of enacting a law, which has its only source in the power of jurisdiction, the power of imposing a precept is inherent not only in the power of jurisdiction but in the dominative power possessed by all religious superiors as well.[11] Depending on its source, the precept may be either a dominative precept or a jurisdictional precept. In the case of the latter, the precept may furthermore be divided into legislative, administrative, or judicial, and can be issued for either the external or the internal forum.[12] The supreme moderator of exempt religious Orders, in view of enjoying jurisdiction and dominative power, can therefore impose precepts of a jurisdictional or of a dominative nature in accordance with the power he chooses to use.

Another basic distinction is that, unlike a law, the precept is not of necessity directed to the promotion of the common welfare of

---

[8] All standard definitions of a precept agree essentially, if not in the specific differences introduced for the sake of clarification. Representative definitions are those of Michiels, *Normae Generales,* I, 507: "Jussum rationabile a competente Superiore singulis datum"; Roelker, *Precepts* (Paterson, N.J., 1955), p. 3: "A precept is a command given by a competent Superior to an individual person;" Wernz-Vidal, *Ius Canonicum,* I, 256: "Iussum ad tempus vel in perpetuum singularibus personis aut absque perpetuitate toti communitati publicatum."

[9] Abbo-Hannan, *The Sacred Canons,* I, 47.

[10] Roelker, *Precepts,* p. 4.

[11] Vermeersch-Creusen, *Epitome,* I, n. 105.

[12] Abbo-Hannan, *The Sacred Canons,* I, 48.

the community, but seeks the good of the individual.[13]   Furthermore, all laws can be judicially enforced and do not cease to bind
with the expiration of the authority issuing them; precepts, on the
other hand, unless certain legal requirements are observed, are not
subject to judicial enforcement, and their obligatory force ceases
with the cessation of the authority of the superior.[14]   Lastly, a
precept also differs from a law in that its obligatory force is not
delimited by territorial boundaries, but the obligation which it
imposes is personal and binds the subject everywhere.[15]

The supreme moderator exercises his jurisdictional power not
only for the common good of the community but also for the
individual and private good of each of the members of his community.   His first duty to the community is discharged through
the medium of laws; the second, through the use of precepts.
Since religious superiors, unlike local ordinaries, do not possess
radical power in the constitution of the Church, but have power
only by the concession of the Supreme Pontiff, the power of imposing a jurisdictional precept is enjoyed by the general superior
in virtue of the concession made in canon 501, § 1.[16]   The scope
of his preceptive power, like that of his legislative power, is to be
exercised simply in accord with the limitations as delineated in the
Constitutions of his Order.

The dominative power of the general superior is also a source
of precepts since it rests upon the free agreement of the religious
to obey their superiors.   The dominative precepts which stem
from its exercise by the supreme moderator extend over all the
provinces, houses and members of the community.[17]   The scope
of the exercise of dominative power in the imposition of dominative precepts is limited only by the specific purpose of the society
itself.   Within this limit the choice of means to achieve the
society's end rests with the superior, who may issue commands
insuring its attainment.

---

[13] Jone, *Commentarium*, I, 44.

[14] Can. 24: "Praecepta, singulis data, eos quibus dantur, ubique urgent,
sed iudicialiter urgeri nequeunt et cessant resoluto iure praecipientis, nisi per
legitimum documentum aut coram duobus testibus imposita fuerint."

[15] Michiels, *Normae Generales*, pp. 510–511.

[16] Wernz-Vidal, *Ius Canonicum*, III, 87.

[17] Can. 502.

These jurisdictional and dominative precepts may be given either to individuals or to an entire community, and thus there is reflected the twofold division of individual precepts, and of common or general precepts.

The canonical legislation concerning individual precepts and the manner of their imposition is contained in canon 24. Whenever the supreme moderator issues a precept, be it jurisdictional or dominative,[18] it is presumed to be personal rather than territorial, and accordingly binds the subject everywhere. Its binding force, however, ceases with the cessation of the authority of the general superior, unless it was given by way of a document or before two witnesses. These precepts can likewise not be enforced juridically unless the same legal formalities were observed.

Common precepts, on the other hand, are those which are imposed upon subjects not as individuals but as collective units. A common precept is not to be understood as a multiplication of individual precepts, so that all the subjects are affected, but must be considered as a command of the superior by which an obligation is imposed upon the subjects considered as a group.[19] In their final analysis common precepts are in reality laws with the emphasis placed upon the person rather than upon the territory, as is the case with laws.[20]

In summarizing the conclusions concerning the preceptive power of the supreme moderator one can set down the following broad principles:

---

[18] Canonists disagree on whether or not canon 24 legislates for dominative as well as jurisdictional precepts. Michiels (*Normae Generales,* I, 510) and Roelker (*Precepts,* pp. 30–41) maintain that canon 24 relates also to dominative precepts. Opposed to this view are the opinions of Vermeersch-Creusen (*Epitome,* I, nn. 106–107), Van Hove (*Commentarium Lovaniense in Codicem Iuris Canonici,* Vol. I, tom. II, *De Legibus* [Mechliniae-Romae, 1930], 362–363 [hereafter cited as *De Legibus*]), Onclin (*De Territoriali vel Personali Legis Indole* [Gemblaci, 1938], pp. 364–365) and Coronata (*Institutiones,* I, 48). The unqualified use of the term *"praecepta"* in the canon and the untoward consequences which would follow from the non-inclusion of dominative precepts under the same rule militates in favor of the opinion that dominative as well as jurisdictional precepts are regulated by the legislation contained in canon 24.

[19] Roelker, *Precepts,* pp. 36–37.

[20] Michiels, *Normae Generales,* I, 519–520.

1. Preceptive power is a necessary adjunct to the principle that all societies require authoritative leadership. It serves as a supplement to the superior's power of enacting laws, especially if for reasons of expediency a precept will serve the desired purpose better than a law will serve it.

2. It is of the utmost importance to determine whether the supreme moderator in expressing his will intends to impose a precept or desires simply to admonish, to counsel and to exhort his subjects. A practical norm may be applied with reference to the content matter of his expression: if the matter deals with religious observance, it may be assumed that a precept was imposed; if the content matter is purely ascetical in nature, most probably a counsel, admonition or exhortation was intended.

3. A command of the supreme moderator may oblige in virtue of the vow of obedience or it may proceed from the jurisdictional or dominative power he enjoys. Unless the contrary is proved, the precept is of a dominative nature.

4. The supreme moderator's precepts when given to individuals are temporary and expire with his death, resignation, transfer or loss of office, unless they are imposed in accord with the prescribed juridic form of canon 24, which then endows these precepts with a perpetual obligation. Common precepts and individual precepts imposed by the supreme moderator not because of personal reasons but in consideration of an office, must of their very nature be vested with some stability and permanence, and hence are generally issued in legal form. The reason for this procedure must be sought in the purpose underlying the issuance of these precepts, namely, the promotion of the general welfare of the Order and the obtaining of good government in the external forum. To secure these ends, the precepts must continue in force even after the general superior has lapsed from office and they must continue to bind those who succeed in the office in consideration of which the precept was imposed.

5. In giving a precept the supreme moderator does not oblige his subject in conscience, unless he specifically and expressly imposes such an obligation. If the existence of such an obligation is verified, then a grave matter presupposes a grave obligation, a slight matter, a light obligation, unless the wording or the circum-

stances favor another interpretation. Even if he commands, however, *in conscientia* or *sub peccato*, the obligation is not in consequence thereof imposed in virtue of the vow of obedience, unless this condition was expressly attached to the command.

C. The Power of Granting Dispensations

Since the granting of dispensations is intimately connected with the legislative power of the general superior and is of the greatest importance in the exercise of the pastoral office of any superior, the question of the power of dispensing is not theoretical, but of utmost practical import. The granting of a dispensation is always an act of jurisdiction, and hence the dispensatory power may be exercised directly over subjects only.[21] It requires an act of the will on the part of a lawful superior, who removes or suspends, in particular cases, the obligation of a law in favor of a physical individual or a moral personality. This jurisdictional quality of a granted dispensation distinguishes it from other juridical relaxations of a law which do not presuppose the power of jurisdiction, e.g., excuse, epikeia, license or permission. Consequently, also, the requirement of the actual intervention of the will of the superior in relaxing the moral bond of the law implies that a dispensation cannot be presumed.[22]

Canon 80 supplies a brief canonical definition of dispensation together with a general indication of those who are empowered by law to grant a dispensation.[23] A dispensation is a relaxation of a law in a particular case, i.e., a freeing or exemption from its observance. Since "law" is not qualified by any restrictive words or clauses, it includes every species of law without reservation. The proper object of this release or relaxation is the dissolution of the legal bond or obligation which is proper to a specific law, be it a preceptive or a prohibitive, a penal or an invalidating law.[24] The phrase "in a particular case" refers not only to an individual single act, but also to a series of acts to be repeatedly performed over the

---

[21] Can. 201, § 1.

[22] Coronata, *Institutiones,* I, 118.

[23] "Dispensatio, seu legis in casu speciali relaxatio, concedi potest a conditore legis, ab eius successore vel Superiore, nec non ab illo cui iidem facultatem dispensandi concesserint."

[24] Michiels, *Normae generales,* II, 453.

period of time (*cum tractu successivo*) for which a dispensation is requested.[25]

Notwithstanding the official definition of dispensation as given in canon 80, the Code persists in using the term loosely, giving it meanings incompatible with its definition.[26] A dispensation, in a less proper meaning, is granted from a vow or from an oath, although neither is a law. Again, they entail obligations binding by divine law, and hence remain outside the scope of a direct human jurisdiction.[27] In both of these instances there is actually no relaxation of the divine law; rather, the object itself or the cause of the obligation subsides, thus obviating the application of the divine law.[28] Similarly the divine law of the indissolubility of marriage is not relaxed when a dispensation is granted in the case of a *ratum non consummatum* marriage.[29] In penal legislation examples of the analogical usage of dispensation are found in the remission of vindictive penalties.[30] Obviously one cannot speak of the relaxation of a law which already has been violated, but one

[25] Cicognani, *Canon Law* (ed., Westminster, Maryland: The Newman Press, Reprint, 1949), 834.

[26] Roelker, "The Use of the Term '*Dispensatio*' in the Code of Canon Law," *The Jurist*, X (1950), 138–151. The author concludes his investigation with the following observation: "By far in the larger number of times the term is used it means a release. In the sense of release from law, the term is extensively used. Considerable use is found also in the sense of release from the bond of contract. More sparing use, however, is found where the term means either release from the bond of penalty or is used to describe an act of administration. The two separate uses of the term in the sense of release and of administration are not univocal. Some analogy, however, can be seen in the meaning of the term in the sense of release and in its classical use in canon 912."

[27] Canons 1311; 1313; 1319, n. 4; 1320.

[28] Canonists differ in their explanations of the manner in which the legal bond is relaxed in a dispensation from a vow or from an oath. Cf. Van Hove, *Commentarium Lavaniense in Codicem Iuris Canonici*, Vol. I, Tom. V., *De Privilegiis—De Dispensationibus* (Mechliniae-Romae, 1939), p. 306 (hereafter cited as *De privilegiis et dispensationibus*); Michiels, *Normae Generales*, II, 453–454; Coronata, *Institutiones*, I, 106; footnote 3; Chelodi-Ciprotti, *De personis*, p. 155, footnote 1.

[29] Canons 1119 and 1985.

[30] Canons 2236, § 1 and 2289.

can seek and intend the removal of a juridic effect which arises
from the violation of a penal law.[31]

According to canon 80 the power of dispensing is vested in the
legislator, in his successor, in his superior, and also in one to
whom any of these has given the faculty of dispensing.[32] The
legislator and his successor dispense in virtue of a proper ordinary
authority (*potestas ordinaria propria*), for a law obtains its binding power from the will of the legislator, and consequently its total
or partial relaxation is also dependent on his will. In accordance
with the rule of law which states that *"omnis res, per quascumque
causas nascitur, per easdem dissolvitur,"* [33] the legislator undeniably possesses full power for dispensing from laws of his own
making. His superior enjoys the same power of dispensing, since
all subordinates in the performance of their acts are dependent on
him,[34] while his successor assumes the same prerogative in virtue
of the legal rule, *"ille qui in ius succedit alterius, eo iure, quo ille,
uti debebit."* [35] A lesser superior may dispense from a law of his
superior either in virtue of his participated ordinary authority
(*potestas ordinaria participata*) which he receives with the office
he holds, or in virtue of a delegated power (*potestas delegata*)
which he obtains as a delegate of the superior. This transference
of dispensatory power is founded on the classical juristic principle
"potest quis per alium, quod potest per seipsum." [36]

---

[31] Michiels, *Normae Generales*, II, 677–678; Ojetti, *Commentarium*, I,
325. Some canonists, however, uphold the position that the remission of
vindictive penalties is a true dispensation. Cf. Van Hove, *De privilegiis et
dispensationibus*, pp. 310–312; Blat, *Commentarium*, VI, 56; Christ, *Dispensation from Vindictive Penalties*, The Catholic University of America
Canon Law Studies, No. 174 (Washington, D.C.: The Catholic University
of America Press, 1943), pp. 67–69.

[32] "   concedi potest a conditore legis, ab eius successore vel Superiore,
nec non ab illo, cui iidem facultatem dispensandi concesserint."

[33] C. 1, X, *de regulis iuris*, V, 41. Cf. also c. 2, I, *de electione et electi
potestate*, 3, in Clem.; c. 16, X, *de maioritate et oboedientia*, 1, 33.

[34] C. 4, X, *de electione et electi potestate*, I, 6.

[35] Reg. 46, *R.J.*, in VIº.

[36] Reg. 68, *R.J.*, in VIº.

1. Dispensation from the General Laws of the Church

a. Pre-Code Legislation

Exempt religious Orders, as represented by the Mendicants in the thirteenth century, claimed certain dispensatory powers for their prelates as a natural consequence not only of their privilege of exemption but also of their status of juridically established institutes. The major superiors of exempt religious Orders assumed, or there were acknowledged for them, episcopal or quasi-episcopal powers, inclusive of the exercise of dispensatory powers enjoyed by local ordinaries.

In Decretal law, prelates subordinate to the Pope possessed dispensatory powers, which they exercised solely in such cases as were tacitly or expressly admitted by law.[37] Alexander III (1159–1181) permitted bishops to dispense priests who had incurred an irregularity by attempting marriage,[38] clerics who had incurred deposition by participating in a duel[39] and clerics who had been subjected to suspension for adultery or also lesser crimes.[40] At the time of Innocent III (1198–1216) the Decretal law formally acknowledged entrenched custom as being sufficient to demonstrate the existence of dispensatory powers for ordinaries.[41] By the end of the thirteenth century the question was no longer *whether* the bishops could dispense *in iure communi,* but *when* they enjoyed this power. The controversy that ensued divided the canonists into two classes: the first contended that the ordinaries were allowed to dispense only in the cases authorized in the law; the second upheld the position that all episcopal dispensations were licit unless they were prohibited by the law.[42]

When Gregory IX on August 21, 1231, conceded the privilege

---

[37] *Glossa ordinaria* ad c. 15, X, *de temporibus ordinationum et qualitate ordinandorum,* I, 11, s. v. *permissa.*

[38] C. 4, X, *de clericis coniugatis,* III, 3.

[39] C. 1, X, *de clericis pugnantibus in duello,* V, 14.

[40] C. 4, X, *de iudiciis,* II, 1.

[41] C. 9, X, *de officio iudici ordinarii,* I, 31; c. 13, X, *de foro competenti,* II, 2.

[42] A brief summary of this controversy is given by Cappiello, *De Ordinariorum Dispensandi Facultate ad normam can. 81,* The Catholic University of America Canon Law Studies, no. 323 (Washington, D.C.: The Catholic University of America Press, 1952), pp. 44–47.

of exemption to the Order of Friars Minor with his Bull *Nimis iniqua*,[43] the episcopal jurisdictional powers on the part of the major superiors of the Order were recognized.[44] Thenceforth the Decretals officially treated of religious law and privilege.[45] Usually the dispensatory powers of the religious prelates were regulated and determined by particular law, though an occasional specific reference to them appeared also in the common law. Regular prelates, for example, could permit the intellectually backward to be ordained.[46] The only restriction upon this dispensatory power was established by Pope Innocent III, who declared that only laws pertaining to the essence of the religious state were not amenable to dispensations granted by regular prelates.[47] The Council of Trent reaffirmed this principle of limitation;[48] it did not grant definite and specific dispensatory powers to any of the major superiors of exempt religious.

The appearance of the Constitution *Romani Pontificis* of Pius V on July 21, 1571, marks the most explicit statement of the power Regular Prelates possessed over the general laws of the Church. In virtue of this constitution religious superiors in the Dominican Order were given powers of absolving and of dispensing which paralleled the powers enjoyed by the bishops over their own subjects.[49] Thenceforth pre-Code canonists were guided by this principle, for through a mutual interparticipation of privileges the superiors of all exempt Orders obtained the same dis-

---

[43] *Bullarium Franciscanum*, I, 74.

[44] C. 24, *de electione et electi potestate*, I, 6 in VI°.

[45] Cf. especially the *Decretales Gregorii IX*, titles 31–32, 34–37 and 50 of the Third Book, and titles 9, 31, 33 of the Fifth Book; *Liber VI Decretalium Bonifacii VIII*, titles 14, 16–18, 23–24 of the Third Book, and titles 5–7 of the Fifth Book; *Extravagantes Communes*, titles 8–9 of the Third Book.

[46] C. 4, *de temporibus ordinationum et qualitate ordinandorum*, I, 9 in VI°.

[47] C. 6, *de statu monachorum*, III, 35.

[48] Sess. XXV, *de regularibus et monialibus*, c. 1.

[49] "Ipsi per se ipso idem omnino possint . . . in subditos, quod possunt Episcopi in clericos sibi subiectos, tam quoad absolvendi et dispensandi huiusmodi, quam alias quascumque facultates . . . etiam perpetuo concedimus, et indulgemus ac etiam declaramus."—*Bullarum Diplomatum et Privilegiorum Sanctorum Romanorum Pontificum Taurinensis Editio* (24 vols. et Appendix, Augustae Taurinorum, 1857–1872), VIII, 931; Piatus, *Praelectiones*, I, 607; Donatus, *Rerum Regularium Praxis*, II, 173.

pensatory authority as that which had been granted to the Dominican prelates.[50]   In 1725 the Premonstratensian Order received a decree from the Holy See whereby the superior's faculties for dispensing were restricted to individual cases within his jurisdiction.[51]   Benedict XIV (1740–1758), however, granted major superiors the faculty of dispensing the entire community from an ecclesiastical law, provided that it was necessitated by a grave and urgent reason.[52]   In case of doubt either concerning the need of a dispensation or the gravity and urgency of the reasons for its granting, the canonists adopted the principle that the reservation of the right to grant a dispensation implied a restriction of one's power, which, in turn, obtained only when a dispensation was certainly not needed.[53]

b. Legislation of the Code

The legislation of the Code does not distinguish between the powers of dispensing as vested in the supreme moderator and the provincial. Since each of these superiors is designated as a major superior,[54] as an ordinary [55] and as a prelate,[56] the same jurisdictional powers and privileges are theirs, with some restrictions, as are granted to bishops. Nowhere in the Code does one find mention of dispensatory powers which are exclusively restricted to the supreme moderator or to the provincial. By reason of his office, however, the extent of the general superior's dispensatory powers is vaster, since it embraces all provinces, houses and members of the Order, while the provincial's powers are circumscribed by the limitations of his charge.[57]

The second great difference in the dispensatory powers of the supreme moderator from those which are enjoyed by the provincial must be sought in the particular legislation and apostolic

---

[50] Donatus, *Rerum Regularium Praxis*, II, 173–175.

[51] S. C. C., 15 dec. 1725—*Fontes*, n. 3306.

[52] Ep. encycl. *Non ambigimus*, 30 maii, 1741—*Fontes*, n. 308.

[53] Reiffenstuel, *Ius Canonicum Universum*, I, 474; Schmalzgrueber, *Ius Canonicum Ecclesiasticum*, I, 59; Piatus, *Praelectiones*, I, 607.

[54] Can. 488, n. 8.

[55] Can. 198, § 1.

[56] Can. 110.

[57] Can. 502.

privileges, wherein the general superior is usually favored. Since, however, in most cases these privileges can, through an act of delegation, be shared with others, and *de facto* are so delegated to the provincial and local superiors by the supreme moderator, no actual difference exists in the exercise of the powers of dispensing. Because of these privileges granted to religious superiors, the jurisdictional powers of the major superior for the granting of dispensations for his subjects is more extensive in many Orders than that possessed by a bishop over his diocese.[58]

The pre-Code teaching of the canonists which denied to ordinaries and to major superiors of exempt religious the power of dispensing from the common law of the Church is upheld in the Code. It, however, recognizes their right to do so in urgent cases under certain conditions.[59] When these prescribed conditions are verified, canon 81 concedes this power in a "particular case," i.e., when a dispensation is granted to particular persons for a just cause.[60] Consequently, the relaxation of a law in favor of all his subjects is definitely not within the competence of the ordinary or of those who enjoy episcopal powers.

A dispensation from the common law of the Church may be given by prelates below the Supreme Pontiff if by law the power was explicitly granted to them. In some instances the Code grants this faculty to local ordinaries only.[61] At other times the Code grants this dispensatory power to all ordinaries indiscriminately.[62] In two instances the Code limits its concession of the dispensatory power to the supreme moderator of exempt religious or to the major superiors of the Order. The supreme moderator has the general faculty, enjoyed also by religious superiors in particular

---

[58] Coronata, *Institutiones,* I, 122.

[59] Can. 81: "A generalibus Ecclesiae legibus Ordinarii infra Romanum Pontificem dispensare nequeunt, ne in casu quidem peculiari, nisi haec potestas eisdem fuerit explicite vel implicite concessa, aut nisi difficilis sit recursus ad Sanctam Sedem et simul in mora sit periculum gravis damni, et de dispensatione agatur quae a Sede Apostolica concedi solet."

[60] Vermeersch-Creusen, *Epitome,* I, n. 174.

[61] Cf. Canons 130, § 1; 131, § 3; 1028; 1043; 1045, §§ 1 and 2. The quinquennial faculties which the Holy See grants to bishops are another example of such a concession in favor of local ordinaries alone.

[62] Canons 15, 972, § 1; 990, § 1; 998, § 1; 1245, § 2; 1313; 1320; 2237.

cases, prudently to dispense students from some communal practices, even from the obligation of nocturnal recitation of the Divine Office in choir.[63]   All major superiors likewise are granted the power to free priests religious from their obligation of the quinquennial examinations for a grave cause.[64]

Secondly, ordinaries may dispense from the common laws of the Church if an implicit concession to do so has been granted by the Code.   An implicit concession is one which, though not specifically conceded, is nevertheless indubitably contained in another faculty explicitly given by law.   Its relation to the explicit concession is that of an effect to a cause, a conclusion to its principle, a part to the whole, a species to its genus, or a *conditio sine qua non* for the understanding or exercise of the explicitly granted faculty.[65]   The interrelationship flows from the very nature of two laws, so that the relaxation of one hinges upon the dispensation granted for another, e.g., if an ordinary is granted the explicit faculty to dispense one of his priests from the law forbidding the plurality of residential benefices, he would also be implicitly authorized to dispense him from the law of continually residing in one or the other of these benefices.[66]

Similarly the power of dispensing is implicitly granted by the Code when its provisions contain such phrases as *"nisi dispensatum fuerit," "donec dispensetur," "dispensari posse,"* or some similar expressions which would be completely unnecessary if the power of dispensing in these instances were restricted to the Supreme Pontiff alone.   In practice, these canons, *servatis ser-*

---

[63] Canon 589, 2: "Studiorum tempore magistris et alumnis officia ne imponantur quae a studio eos avocent vel scholam quoque modo impediant; supremus autem Moderator et in casibus particularibus alii quoque Superiores possunt pro sua prudentia eos a nonnullis communitatis actibus, etiam a choro, praesertim nocturnis horis, eximere, quoties id studiis excolendis necessarium videatur."

[64] Can. 590.

[65] Michiels, *Normae Generales,* II, 481: "Implicita concessio potestatis dispensandi tunc habetur, quando collatio potestatis est in plico verborum occulta, de facto tamen contenta, vel ut effectus in causa, conclusio in principio, vel ut pars in toto, species in genere, vel ut conditio, sine qua potestas explicite concessa intelligi vel exerceri nequeat."

[66] Canons 1411, n. 3 and 1439.

vandis, are also applicable to the supreme moderator's power of dispensing for the benefit of the religious under his care.[67]

In the absence of an explicit or of an implicit concession of dispensatory power over the common laws of the Church, the Code provides for an extension of this faculty to urgent cases. Provision is made in canon 81 whereby ordinaries are empowered to grant any dispensation which the Holy See itself is wont to grant, if a situation arises in which it would be difficult to have recourse to the Holy See to obtain the required dispensation and at the same time there would be danger of serious harm in case of delay. For validity all three of these conditions must be fulfilled before the ordinary can grant a dispensation from a common law of the Church.

Some specific powers for dispensing as mentioned in the Code are shared by all religious superiors, major and minor. Within their own sphere of competence all religious superiors may dispense from the common law of the observance of the feasts and days of fast and/or abstinence.[68] This dispensation may be granted in favor of all their subjects who fall under the extension of canon 514, § 1, as well as individual families or groups within their jurisdiction. Canonists hold the opinion that, given a sufficient cause, a provincial may dispense individual religious houses of his province, since each house can be considered to constitute a family within the province.[69] On the basis of reasoning *a pari,* the supreme moderator is able to grant a similar dispensation to an entire province under his jurisdiction, since it comprises a small family within the Order.

All religious superiors may dispense from the non-reserved vows of their subjects, inclusive of the persons mentioned in canon 514, § 1, whenever a just cause exists and the rights of a third party are not violated.[70] This faculty includes the power to

---

[67] An excellent summary of the implicit concession of dispensatory power in the Code is found in Reilly, *The General Norms of Dispensation,* The Catholic University of America Canon Law Studies, No. 119 (Washington, D.C.: The Catholic University of America Press, 1930), pp. 68–72.

[68] Can. 1245, §§ 1 and 3.

[69] Vermeersch-Creusen, *Epitome,* II, n. 556; O'Brien, *The Provincial Superior,* p. 46.

[70] Can. 1313, n. 2.

modify or to mitigate the obligation of the vow, even though a sufficient cause to justify the granting of a dispensation does not exist.[71] Similarly obligations arising from a promissory oath may be set aside through an act of annulment, dispensation or commutation by religious superiors.[72] As a rule, however, particular legislation reserves the power of relaxing vows and oaths by way of dispensation to the major superiors of the Institute.

In the legislation of the Code which grants specific dispensatory powers to the major superiors of religious Orders, the right is a cumulative right, which either the supreme moderator or the provincial may exercise, unless particular law imposes a limitation on the competence of one or the other superior. Common law grants such general faculties to major superiors in several specific canons. These may be summarized as follows:

1. Ordinaries, inclusive of the ecclesiastical superiors named in canon 198, § 1, are empowered to dispense from laws, even invalidating and disqualifying laws, in the case of a doubt of fact, provided that the Holy See is wont to grant dispensations in this matter.[73] In virtue of this faculty the major superior can render a decision regarding the existence as well as the cessation of infamy of fact,[74] or dispense from the irregularity arising from a bodily defect concerning which there is a positive objective doubt.[75]

2. The major superior and his delegate have the faculty to dispense their subjects from all irregularities arising from an occult delict, with the exception of the ones mentioned in canon 985, n. 4 (voluntary homicide or the procuring of an abortion) and of such as have been brought to the judicial forum's attention.[76]

3. In occult cases, without prejudice to canons 2254 and 2290, the major superiors of exempt religious, and also their delegates, can remit all *latae sententiae* penalties established by the common

---

[71] Can. 1314.

[72] Can. 1320.

[73] Can. 15.

[74] Canons 2293, § 3 and 2295.

[75] Can. 984, n. 2.

[76] Can. 990, § 1.

law, except the censures which are reserved to the Apostolic See in a most special manner (*specialissimo modo*) or in a special manner (*speciali modo*).[77]

4. In public cases, not only ordinaries but also the major superiors [78] can remit all *latae sententiae* penalties established by the common law, with the exception of the following:

(1) cases already brought to trial; [79]

(2) censures reserved to the Holy See;

(3) penalties entailing disqualification for benefices, offices, dignities and posts in the Church, depriving one of electoral rights both active and passive, involving perpetual suspension, legal infamy (*infamia iuris*), and the deprivation of the right of patronage and of a privilege or favor granted by the Apostolic See.[80] In these cases, since the major superiors exercise ordinary power, they may delegate their faculties to others.[81]

5. The major superior, either personally or through a delegate, can dispense his subjects from the prohibition of reading individual books which are forbidden by the general law of the Code or which are condemned in a decree of the Holy See, but only in individual and urgent cases.[82]

More numerous are the supreme moderator's powers of dispensing from the general laws of the Church when one looks to the powers that receive mention in the canonically approved particular Constitutions or that are acquired by way of privilege or indult. Unless these powers have been expressly revoked in the Code, they may be used by the superior general.[83] In view of their great multitude and diversity they lie outside the scope of

---

[77] Can. 2237, § 2.

[78] Augustine, *Commentary*, VIII, 110.

[79] Canons 1725, nn. 1 and 2; 2210, § 1. Some canonists contend that the competence of the major superiors in such cases is excluded even if the trial is instituted before a secular judge endowed with competent jurisdiction. Cf. Abbo-Hannan, *The Sacred Canons*, II, 816, footnote 6.

[80] Can. 2237, § 1, nn. 1–3.

[81] Canons 197, § 1 and 199, § 1; Beste, *Introductio*, p. 920; Coronata, *Institutiones*, IV, 140.

[82] Can. 1402, § 1. Cf. Coronata, *Institutiones*, II, 346; Vermeersch-Creusen, *Epitome*, II, n. 736.

[83] Can. 4.

interest for the present dissertation, but one may ascertain them in the many excellent *Compendia* of privileges of regulars which are readily available for reference.[84]

In fine, it can be said that the present law of the Code retains the historical powers of the supreme moderator for dispensing from the common law of the Church under certain express conditions. The juridic identification of the general superior's office with that of an ordinary warrants for the supreme moderator all the powers of dispensing which by law are granted to ordinaries. In specific canons of the Code wherein major superiors cumulatively share the faculty of dispensing their subjects, the powers of the supreme moderator differ from those of the provincial only in their extension, as it is circumscribed by the segment or the whole of the community they govern. Nowhere does the Code grant peculiar dispensatory powers to the supreme moderator to the exclusion of the provincial, or *vice versa.* Particular law, however, does provide instances wherein the supreme moderator receives specific dispensatory powers over and above those which are granted to other superiors within the community, or it reserves for the higher superior simply a competency that is shared equally by all major superiors according to the common law.

2. Dispensation from the Special Law of the Order

The special law of an exempt religious Order is to be found in its Rule, its Constitutions and its general or provincial Statutes. If the Rule and the Constitutions are approved *in forma specifica* by the Holy See, and this occurs without exception in all exempt religious Orders, they become true pontifical or ecclesiastical laws. Consequently their obligation within their respective jurisdictional areas is parallel to the obligation of the Code for the universal

---

[84] Among the more notable comprehensive works delineating the privileges of regulars for dispensing from the common law of the Church, the following are of primary importance: Rodericus, *Nova Collectio et Compilatio privilegiorum Apostolicorum Regularium Mendicantium et Non-Mendicantium, praesertim in quibus ipsae Religiones communicant* (Venetiis, 1611); Lezana, *Mare Magnum Ordinum Praedicatorum, Minorum, Eremitarum Sancti Augustini, Carmelitanorum cum ipsorum Regula, Servitarum et Minimorum* (Venetiis, 1653); Alvissenet, *De privilegiis Ordinum Regularium* (Venetiis, 1661); Capobianco, *Privilegia et Facultates Ordinis Fratrum Minorum* (Nuceriae, 1946).

Church. The general norms of interpretation of the Code, and particularly the application of canon 81 with relation to the common law of the Church, is equally applicable to the pontifically approved special law of the Rules and Constitutions. The same may be said of the general chapters in clerical exempt institutes which are endowed with jurisdictional authority, and hence any true legislation passed and promulgated by them automatically becomes an ecclesiastical law with its juridic consequences.

Several fundamental notions about the special law of exempt Orders must be kept in mind. Although religious Rules and Constitutions are not technically synonymous,[85] the Code does not distinguish between their obligatory force.[86] Secondly, contrary to the common law of the Church, which is territorial in nature, the Rules and Constitutions of religious Orders are personal, and hence oblige the individual everywhere.[87] Thirdly, the transgression of a Rule or of the Constitutions does not constitute, in most instances, a venial sin, and much less, a mortal sin.[88]

---

[85] A Rule is always a brief document delineating the general lines of religious life in a very limited number of maxims and precepts, usually of a spiritual or disciplinary character. In view of their sketchiness, monastic Rules are insufficient for regulating and ordering successfully the daily monastic life of the religious. This lack is supplemented by the more extensive legislation of the Constitutions, Statutes and Custom Books of the given Institute. Cf. Mazon, *Las Reglas,* p. 102. Maroto (1875–1937) provided excellent workable definitions of a Rule and Constitutions. He wrote : "*Regula* dici potest, in re nostra, brevior, adstrictior et generatim vetustior collectio complectens primarias aut fundamentales seu principales et communes ordinationes vel normas, quibus fertur ordo seu forma vivendi in religione, itemque pauca quaedam et praecipua documenta tradita ad moderandam perfectionis religiosae semitam. *Constitutiones* dicuntur amplior, latior et generatim recentior collectio normarum et ordinationum vitae religiosae, quibus distinctius, plenius, magis determinate et particulariter feruntur praescripta etiam minutiora et diffusiora ad religiosam observantiam et vitam perfectam spectantia, atque definiuntur finis, institutum, regimen, munera, obligationes, iura et cetera, alicuius peculiaris Religionis propria."—"Regulae et Particulares Constitutiones Singularum Religionum ex Iure Decretalium usque ad Codicem," *Acta Congressus Iuridici Internationalis,* IV (1937), 214.

[86] Canons 578, n. 2 ; 593 ; 595.

[87] Can. 8, § 2.

[88] E.g., the Constitutions of the Friars Minor are representative of the wording adopted in most Constitutions. "Hae Constitutiones, excepto contemptu formali vel habituali transgressione ex qua scandalum oriatur, non

a. Pre-Code Legislation

Before the promulgation of the Code the common doctrine of the canonists and the practice in the Church followed the principle that religious prelates possessed the power of dispensing from the precepts of the Rule and the Constitutions in individual cases.[89] The canonical formulas adopted to indicate any restriction on the dispensatory power of the religious superiors differed considerably in canonical literature. Following the principle laid down by Innocent III (1198–1216), the Council of Trent introduced the formula that superiors were prohibited from granting dispensations in matters which pertained to the essence of the religious life (*ad substantiam regularis vitae*).[90] The Constitutions and customary usage, itself the best interpreter of laws,[91] sufficiently circumscribed the extent of the dispensatory power of the superiors. Vows and the laws relating to the constitution and regimen of the Order were generally considered as referring to the common good of the community rather than to the private good of the individual, and hence were included in the notion of the *"bases et fundamenta totius regularis disciplinae,"* which the

---

obligant sub peccato, sed ad subeundam tantum poenam a Superiore in casu transgressionis impositam, nisi aliquid in ipsis sub poena canonica aut obedientiae praecepto praescriptum sit, salva semper obligatione legum iuris divini et canonici necnon praeceptorum S. Regulae."—*Regula et Constitutiones Generales Ordinis Fratrum Minorum* (Romae, 1953), art. 9, § 3. With regard to the Rules of the individual Orders some divergence of obligation is noted. The Rules of the Dominican Order and of the Society of Jesus do not oblige under pain of sin; the Rule of the Carmelites obliges under venial sin; the Rule of St. Francis has its precepts divided into classes, some of which oblige under mortal sin. Cf. Pejška, *Ius Canonicum Religiosorum* (3 ed., Friburgi Brisgoviae, 1927), p. 147; Kazenberger-Iglesias, *Liber Vitae seu Regulae S. Francisci Expositio* (Romae, 1948), pp. 34–40.

[89] Vermeersch, *De Religiosis Institutis et Personis* (2 vols., Romae-Ratisbonae, 1902), I, 251–252 (hereafter cited as *De Religiosis*): "Non ergo cum tota communitate (nisi gravissima urgente necessitate, et cum facilis non est recursus ad legislatorem), sed cum singulis personis dispensare possunt . . . per se in praeceptis Regularum et Constitutionum." Piatus (*Praelectiones*, I, 608) was of the same opinion and adduced the testimony of many other authorities.

[90] Sess. XXV, *de regularibus et monialibus,* c. 1.

[91] Can. 29.

Tridentine legislation excepted from the competence of the dispensatory powers of superiors.

The power to change the provisions of the Rule and the Constitutions always was considered to reside solely in the general chapter.[92] Consequently, the supreme moderator was not competent for dispensing the entire community collectively, although he could dispense individuals, from the observance of a precept of the Rule and the Constitutions, for such a procedure would have amounted to effecting a change in the Rule, which was forbidden under any circumstances.[93]

b. Legislation of the Code

According to canon 80, a dispensation may be granted by the legislator, by his successor, by his superior, or by one to whom any of these have given the faculty of dispensing. Hence, the power of dispensing from the Rules and Constitutions of exempt Orders belongs to the Roman Pontiff and to the General Chapter, for they alone have legislative powers in religious communities, and to those superiors who by law (the Code, or the pontifically approved Rules and Constitutions) or privilege were conceded this faculty.

The Code frequently grants the determining of the competent superior to the respective Constitutions of the Order by adding to their provisions the clause *"nisi aliud constitutiones caveant,"* or its equivalent.[94] In virtue of this clause the special law of the Constitutions often reserves the power of dispensing to the general superior. In canon 589, § 2, the Code expressly grants to the supreme moderator, and in particular cases to other superiors, the prudent dispensing of teachers and students from certain community acts, inclusive of the nocturnal choir obligations, if it is necessary to foster studies.[95]

---

[92] Vermeersch, *De Religiosis,* I, 252.

[93] Donatus, *Rerum Regularium Praxis,* II, pars 1, tract. XI, q. 3, p. 190; Miranda, *Manualis Praelatorum Regularium* (2 vols., Placentiae, 1616), II, q. xxxi, p. 279 (hereafter cited as *Manualis*).

[94] E.g., can. 494, § 2.

[95] "Studiorum tempore magistris et alumnis officia ne imponantur quae a studio eos avocent vel scholam quoquo modo impediant; supremus autem Moderator et in casibus particularibus alii quoque Superiores possunt pro sua

Since the promulgation of the Code canonists no longer apply the Tridentine formula, which excluded from the dispensatory powers of superiors all matters which pertain *"ad substantiam regularis vitae,"* but rather agree upon the distinction which permits superiors to dispense from purely disciplinary laws to the exclusion of what they call "constitutive laws" (*leges constitutivae*).[96] Thus, the supreme moderator may dispense individuals, even habitually, from any disciplinary law contained in the Constitutions. He cannot, however, without a special grant from the Holy See, dispense from the laws governing the establishment and election of superiors, or change the prescribed time for the holding of general chapters.

Modern canonists subscribe to the opinion that the major superiors of exempt Orders, unless they are expressly forbidden by law, enjoy the tacit concession on the part of the Supreme Pontiff of dispensatory powers with reference to the special laws of their Institutes.[97] Cicognani points out that right government requires this procedure, but only in minor observances which do not pertain to the substance of religion.[98]

Nevertheless, since the office of the supreme moderator must

---

prudentia eos a nonnullis communitatis actibus, etiam a choro, praesertim nocturnis horis, eximere, quoties id studiis excolendis necessarium videatur."

[96] Goyeneche, "Consultationes," *CpR,* III (1922), 56: "Iam vero possunt Superiores dispensare, iuxta dicta, in illis observantiis minoribus quae ad substantiam religionis non pertinent . . E contra, nequeunt in iis quae essentialia religioni vocantur, ut vota, licet peculiaria religionis; neque in illis articulis qui constitutivi eiusdem religionis sint." Cf. also Schaefer, *De Religiosis,* p. 240; Van Hove, *De privilegiis et dispensationibus,* p. 390; Ledwolorz, "De potestate Superiorum O.F.M. dispensandi a legibus Constitutionum Generalium Ordinis," *Antonianum,* XXX (1955), 250–251.

[97] Ledwolorz, "De superiorum potestate dispensandi in iure particulari Ordinis Fratrum Minorum," *Antonianum,* XIII (1938), 43. This author restricts himself to the tacit concession, even though a *viva voce* express concession to this effect was granted to the Superiors of the Franciscan Order by Pope Pius II. Goyeneche ("Consultationes," *CpR,* III [1922], 55) states his position as follows: "Verumtamen, auctores iuris regularis communiter tenebant—quod et nunc tenendum censeo—praelatos, ni eis expresse prohibeatur, pollere tacita auctoritate in praeceptis regulae (in aliquo particulari discrete dispensandi)." Cf. also Michiels, *Normae Generales,* II, 490; Schaefer, *De Religiosis,* p. 240.

[98] Cicognani, *Canon Law,* p. 839.

primarily seek to promote the observance of the Rule and the Constitutions, the granting of dispensations from their provisions is of rare occurrence, either because the power of dispensing is restricted, or because a dispensation in the strict sense is unnecessary, inasmuch as a permission or an authoritative declaration on the part of the superior suffices.[99]

---

[99] Ledwolorz, *"art. cit."*—*ibid.*, pp. 48 and 57.

CHAPTER VII

THE JUDICIAL POWER OF
THE SUPREME MODERATOR

An indisputable adjunct to any legislative authority is the concomitant possession of judicial power. If legislation is necessary for the preservation of the moral and physical unity of any society, it is of the utmost importance to have the means to enforce it. Efficacious government does not cease with the enactment and promulgation of laws, nor even with the functions of the executive power, which seeks to put these laws into execution. For the achieving of the common end of the society there must be a supervisory agency which will insure the conformity of the acts of the members of the society to the legally established order. This application of the law to concrete cases, its interpretation, the judgment and settlement of disputes, and the prosecution and punishment of violators of the law, are the function of the judicial power.

Judicial power is commonly defined by jurists and canonists as the right to declare or pronounce in an obligatory fashion which actions of the subjects are, in the concrete, in conformity or at variance with the law, and the legal effects of this conformity or variance.[1]

Major superiors of clerical exempt Orders are vested with judicial powers which were transferred to them simultaneously with the granting of the privilege of exemption. This served to prevent the religious from being outside the sanction of law.[2]

---

[1] Ottaviani, *Institutiones*, I, 102: "Ius declarandi seu proponendi modo obligatorio, quaenam subditorum actiones in concreto sint iuri conformes, quaequae eidem difformes, et effectus legitimos eiusdem conformitatis aut difformitatis." Cf. also Cappello, *Summa Iuris Publici Ecclesiastici* (2 ed., Romae, 1928), p. 74; Marchesi, *Summula Iuris Publici Ecclesiastici*, p. 26.

[2] Lega, *Praelectiones in Textum Iuris Canonici—De Iudicis Ecclesiasticis*, IV, 518: "Ast Romani Pontifices Ordines religiosos donare coeperunt *exemp-*

As a result of this transference of judicial power another link was forged in the quasi-episcopal jurisdiction of the major superiors of religious Orders, which culminated in the recognition by the Code of their legal rank as ordinaries. The nature and extent of the judicial power of the general superior underwent a gradual historical development, keeping pace with the numerical growth of exempt Orders and the resulting inevitable increase of violations of the law by which religious were bound.

A. Pre-Code Legislation

The Decretals did not expressly state that religious superiors were endowed with judicial power, but clearly implied its possession when granting to regular prelates the right to inflict canonical censures upon their subjects.[3] With the rise of the Mendicant Orders in the early thirteenth century and the increasing number of exemptions, the judiciary power of Regular Prelates became fortified with additional privileges. Among the greatest of these, granted to the Franciscan Order, was that of Pope Boniface VIII (1294–1303), which permitted the superiors to inflict punishment upon their subjects without observing the canonically required judicial procedure but heeding only the customs and statutes of the Order.[4] The *"rimulae et apices"* of the judicial procedure from which the regular prelates were freed were the solemnities and accidental circumstances which accompanied trials in the lay and ecclesiastical courts.[5]

---

tione a potestate Ordinariorum et tunc factum est ut potestas *coactiva iudicialis* transferretur in Praelatos regulares ne homines regulares fierent exleges et poenalium sanctionum expertes."

[3] C. 26, X, *de accusationibus, inquisitionibus et denuntiationibus,* V, 1; c. 2, *de verborum significatione,* V, 11, in Clem.; c. 24, X, *de regularibus et transeuntibus ad religionem,* III, 31.

[4] Constitution *Ad augmentum,* 12 nov. 1295: ". . . indulgemus ut ad correctiones, et punitiones Fratrum ejusdem Ordinis delinquentium infligendas, Praelati Ordinis supradicti, ad quos eaedem spectare noscuntur, rimulis et apicibus ipsis postpositis, libere procedere valeant secundum consuetudines approbatas, et generalia facta . . ."—*Bullarium Franciscanum,* IV, 371. The following year, on the 16th of May, this same privilege was extended to the Dominican Order. Cf. *Bullarium Romanum Taurinense,* I, 134.

[5] Emmanuel a Conceptione, *Enchiridion Judiciale Ordinis Fratrum Minorum* (Ulyssipone, 1693), pp. 33–35; Bouix, *De Iure Regularium,* II, 442.

This unusual privilege was preceded by many other pontifical documents in which specific permission was granted to religious superiors to exercise judicial powers. As early as 1223, Honorius III (1216–1227) insisted that bishops recognize the censures inflicted by religious superiors for unlawful egress from the Order.[6] Some twenty years later Innocent IV (1243–1254) reaffirmed this power of inflicting censures. In the form of sanctions, he added a series of coercive measures which could be used by the authorized superiors.[7] In view of the prevalent mutual sharing in granted privileges these same powers were subsequently shared by the other Mendicant Orders.

These privileges, however, were to be enjoyed within the limitations of the Decretal law. Suspension or excommunication always presupposed that the superior would issue a canonical warning unless the gravity of the crime or a papal pronouncement to that effect obviated all need of the prescribed warnings.[8] The common law also provided severe penalties for Prelates who abused their judicial power by threatening their subjects with penalties for revealing their shortcomings or transgressions during canonical visitation.[9] Similarly, the penalty of excommunication was incurred by a Provincial who neglected to depose a negligent local superior.[10]

Since the common law generally conceded judicial power to exempt religious superiors as such, the particular constitutions of the respective Orders determined the extent and the limitations of the competence of the various superiors.[11] No circumscription

---

[6] Apostolic Brief, Fratrum Minorum, 18 dec. 1223: "Nosque Prioribus et Custodibus Fratrum ipsorum concessimus, ut in discendentes liceat, donec resipuerint, ecclesiasticam exercere censuram   nunc autem non sine admiratione accepimus .   hos aliqui vestrum tanquam excommunicatos evitare non curant."—*Bullarium Franciscanum*, I, 19.

[7] Constitution, *Provisionis Nostrae:* "   . ut apostatas vel insolentes vestri Ordinis, nisi salutaribus monitis acquiescant, excommunicare, ligare, capere, carceri tradere, mancipare (si videbitur expeditus) possitis, auctoritate praesentium, facultatem concedimus."—*Bullarium Franciscanum*, I, 410.

[8] C. 26, X, *de appellationibus, recusationibus et relationibus*, II, 28.

[9] C. 4, *de officio iudicis ordinarii*, I, 16, in VI°.

[10] O'Brien, *The Provincial Superior*, p. 56.

[11] Rodericus, *Quaestiones Regulares*, IV, tit. ii, c. ii, p. 5.

of the general superior's authority in these matters is encountered in the available canonical literature. As a rule the same degree of authority in judicial affairs is conceded to the provincial superior. Only a few Constitutions, however, of exempt religious communities vindicate the same right for the local superior. The early Constitutions of the Dominicans granted judicial power to the local superiors or priors, for they were considered as partaking of the quasi-episcopal powers of the major superiors.[12] In the Carmelite Constitutions the power of inflicting censures was specifically reserved to the provincial with the provision that the local superior with the consent of the majority of his community represented by the older religious would likewise be empowered to inflict these penalties.[13] The earliest Franciscan Constitutions, the *Constitutiones Narbonnenses* of 1260 as edited by St. Bonaventure, acknowledged this authority as ordinary for the Minister General, and also as ordinary for the Provincial, but the lesser superiors were capable of exercising the same only in cases of urgent necessity.[14]

With the reforms instituted by the Council of Trent certain limitations were imposed upon the exercise of judicial powers on the part of religious superiors. Since it appeared incongruous to consider local superiors of very small religious houses to be on a par with local ordinaries in view of the very limited numbers of subjects, the natural consequence was the curtailment of some judicial authority as resulting from the privilege of exemption. If the number of religious in a monastic house was less than twelve, they were subject to the judicial power of the local ordinary in disciplinary matters rather than to their own superiors.[15] In keeping with the revocation of many of the privileges of

---

[12] *Constitutiones Fratrum S. Ordinis Praedicatorum* (Parisiis, 1886), pp. 307–315. But the constitutions as revised in 1932 reserve these judicial rights to the provincial. Cf. Clancy, *The Local Superior,* p. 52, footnote 7.

[13] O'Brien, *The Provincial Superior,* p. 55.

[14] "Quilibet Minister Provincialis habeat ordinariam jurisdictionem auctoritate generalis Ministri excommunicandi, capiendi et incarcerandi et alia poena puniendi super apostatas aliarum Provinciarum in Provinciis suis. Idem possint Custodes et Guardiani in casu necessitatis."—*Opera Omnia S. Bonaventurae,* VIII, 458.

[15] Urbanus VIII, const. *Cum saepe contingat,* 21 iun. 1625—*Bullarium Romanum Taurinense,* XIII, 336.

exempt Orders, the Council of Trent also subjected the Regulars to the local ordinaries in matters pertaining to the care of souls.[16] Subsequently, Pope Gregory XV (1621–1623) reiterated the same restriction.[17] Pursuing the same restrictive policy, in consequence of the serious inroads of the Protestant Reformation, the Holy See included in its restrictions upon religious superiors, under heavy penalties, the undertaking of judicial procedure in cases involving heresy.[18] Thenceforth heretics were to be denounced before the duly appointed Inquisitors or local ordinaries.

Regular prelates, following the rules enacted by Benedict XIV (1740–1758) in the Constitution *Si datam,* were empowered to undertake criminal causes and also those which involved the nullity of profession.[19] As a result of these concessions to institute judicial procedures, the major superiors were enabled to excommunicate their subjects and to inflict other censures within the inflictive rights of ordinaries with the exception of the local interdict, since it would affect also other persons than their own subjects. A criminal process did not need to be introduced in causes wherein the punishment to be imposed did not outmatch the dominative power of the superior. When, however, punishments of a grave nature were to be inflicted, such as excommunication, suspension, dismissal from the Order, or deprivation of electoral rights both active and passive, then a canonical process which was conducted according to the norms enacted for religious had to be instituted.[20]

The judicial powers of the supreme moderator were usually exercised in accordance with the provisions of the particular Constitutions. Notwithstanding this general principle, modifications were introduced by the Holy See whenever the emergence of serious problems affected the universal status of religious irre-

---

[16] Sess. XXV, *de regularibus et monialibus,* c. 11.

[17] Const. *Inscrutabili,* 5 febr. 1622—*Fontes,* n. 199. Cf. also *Bullarium Romanum Taurinense,* XII, 656.

[18] Paulus V, const. *Romanus Pontifex,* 1 sept. 1606—*Fontes,* n. 194. Cf. also *Bullarium Romanum Taurinense,* XI, 346.

[19] C. 24, X, *de accusationibus, inquisitionibus et denuntiationibus,* V, 1; c. 3, X, *de appellationibus, recusationibus et relationibus,* II, 28; Bouix, *De Jure Regularium,* II, 436–440; Wernz, *Ius Decretalium,* III, 395.

[20] Bouix, *De Jure Regularium,* II, 441–442.

spective of the particular Institute involved. The question of expulsion from the Order was a matter of such magnitude that legislation concerning the judicial process proved of immediate concern to the Holy See. Urban VIII (1623–1644) decreed that an incorrigible religious who continued in his obstinacy after an incarceration of one year was to be expelled after a formal trial. The sentence of expulsion was to be pronounced by the supreme moderator with the assent of six other priests selected from the Order.[21] Innocent XII (1691–1700), after making some modifications in the stringent requirements of the trial, extended the faculty of expulsion to the Provincial with the assent of six other religious of the Order approved by the supreme moderator. The sentence became effective only after the review and approval of the general superior.[22]

No alteration was induced in this matter until shortly before the promulgation of the Code, when the Sacred Congregation for Religious restricted the power of expulsion to the supreme moderator exclusively. The general superior, together with at least four of his counsellors, constituted the tribunal before which a summary procedure was to be held. In particular cases provision was made for dismissals to be effected by means of a declaratory sentence on the part of the superiors.[23]

B. Legislation of the Code

1. Commentary on Canon 1579, § 2

Canon 1579 determines the competent court of the first instance for deciding disputes among religious in line with their exemption.[24] In the first paragraph the general principle is established that, unless the Constitutions of the respective Orders rule otherwise, causes involving exempt religious of the same Institute are to be tried before the Provincial, who is the competent judge of

---

[21] S. C. C., decr. 21 sept. 1624—*Fontes*, n. 2454.

[22] S. C. C., decr. 24 iul. 1694—*Fontes*, n. 2942.

[23] S. C. de Religiosis decr. 16 maii, 1911—*Fontes*, n. 4409; *AAS*, III (1911), 236–238.

[24] Cf. Lega-Bartoccetti, *Commentarius in Iudicia Ecclesiastica iuxta Codicem Iuris Canonici* (3 vols., Romae: Anonima Libreria Cattolica Italiana, 1950), I, 137.

the first instance. An exception is made to this rule by the common law in the next paragraph, which declares that in a controversy between two Provinces, the supreme moderator judges the cause in the first instance either in person or through a delegate, unless the Constitutions prescribe otherwise.[25]

Since the particular Constitutions are privileged to determine another judge for the first instance in these controversies, it seems logical that they also be required to establish the court of appeal if they introduce a change in the common law by the exercise of their prerogative. According to the principle accepted among canonists, the judge of the second instance should then be the immediate superior of the judge of the first instance.[26]

The phrase *"salvo diverso constitutionum praescripto"* includes all approved special legislation of religious Orders. Hence, the divergence between the law of the Code and the law of the religious may be found in the Rule, the Constitutions of the Order properly so called, the ordinances of the general chapters functioning as the sole legislative body of the Order, or the procedural manual specifically drawn up for the conducting of trials.[27]

The competence of the supreme moderator as judge of the first instance extends to controversies *"inter duas provincias."* The term "province" is taken in its official designation of a subdivision of a religious Institute as formed by the union of religious houses under one superior.[28] Under this term would fall all the subdivisions of the Order which are constituted not strictly as a religious house (*domus*) within a province. Hence, the supreme moderator would be the judge of the first instance, unless special legislation existed to the contrary, in disputes between independent

---

[25] Can. 1579, § 2, "Salvo diverso constitutionum praescripto, si res contentiosa agatur inter duas provincias, in prima instantia iudicabit ipse per se vel per delegatum supremus religionis Moderator."

[26] Noval, *Commentarium Codicis Iuris Canonici,* Lib. IV, *De Processibus* (2 vols., Romae, 1920–1932), I, 88 (hereafter cited *De Processibus*).

[27] E.g., the Capuchin Order has drawn up precisely such a manual containing the general norms of procedure to be followed in trials. Cf. *Modus Procedendi in Causis Disciplinaribus, Contentiosis, Criminalibus Ordinis Fratrum Minorum Capuccinorum auctoritate Capituli Generalis LXXII Promulgatus* (Romae, 1945).

[28] Can. 488, n. 6.

commissariats and custodies as well as religious houses withdrawn from the jurisdiction of the provincial and placed directly under the surveillance of the general superior. In view of the wording of the preceding and subsequent paragraphs of canon 1579, it is understood that the controversy is between two provinces of the *same* religious Institute, for the local ordinary serves as the judge of the first instance in controversies between physical and moral persons of different organizations.[29]

None of the Constitutions of the Mendicant exempt Orders exercise their privilege of changing the legislation of the Code in depriving the supreme moderator of his competence as judge of the first instance. On the contrary, since the same privilege is accorded to particular Constitutions with reference to the general principle enunciated in canon 1579, § 1, some special legislation is to be found wherein the judicial power is withdrawn from the competence of the Provincial in favor of the provincial or the general chapter, or of the supreme moderator. This is achieved through the empowering of the general superior, for a grave and just reason, to reserve for his own adjudication in the first instance any judicial cause that may arise in the Order.[30]

The supreme moderator may delegate another to function as the judge of the first instance. If the Constitutions prescribe the consent of his council for delegation or for the designation of delegated judges, as sometimes occurs in causes involving the dismissal of religious after solemn profession, then this must be observed for validity.[31] If the trial is to be held in distant countries, even amid normal and ordinary contingencies, then the superior general may, with the consent of his council or chapter, delegate to at least three trustworthy and prudent religious the

---

[29] Can. 1579, § 3.

[30] E.g., the special legislation of the Capuchin Order in their *Modus Procedendi in Causis Disciplinaribus, Contentiosis, Criminalibus* (cited above) provides for such a reservation on the part of the general superior in art. 79, § 3, which states: "Minister generalis tamen causam quamcumque ad se ex gravi et iusta causa advocare et Superiores provinciales ad ipsum deferre valent; ac in utroque casu Minister generalis causam ad se ut supra advocatam vel delatam definire valet in prima instantia per tribunal delegatum generale, in altera autem instantia per suum tribunal ordinarium vel per tribunal delegatum supremum."

[31] Can. 105, n. 1.

faculty of dismissing the subjects.[32] Countries overseas or those with which intercommunication is difficult for any reason whatsoever may be considered as distant regions.[33]

2. Commentary on Canon 1594, § 4

In exempt religious Orders the appeal from all causes tried before the Provincial goes to the supreme moderator of the Institute as the court of the second instance.[34] This designation of the court of appeal for religious presupposes that the Provincial or his delegate was the judge of the first instance. Since special legislation is at liberty, according to canon 1579, § 1, to depart from the general legislation regarding the judge of the first instance, some causes would, therefore, not be tried before the supreme moderator as the judge of the second instance. If the cause was originally tried before an ordinary judge lower in rank than the Provincial, but not his delegate, the appeal is made to the immediate superior of the judge of the first instance.[35] If, on the other hand, in accordance with special legislation, the cause was tried before the supreme moderator, then the appeal is made to the Sacred Rota in view of the ruling as stated in canon 1599, § 1, n. 1.[36] Unless the Constitutions prescribe otherwise, a cause delegated by the supreme moderator himself to another is appealed to the general superior as judge of the second instance.[37]

3. Supreme Moderator's Judicial Rights and Duties

Having determined the supreme moderator's competence as the judge of either the first or the second instance, one must now examine other facets of his judicial power.

The common law requires the participation of a notary, who acts as a secretary or clerk, in every ecclesiastical trial.[38] The

---

[32] Can. 667.

[33] Schaefer, *De religiosis*, p. 1021; Beste, *Introductio in Codicem*, p. 457.

[34] Can. 1594, § 4: "Inter religiosos exemptos, pro omnibus causis coram Superiore provinciali actis tribunal secundae instantiae est penes supremum Moderatorem . . ."

[35] Lega-Bartoccetti, *Commentarius in Iudiciis Ecclesiasticis*, I, 170.

[36] Noval, *De Processibus*, I, 88; Lega-Bartoccetti, *op. cit.*, I, 171.

[37] Lega-Bartoccetti, *op. cit.*, I, 171.

[38] Can. 1585.

supreme moderator may constitute notaries for trials involving religious.[39]   Since all major superiors of clerical exempt religious are endowed with this power, the designation of a major superior by the supreme moderator as a delegate judge does not raise any difficulties in this regard.   If, however, he should delegate as judge one who is not a major superior, then it follows that he must designate a notary as well.   These notaries may be appointed to serve in all trials, i.e., as having the *office* of a notary, or they may be designated for a particular trial only.[40]   Consequently, a delegated judge may choose a notary from those who are appointed for that task by the supreme moderator, unless a special notary is designated by him for a particular trial.   In either event, the appointment of the notary should be made in writing.[41]

The supreme moderator functioning as a judge or delegating another to exercise this office is obliged to follow all the provisions (rules) of the common law governing ecclesiastical judges as contained in canons 1608–1626 as well as in the general provisions for the judicial dismissal of religious or the infliction of judicial penalties.   He is deprived of competency with reference to religious who are involved in causes directly or indirectly connected with the faith, for such causes are by law reserved to the Holy Office.[42]

Before functioning as a judge, the supreme moderator must take an oath to fulfill his office properly and faithfully.[43]   Since the Code specifies that this oath should be taken at the beginning of the tenure of their office if they are regular officials, or before the beginning of the trial if they are appointed for a particular cause only, it seems sufficient for the supreme moderator to take this oath only once.[44]   This oath is to be taken in the presence of

---

[39] Can. 503.

[40] Fanfani, *De iure religiosorum,* p. 73.

[41] Abbo-Hannan, *The Sacred Canons,* I, 513.

[42] Can. 501, § 2. Cf. also can. 247, § 2; Schaefer, *De religiosis,* pp. 223–224.

[43] Can. 1621, § 1.

[44] Canonists are divided in their opinions concerning the taking of this oath. Noval (*De Processibus,* I, 126) holds for the repeated taking of this oath, since a religious superior is not a public magistrate in the Church. Coronata (*Institutiones,* III, 60) offers the lesser frequency of judicial trials among religious as a sufficient reason for the repeated taking of the oath.

the notary of the tribunal, and is also to be duly recorded in the acts.[45]

The court of appeal must consist of the same number of judges as the tribunal of the first instance.[46] All contrary privileges and customs being revoked, criminal trials of religious that involve the infliction of excommunication are removed from the jurisdiction of the supreme moderator and must be tried before a tribunal of three judges.[47] Causes involving deposition, perpetual deprivation of the wearing of the habit, or degradation are reserved to a tribunal of five judges.[48] Any other causes that involve notable difficulties may also be tried before a collegiate tribunal rather than by the supreme moderator alone.[49]

The particular Constitutions must be examined if one is to determine the superior competent to exercise many of the powers the Code grants to religious superiors as such in ecclesiastical trials. The common law authorizes all superiors to permit their subjects to act as plaintiffs,[50] procurators and advocates,[51] or also arbiters.[52] Special legislation, however, generally restricts the jurisdiction of the superiors in favor of either the provincial or the supreme moderator with the consent of their councils or the permission of the supreme moderator.

According to the common law, religious superiors represent their respective houses, Provinces or entire Institutes in ecclesiastical trials, but only in accordance with the provisions of their Constitutions.[53]

Coronata cites Torrubiano as favoring the opposite opinion. Unless an authentic interpretation is forthcoming, there seems to be sufficient doubt concerning the interpretation of the canon to justify the acceptance of either of these opinions.

[45] Can. 1621, § 2.
[46] Canons 1595 and 1596.
[47] Can. 1576, § 1, n. 1.
[48] Can. 1576, § 1, n. 2.
[49] Can. 1576, § 2.
[50] Can. 1652.
[51] Canons 1657, § 3 and 1658, § 4.
[52] Can. 193.
[53] Can. 1653, § 6.

4. Beatification and Canonization Processes

It is customary for all exempt religious institutes to appoint a postulator for the introduction of beatification and canonization processes.[54]   His office, as a rule, is under the immediate supervision of the supreme moderator.[55]   Once appointed, according to the provisions of the canonically approved Constitutions, he generally may not be removed from office unless the Sacred Congregation of Rites has been previously notified.[56]

Should necessity dictate it, the supreme moderator may permit a religious to function as a notary in these processes, with the exception of those causes that involve a religious of his own Institute.[57]   Once the process is introduced, all religious are bound, immediately and directly, to forward to the ordinary or the promoter of the faith sealed letters testifying to their special knowledge which may contribute to the investigation of the person proposed for beatification or canonization.[58]   An obligation is imposed upon the supreme moderator and other superiors to attend to these depositions by their subjects without, however, inducing them, directly or indirectly, to render favorable or unfavorable testimony.[59]

If the cause for beatification or canonization refers to a member of the Institute, this must be made known to all the religious houses through the customary official channels (usually a circular letter or the insertion of a notice to this effect in the official organ

---

[54] Blaher, *The Ordinary Processes in Causes of Beatification and Canonization*, The Catholic University of America Canon Law Studies, No. 268 (Washington, D.C.: The Catholic University of America Press, 1949), p. 75.

[55] E.g., in the Franciscan Order he must render a yearly account of the actual status of the processes as well as the expenses involved. Furthermore, the Constitutions contain a prohibition that "nihil maioris momenti postulator agat inconsulto Ministro generali, neque sine eius licentia causas tractandas assumat, quae scilicet ad primum, secundum vel tertium Ordinem non pertineant."—*Regula et Constitutiones Generales Ordinis Fratrum Minorum* (Romae, 1953), art. 448, § 1.

[56] Blaher, *loc. cit.*

[57] Can. 2014.

[58] Can. 2025, § 2.

[59] Can. 2026.

of the Institute) and the supreme moderator and other superiors are obliged to remind their subjects to submit all information and writings in their possession to the proper authorities.[60]

---

[60] Can. 2043, § 2.

CHAPTER VIII

THE EXECUTIVE POWER OF
THE SUPREME MODERATOR

Having treated the legislative and judicial aspects of the jurisdictional authority of the supreme moderator in the preceding
chapters, the writer now proposes to analyze the supreme moderator's executive powers. With consideration given to the broad
personal aspects of the executive power of the general superior in
the first section, all his remaining executive rights and obligations
will receive special consideration in the second section under the
headings suggested by canon 502, namely, his jurisdiction over the
provinces, the houses and the members of his Institute.

A. Personal Aspects of the Executive Power

Under the heading of the personal aspects of the executive
power will be considered those obligations and relationships which
determine the status of the power of the supreme moderator in
virtue of the tenure of his office even prior to the exercise of any
of his powers. The fulfillment of these obligations and the correct
understanding of the relationships will facilitate and expedite the
solution of many problems of government which the supreme
moderator must solve if he is to execute fruitfully the legislation
of the Code and of the Constitutions.

1. Profession of Faith

Upon assuming his office the supreme moderator is bound to
make a profession of faith, in accordance with the formula
approved by the Apostolic See, in the presence of the electing
chapter.[1] He is furthermore obliged to take the oath against

---

[1] Can. 1406, § 1, n. 9. The formula which is prescribed is printed in the
Vatican editions of the Code just preceding the text of the canons.

modernism as prescribed by Pope Pius X (1903–1914).[2] Although the grave obligation which looks to the taking of the oath and the making of the profession of faith rests primarily on the superior before whom these acts are to be performed,[3] nevertheless a similarly grave obligation rests on the general superior who is required to take it. If he should neglect to fulfill this obligation, he is to be warned and be granted a definite time for compliance. Upon failure to comply, he is subject to canonical punishments even to the extent of loss of office.[4] Despite the severe tenor of this injunction, the profession of faith is not required for the valid assumption of the office of general superior.[5] However, a document attesting to the fulfillment of this obligation must be preserved in the files of the Curia.[6]

2. Residence

Nowhere in the Code is residence at a specific place imposed as mandatory for the supreme moderator. According to the common law, all superiors shall live in their respective houses, which they are not permitted to leave except in accordance with the terms of their Constitutions.[7] Hence the Code presupposes a permanent residence for the supreme moderator, but refrains from specifying the place where he should habitually reside, implying that the Constitutions legislate in this matter or that custom is to be followed.

Upon assumption of office the supreme moderator should make his residence in the generalitial house in which the other administrative offices for the entire institute are located. It is true that he is not bound by the same limitations of residence as is the local superior, or even the provincial, for whom the legislation concerning residence was always severe.[8] The necessity of an immediately manifest subject-superior relationship with constant

---

[2] S. C. S. Off., decr. *Cum in Codice,* 22 martii, 1918—*AAS,* X (1918), 136; Bouscaren, *Digest,* I, 50–51.

[3] Vermeersch-Creusen, *Epitome,* II, 460.

[4] Can. 2403.

[5] Goyeneche, "Consultationes," *CpRM,* XVIII (1937), 95–96.

[6] Abbo-Hannan, *The Sacred Canons,* I, 645.

[7] Can. 508.

[8] C. 1, *de statu monachorum vel canonicorum regularium,* III, 10, in Clem.

availability on the part of the superior, as it is demanded of the local and the provincial superiors, is not so apparent with regard to the general superior. Nevertheless, to a certain degree, the nature of the supreme moderator's office with its supervisory and managerial duties seems to indicate a determined and permanent residence, which the particular Constitutions usually designate as the generalitial curia (*curia generalitia*).

The location of the generalitial curia was ordinarily determined by the place of origin of the Institute or by the preference of its founder, and was commonly identified with the mother-house of the Institute. Although the Code provides for the appointment of a Procurator General, whose duty it is to conduct the business of the Institute with the Holy See [9] and who is required to reside in Rome, even though the Order has no house there,[10] it seems advisable that the general superior make his residence there also. The center of Christendom is likewise the center of the Order. That this is the desire of the Holy See is evident from the papal brief by which the confederation of all Benedictine congregations was established and the office of the *abbas primas* created with the instruction that he make his residence in Rome.[11]

Since the requirement of residence is not as rigid for the supreme moderator as for the local and provincial superiors, the reasons justifying his absence from the curia also need not be as grave.[12] Again, the Constitutions are the proximate source of law regarding the limitations affecting the frequency and duration of the absences. At other times the nature of the supreme moderator's office, which demands the visitation of the provinces and the presence at many, often far-distant, affairs, is a sufficiently grave reason for his absence. In practice, however, the general superior should not absent himself with great frequency nor for a lengthy duration of time. It is not unusual, if one has exceeded herein, that he be called before the Holy See to render an account

---

[9] Can. 517, § 1.

[10] S. C. de Religiosis, *monitum*, 4 iunii, 1920—*AAS*, XII (1912), 301; Bouscaren, *Digest*, I, 294–295.

[11] Leo XIII, brief *Summum semper*, 12 iulii, 1893—*AAS*, XXVI (1893), 372.

[12] Schaefer, *De religiosis*, p. 293; Larraona, "Commentarium Codicis," *CpR*, VIII (1927), 167.

for his excessive absences. Penalties for negligence in the observance of the law of residence are provided in the Code for superiors below the rank of the supreme moderator,[13] but his own transgression is penalized only upon the immediate intervention on the part of the Holy See.

3. The Definitorial Council

The supreme moderator of an Institute must have a body of counselors, whose consent or advice he must seek in accordance with the Constitutions and the sacred canons.[14] This body of the general superior's counselors is called a general council, a definitorial council, or simply a *definitorium.* The nature of the counselors' office is manifest from the text of canon 516, wherein their auxiliary rôle in government is indicated in that, by consent or counsel, they moderate the powers of the superior in specific matters, without, however, being granted any power of government themselves, since this resides in the superior alone or also in the general chapter.[15]

To avoid confusion, the distinction between the general council and the general chapter must be constantly kept in mind. The council differs from the chapter in the number of its members, stability, powers and juridic character. As a rule it consists of fewer members than the chapter, but its stability is more pronounced, since it is permanently attached to the supreme moderator even to the extent of residing with him in the same house. The power of the counselors is less than that of the capitulars not only in degree but also in kind, for their aid is sought in the ordinary affairs of government rather than in the grave matters reserved to the general chapters. Finally, chapters are always truly collegiate moral persons, while councils, except for specific cases indicated in the Code or the Constitutions, lack this juridic character.[16]

The common law leaves it to special legislation to determine the

---

[13] Canons 2381, n. 2 and 2222, § 1.

[14] Can. 516, § 1.

[15] Wernz-Vidal, *Ius Canonicum,* III, 128.

[16] Larraona, "Commentarium Codicis," *CpR,* VI (1925), 428–430; Goyeneche, "Consultationes," *CpRM,* XXII (1941), 199–201.

number of the counselors, the manner of their appointment, their term of office and their personal qualities. It seems necessary, however, that the council of the supreme moderator consist of at least four members, since the Code requires at least four religious in the council or the chapter for passing a sentence which calls for the dismissal of a religious from the Institute.[17] Their election or nomination is to be made according to the norms of the Constitutions which normally exclude appointment by the general superior himself in order to forestall the creation of a benevolent *definitorium.*[18]

Though the council does not possess any jurisdiction, its advisory function is performed by means of a vote which may be either binding upon the superior, i.e., a deliberative vote, or nonbinding, i.e., a simply consultative vote.[19] The common law and the Constitutions determine the specific cases in which the general superior is to seek consent from his counselors, who by their deliberative vote, generally given in secret, decide his course of action.[20] Should the supreme moderator act without securing the council's consent or perform any act contrary to the deliberative vote of the council, the act is invalid.[21] If, however, their decision is displeasing to him he may refrain from acting entirely, since the vote does not oblige him to act.

In all matters, except the enumerated ones in the Code for which the deliberative vote of the council is required, the Code merely requires that the superior consult his *definitorium* when he is commanded to act jointly with council.[22] Upon consultation, however, the supreme moderator does not for the sake of validity need to follow the resultant counsel, but prudence urges him to follow the unanimous opinion of his counselors unless he has

---

[17] Can. 655, § 1.

[18] Schaefer, *De religiosis,* p. 325.

[19] Can. 516, § 1.

[20] In the Code the consent of the council is required for admission to the first temporary profession (can. 575, § 2) ; for dismissal of professed religious (canons 647, § 1 ; 650, § 1 ; 653 ; 655 ; 668) ; for the election of an econome (can. 516, § 4), and for the alienating of goods and the contracting of debts (can. 534, § 1). The particular Constitutions must be consulted for other matters requiring the deliberative vote and consent of the council.

[21] Can. 105, n. 1.

[22] E.g., canons 543 ; 896 ; 1395, § 3.

grave and prevalent reasons to the contrary.[23] Whenever the Code or the Constitutions fail to specify the type of vote that is required, the supreme moderator is presumed to enjoy the favor of the law, so that only a consultative vote seems to be indicated, particularly since a deliberative vote implies a restriction on his powers.[24] Although the opinions of canonists vary, it is probable that, even if the superior general failed to consult his council when consultation is required, his act would be valid, though of course illicit.[25]

It is important to note the manner in which the consent or the consultation of the council should be sought by the supreme moderator. Since the council juridically is not a collegiate moral person, it is not obligatory that it follow the laws in the Code governing the deliberation of such bodies, although these could serve as indicative norms. Usually the method of procedure is detailed in the particular Constitutions. If, however, they contain no such determination, then it seems that the advisory-board nature of the council would demand that it meet collectively and that the general superior seek its consent or advice as from a group rather than by approaching the members individually.[26]

Problems may arise if the council refuses to respond to the general superior's request for consent or counsel. If their consent is required by law, but has not been furnished either affirmatively or negatively, then the supreme moderator could not proceed to perform the action as if consent had actually been given.[27] Since a positive consent is required for validity, recourse could then be had to the general chapter or to the Holy See. If only advice or counsel is prescribed, then the supreme moderator has substantially fulfilled his obligation by giving his council an opportunity to express its opinions, and he may proceed to act even if their

---

[23] Can. 105, n. 1.

[24] Fanfani, *De iure religiosorum*, p. 79.

[25] For a detailed study of the controversy in which the arguments of the canonists are critically examined see Michiels, *Principia Generalia de Personis in Ecclesia* (Lublin, 1932), pp. 406–418; De Carlo, *Jus Religiosorum*, pp. 81–82; Clancy, *The Local Superior*, pp. 64–65.

[26] Chelodi-Ciprotti, *De personis*, pp. 169–170.

[27] Ojetti, *Commentarium*, II, 184.

counsel is withheld.[28]   It is presumed in this case that the counselor's silence, when they were given the opportunity to express their opinion, indicates that either they had nothing to contribute or they were not opposed to the proposed plan of the general superior.

Finally, attention must be called to the phrase which is occasionally found in the Constitutions or in rescripts emanating from the Holy See, and which permits the superior to act with the consent of the community (*cum consensu communitatis*). Such a provision (requirement) is not fulfilled if the supreme moderator simply seeks the consent of his council; he is obliged to seek permission from all the members of the community who enjoy active electoral rights.[29]   The obvious reason underlying this conclusion is that the general superior's council is not a body representative of all the members of the community but simply an auxiliary group of religious who aid the supreme moderator in the performance of his duties.

4. The General Chapter

Although a modified ascetical concept of general chapters existed from the very beginnings of religious and cenobitical life, and was even incorporated in the Benedictine Rule in the sense of a body of counselors,[30] its modern juridic counterpart has its origin in the fully organized machinery of centralized government as introduced by the Cistercian and Mendicant Orders in the twelfth and thirteenth centuries.[31]

The general chapters during the reform movements were designed to serve as a check and balance system with reference to the powers of the supreme moderator, and to democratize the form

---

[28] Toso, *Commentaria Minora*, II, 54.

[29] Goyeneche, "Consultationes," *CpRM*, XVII (1936), 247.

[30] *Regula*, c. III. "Quotiens aliqua praecipua agenda sunt in monasterio, convocet abbas omnem congregationem, et dicat unde agitur. Et audiens consilium fratrum tractet apud se, et quod utilius iudicaverit faciat. Ideo autem omnes ad concilium vocari diximus, quia saepe iuniori Dominus revelat quod melius est . . . Si qua vero minora agenda sunt in monasterii utilitatibus, seniorum tantum utatur consilio . . ."

[31] Neukirchen, *De Capitulo Generali in Primo Ordine Seraphico*. Bibliotheca Seraphico-Cappucina, Sectio Historica, Tom. XII (Romae, 1952), p. 7.

of government in religious Institutes, in order to prevent inept superiors from performing acts detrimental to the common good of the Institute. Subsequent monastic and canonical legislation developed the juridic nature of general chapters into collegiate moral persons, which became electoral bodies in which many of the jurisdictional powers within religious communities were vested, and to which most of the legislative powers were reserved, and, finally, from which the major superiors had to seek decisions in matters of greater importance. From a merely consultative institute the general chapter evolved into a deliberative body of representatives possessing a decisive vote in the grave affairs of the community.

Surprisingly the Code does not officially command the regular holding of general chapters. Nevertheless, the Holy See insists upon the inclusion of legislation to this effect in the particular Constitutions of religious Institutes.[32] Furthermore, frequent mention of the general chapter in the Code, with indications of its competence in numerous affairs of the Institute, implies its existence and furnishes an insight into its juridic nature.[33] In view of this, many of the powers of the supreme moderator and the exercise of his authority are intimately connected with the functioning of the general chapter.

The general chapter of exempt religious Institutes enjoys jurisdictional powers.[34] Its specific jurisdictional competence is at times indicated in the Code, but a full delineation of its powers must be sought in the special legislation. As a rule its powers are greater than those of the general superior, and hence matters of greater importance are reserved for its decision.[35] In fact, while it is in session it exercises full and supreme power within the Institute.[36] If, however, the general chapter cannot be held, or if

---

[32] Neukirchen, *op. cit.*, p. 15.

[33] Cf. especially canons 494, § 2; 501, § 1; 506, § 1; 597, § 3; 655, § 1.

[34] Can. 501, § 1.

[35] Coronata, *Institutiones*, I, 636; Lewis, *Chapters in Religious Institutions*, The Catholic University of America Canon Law Studies, No. 181 (Washington, D.C.: The Catholic University of America Press, 1943), p. 54.

[36] Schaefer, *De religiosis*, p. 232.

problems arise in the interim between chapters, its powers devolve upon the supreme moderator with his council.[37]

The right to convoke a general chapter, to determine the place of its meeting, and to preside over its sessions belongs to the supreme moderator, unless the Constitutions rule otherwise.[38] Not infrequently the Cardinal Protector or some appointee of the Holy See presides over the general chapters of exempt religious Institutes.[39] Once convoked, the general chapter is divided for the sake of convenience, into two sections, the general chapter of elections and the general chapter of affairs. During the sessions of the former, the election of the supreme moderator and of other officials takes place; during the latter, important religious and business matters are transacted. In electing the supreme moderator the general chapter must observe the provisions of canons 160–182.[40] Unless special law makes other provisions, the general superior is subject to correction, punishment and even deposition by the general chapter.[41]

The exercise of legislative authority within an exempt Institute is principally vested in the general chapter. Obviously it cannot enact laws contrary to the common law, the Rule or the Constitutions, nor even can it interpret them authentically, since these proceed from a higher authority than its own. With reference to the laws enacted by previous chapters, except such as have been approved by the Holy See *in forma specifica,* the chapters enjoy the power to interpret or even abrogate them, since the authority of all general chapters in the Institute is the same.[42] Laws enacted by the chapter are intended for the whole Institute and bind everyone, including the supreme moderator.

Some of the general superior's executive and administrative powers are considerably curtailed by the common law and notably by special legislation in favor of the general chapter. While the

---

[37] Can. 494, § 2.

[38] De Carlo, *Jus Religiosorum,* p. 78.

[39] Piatus, *Praelectiones,* I, 657.

[40] Can. 507, § 1.

[41] Coronata, *Institutiones,* I, 637. Pejška (*Ius Canonicum Religiosorum,* p. 219), however, contended that the deposition of a general superior is a major cause reserved to the Holy See. Cf. Lewis, *op. cit.,* pp. 63–65.

[42] Canons 17 and 22.

chapter is in session it decides the disposition of the goods of a province which has ceased to exist; outside the chapter, however, the supreme moderator together with his council exercises the same power.[43]   Disjunctively with the supreme moderator, the general chapter is vested with the right to approve houses of study [44] and, disjunctively with all major superiors, with the right to determine and change the limits of the cloister in exempt religious Institutes.[45]

More easily recognizable is the restriction of the general chapter's power in those canons of the Code wherein the supreme moderator is enjoined to seek the advice or the consent of the general chapter in order to act.   Thus, in the alienating of goods and in the contracting of debts, the supreme moderator needs the consent either of the general chapter or of his council; [46] if the right to receive novices and to admit them to religious profession is granted to the general superior by special law, he must nevertheless seek the vote of the chapter or of his council; [47] for issuing a declaration of an *ipso facto* effected dismissal of a religious, he, as well as other major superiors, must act jointly with the chapter or the council; [48] in order to pass sentence in a process of the dismissal of a solemnly professed religious, or in order to confer upon other trustworthy and prudent religious in distant lands this faculty of instituting a process of dismissal, he also needs the consent of the chapter or his council.[49]   Finally, the common law forbids the general superior to enter or to defend a suit in the name of his community without the consent of the chapter.[50]

Despite the extensive legislative, judicial and coercive powers wielded by the general chapter, the supreme moderator retains considerable control over it and, in some cases, possesses the exercise of these powers exclusively.   His control over the chapter stems from his chairmanship at the chapter.   As the presiding officer he

---

[43] Can. 494, § 2.

[44] Can. 587, § 1.

[45] Can. 597, § 3.

[46] Can. 534, § 1.

[47] Can. 543.

[48] Can. 646, § 2.

[49] Can. 667.

[50] Can. 1653, § 3.

enjoys not only prestige and dignity, but also real authority. Canonists concede to him the right and the obligation to decide an issue by casting his decisive vote if, after the third ballot, a relative majority is not obtained as the result of an equal division of the votes.[51]   An example of the second is found in the common law when the Code restricts to the supreme moderator alone the power to reserve sins, although the general chapter, like the general superior, by reason of its jurisdictional power can inflict all canonical penalties.[52]   Nevertheless, the general chapter ultimately wields the greater power, for it can take up and discuss matters, even against the will of the general superior who is its moderator, and may even arrive at decisions which are not acceptable to him.[53]   Finally, the supreme moderator is bound to see to the prompt and faithful execution of the decrees of the general chapter, and to give good example to all the religious under his care by being the first to give obedience to them.[54]

5. Canonical Visitation

Canonical visitation of religious by their superiors dates back to the origins of monastic life.   It was perfected during the Middle Ages with the reform movements within monasticism and the rise of the highly centralized Mendicant Orders.[55]   Compared with the vast legislation of the past centuries on the visitation of religious, the Code offers but little.   No treatment is given to the nature or the scope of a canonical visitation beyond the simple affirmation of the right and duty of some major superiors to conduct one within their spheres of jurisdiction.   The details of a visitatorial system are to be provided by special legislation, since

---

[51] Can. 101, § 1, n. 1. Cf. De Carlo, *Jus Religiosorum,* p. 78.

[52] Can. 896.

[53] Vromant, *De Bonis Ecclesiae Temporalibus* (Louvain, 1927), p. 56.

[54] Heston, "Some Aspects of Government in Religious Communities," *The Jurist,* X (1950), 47.

[55] For the historical development of visitation see the earlier chapters of this dissertation. Further extensive historical material is to be found in Reilly, *The Visitation of Religious,* The Catholic University of America Canon Law Studies, No. 112 (Washington, D.C.: The Catholic University of America, 1938), pp. 3–64; O'Brien, *The Provincial Superior,* pp. 66–69.

it can best reflect an understanding of the particular problems and needs of the organization.

The Code, following the legislation of the Council of Trent,[56] imposes the obligation upon the major superiors designated by the constitutions to visit, at appointed times, either in person or through others, if they are legitimately impeded from doing so, all the houses subject to their jurisdiction.[57]   Hence, not all superiors have the duty to make a canonical visitation of their subjects, but only those major superiors whom the constitutions designate.   In exempt religious Institutes this right is generally reserved to the provincial superior and the supreme moderator, or their delegates.   The common law also does not determine the frequency, the time, or the duration of the visitation.   In practice, annual visitations by the provincial, and triennial or sexennial visitations by the general superior, are prescribed by special law.[58]

The obligation incumbent upon the supreme moderator to conduct a visitation of the Institute is a personal one.   Since, however, the Code permits the general superior to delegate a visitor if for some legitimate reason he himself is hindered from performing the task, the usual practice is to appoint a *visitator generalis.* Such procedure is sometimes counseled by the respective Constitutions, inasmuch as they give the general superior the liberty to undertake the visitation himself or by way of a duly appointed visitor.   This faculty is granted to the Constitutions by the Code, and they exercise it by way of the disjunctive designation of a visitor, with the specification that the visitation be conducted by either the general superior or his appointee.   Furthermore, a legitimate cause for delegation seems to be always existent in view of the tremendous expansion of the Orders, numbering many provinces and thousands of members, and extending throughout

---

[56] Sess. XXV, *de regularibus et monialibus,* cc. 1 and 20.

[57] Can. 511: "Maiores religionum Superiores quos ad hoc munus constitutiones designant, temporibus in eisdem definitis, omnes domos sibi subiectas visitent per se, vel per alios, si fuerint legitime impediti."

[58] The Constitutions of the Franciscan Order impose the obligation of a triennial visitation upon the Minister General. "Provincias Ordinis per se, vel per Visitatores generales . . . Minister generalis tertio et sexto anno a celebrato Capitulo provinciali visitare debet."—*Regula et Constitutiones Ordinis Fratrum Minorum,* art. 417.

the world. A personally conducted visitation, even every three years, would leave the supreme moderator unable to fulfill his many other obligations. In general, as long as a grave moral or physical excusing cause exists, the supreme moderator may delegate his power of visitation to another.[59]

Although the Code is silent about it, particular Constitutions commonly enjoin upon the visitor a personal interview with each member of the community. This is a logical consequence of the very nature and purpose of the visitation, namely the examination of the spiritual and temporal administration of the religious houses and the provision of adequate corrective measures. Unless he be restricted by the special law or, in the case of a delegated visitor, unless his faculty is curtailed by the ordinary visitor,[60] the visitor of religious may inquire and personally investigate all matters he judges to have a bearing on his task. He has a right and a duty to question any of the religious who in his opinion should be questioned, and to inform himself on those matters that pertain to the visitation. All religious are placed under the obligation to reply truthfully, and superiors are forbidden to divert them in any way from fulfilling this obligation or otherwise to impede the purpose of the visitation.[61]

Special law and lists privately drawn up by recognized canonists indicate the matters pertaining to the scope of a general visitation. Usually the inquiries in a visitation embrace the place (local visitation), documents and books (real visitation), persons (personal visitation) and any extraordinary and particular circumstances and problems for which the visitation is ordered.[62]

---

[59] Larraona, "Commentarium Codicis." *CpR*, VIII (1927), 357–358.

[60] According to the principles of delegation, a delegated visitor may receive faculties extending to all that an ordinary visitor is empowered to do (*ad universalitatem causarum*), or for certain matters only (*ad singulos et determinatos casus*). Cf. Coronata, *Institutiones*, I, 335.

[61] Can. 513, § 1: "Visitator ius et officium habet interrogandi religiosos quos oportere iudicaverit et cognoscendi de iis quae ad visitationem spectant; omnes autem religiosi obligatione tenentur respondendi secundum veritatem, nec Superioribus fas est quoquo modo eos ab hac obligatione avertere aut visitationis scopum aliter impedire."

[62] In the Franciscan Order the visitation is undertaken according to the detailed norms enacted in the *Synoptica Instructio pro Visitatore Generali et Praeside Capituli Provincialis* (Quaracchi, 1923). Representative lists are

In many instances the Constitutions of the different Institutes specify the matters to which the visitor is obliged to attend, and clearly outline the limitations of his powers.

During the visitation, the dominative power of the local superior and the dominative and jurisdictional powers of the provincial are more or less suspended. Above all is this true in those matters in which the visitor has taken a hand.[63] It is for this reason that the seal of the superior is officially placed in the custody of the visitor at the time of the visitation. The conducting of a visitation by the supreme moderator is, therefore, an act of government. Canon 513 implicitly states that visitors possess the right to issue decrees, to remedy the abuses discovered in the course of the visitation, and to promote the good of the Order. In doing so they are not using a merely dominative power but, being ordinaries and prelates, are exercising jurisdiction or judicial authority over their subjects. In keeping, however, with the injunction of canon 345, and also in harmony with long-established monastic customs, the visitation of the general superior is primarily a paternal rather than a judicial procedure, especially since canon 513, § 2, indicates that judicial procedure reflects an exceptional occurrence. Nevertheless, if a denunciation is made to the general visitor, he is obliged to institute or have instituted a judicial investigation or criminal process.[64]

6. The Decrees of the Holy See

In addition to the promulgation of its own decrees in the *Acta Apostolicae Sedis*, the Holy See imposes upon all superiors the obligation of promoting among their subjects the knowledge and execution of those decrees of the Holy See which concern religious.[65] The word "decree" is here taken in its generic sense rather than in reference to any specific decree [66] and includes,

---

furnished by Schaefer (*De religiosis*, p. 312), Mothon (*Institutions Canoniques* [3 vols., Paris, 1922]) and Gallen, "Canonical Visitation of Higher Superiors," *Review for Religious*, XII (1953), 28–29.

[63] Schaefer, *De religiosis*, p. 313.

[64] Can. 1935, § 2. Cf. De Carlo, *Jus Religiosorum*, p. 85; Fanfani, *De iure religiosorum*, p. 92; Vermeersch-Creusen, *Epitome*, III, 116.

[65] Can. 509, § 1.

[66] Schaefer, *De religiosis*, p. 293.

therefore, any and all decrees having a direct bearing upon the religious life, and especially such as refer to the superior's own institute. Papal documents directed to religious, be they priests, clerics, or brothers, or containing instructions concerning their spiritual life, or detailing norms for those who are engaged in work among the faithful, would definitely be included among the decrees to be read in an exempt institute. It is, furthermore, advisable to include not only the decrees emanating from the Sacred Congregation of Religious, but also those that are issued by other Roman Congregations or Offices which have an immediate interest for religious, e.g., decrees regarding the liturgy, indulgences, or privileges granted to all the faithful.[67]

The proximate obligation to promote and execute the decrees of the Holy See is incumbent upon the local superior, inasmuch as the usual procedure in making them known to the religious is by reading them publicly (in the refectory, chapter room or oratory) or by displaying them in some appropriate place, such as the community bulletin board.[68] If the local superior is remiss in fulfilling this obligation, the provincial is obliged to call his attention to this failure, and to direct him to inform his subjects of the decrees.[69] The supreme moderator, in the final instance, has the gravest obligation to supervise the fulfillment of this obligation in all the houses and provinces of the Institute, and to ascertain in his official visitation whether it has been done.[70] In practice, he facilitates the dissemination of the decrees among the provinces by having them inserted in the institute's official publication or by having the generalitial curia transmit printed copies of the pertinent decrees to all concerned.

Which specific decrees are to be read, and how often, is not determined in the Code. Prior to the promulgation of the new Code, three decrees of the Holy See were to be read yearly in every community of exempt religious, and were usually printed

---

[67] Piatus, *Praelectiones,* I, 634–637.

[68] Clancy, *The Local Superior,* p. 58; Fanfani, *De iure religiosorum,* p. 138.

[69] O'Brien, *The Provincial Superior,* p. 65.

[70] Wernz-Vidal, *Ius Canonicum,* III, 121. Question 92 of the *Elenchus Quaestionum* to be answered in the Quinquennial Report deals with the observance of Can. 509, § 1.

together with the approved Rule and Constitutions. These decrees dealt with the manifestation of conscience (*Quemadmodum* of Leo XIII), the confessions of religious (*Cum de sacramentalibus* of Pius X) and the frequent reception of Holy Communion (*Sacra Tridentina Synodus* of Pius X). Since their provisions have been incorporated into the new Code, they need no longer be read.[71] Hence canon 509, § 1, refers only to new decrees which have been or will be issued since the present Code is in effect. At present, when the Holy See issues a decree regarding religious Institutes, a notation is inserted that it be read publicly in each community at least once, or repeatedly at yearly intervals. Only one such decree dealing with the clerical and religious training of candidates for the priesthood is at present to be read in its entirety to religious clerics at the beginning of each year.[72]

7. The Quinquennial Report

The Holy See, always solicitous for the welfare of the members of religious communities and desirous to be well informed concerning their status, has ordained that the supreme moderator of all pontifical institutes shall send to the Sacred Congregation for Religious every five years, or more frequently if the Constitutions so demand it, a report concerning the state and condition of the organization, signed by him and his council.[73] A few years after the promulgation of the Code some supplementary legislation to this effect was introduced, to be effective January 1, 1923.[74]

---

[71] Vermeersch-Creusen, *Epitome,* I, 363; Creusen, *Religieux et Religieuses d'après le Droit Ecclésiastique,* p. 61.

[72] S. C. de Religiosis, instr. *Quantum Religiones,* 1 dec. 1931—*AAS,* XXIV (1932), 74–81. Pejška (*Ius Canonicum Religiosorum,* p. 233) arbitrarily asserted without adducing any juridic reasons that the *Sacra Tridentina Synodus* of December 20, 1905, in which Pius X exhorted the faithful to the frequent and daily reception of Holy Communion, must still be read in religious communities.

[73] Can. 510. The *"status religionis"* in the canon includes the disciplinary, material, personal and economic state of the institute. Cf. Schaefer, *De religiosis,* p. 296, footnote 369.

[74] S. C. de Religiosis, decr. *Sancitum est,* 8 martii, 1922—*AAS,* XIV (1922), 161–163. The form to be used in the making of this report was issued March 25, 1922—*AAS,* XIV (1922), 278–286. An official English translation of the list of questions was made by the Congregation and printed in the

The numerous modern problems which beset religious subsequent to the upheavals of the second world war have induced the Holy See to issue a new instruction regarding the quinquennial report.[75] Its provisions change and amplify the original legislation of canon 510 and the decree *Sancitum est* of 1922, and must be joined with the list of questions provided by the Sacred Congregation of Religious for the Quinquennial Report of Papal Institutes.[76]

In accordance with the instructions of the decree *Cum transactis*, the supreme moderator must send directly to the Sacred Congregation of Religious a report of the state of the Order every five years, even if the year assigned for sending the report falls wholly or partly within the first two years from the time when he assumed his office.[77] Sincerity and completeness in the replies are demanded, and these demands bind in conscience. If the replies are deficient, uncertain or unreliable, the Sacred Congregation of Religious will *ex officio* see to it that they are completed and, if need be, will itself directly conduct the investigations.[78] The report must be signed not only by the general superior, but also by the members of his council after a careful, personal, and collective examination of its contents.[79]

In the same decree an Annual Report which is independent of the Quinquennial Report is required for statistical purposes. The supreme moderator of exempt religious is obliged to fill it out, in Latin, on the very forms he receives, and to return it directly to

---

AAS, XV (1923), 459–466. According to the new regulations the report is to be made every five years, with the superiors of monastic Orders sending their report in the first year (1928), the Mendicant Orders in the second (1929), the Regular Clerics in the third (1930), etc.

[75] S. C. de Religiosis, decr. *Cum transactis*, 9 iulii, 1947—*AAS*, XL (1948), 378–381.

[76] These Questions, issued by the S. C. of Religious on December 9, 1948, are of a private nature and did not appear in the official *AAS*. The official English version is entitled: "The List of Questions which are to be answered by Religious Institutes and Societies in the Report to be sent to the Holy See every Five Years according to the Decree *Cum transactis*," is to be found in Bouscaren, *Digest*, III, 158–207.

[77] No. I.

[78] No. VI.

[79] No. VII.

the Sacred Congregation of Religious. This report must be of the greatest possible precision and up-to-date as of the 31st of December of the year preceding the one in which the report is sent.[80]

8. Participation in the Ecumenical Council

Among those clerics who are entitled to be invited to an ecumenical council with a decisive voice in its proceedings are the supreme moderators of clerical exempt religious Institutes.[81] In this they have greater rights than titular bishops, who obtain the deliberative vote only if they are called to the council and the decree of convocation does not provide otherwise.[82] Since the deliberative vote is essentially a jurisdictional act, this provision is in keeping with the general superior's extensive jurisdiction in the external forum, which titular bishops lack altogether.[83]

As a member who is present at the council with a decisive vote, the supreme moderator becomes a father of the council.[84] Furthermore, in virtue of his decisive voice, he participates in the character of a true judge in all the transactions and proceedings of the council, and hence in signing the conciliar decrees he uses the formula *"definiens subscripsi,"* rather than the *"consentiens subscripsi"* that is used by those who enjoy the consultative voice only.[85]

Since the supreme moderator is one of the members of the council who are officially invited to participate, he must, if he is lawfully prevented from attending, send a procurator and prove his inability to attend.[86]

---

[80] A private Circular Letter, dated February 9, 1950, on how to fill the Annual Report was sent by the S. C. of Religious to all Superiors General. An English translation was made and published by the same Congregation. Its text is to be found in Bouscaren, *Digest*, III, 207–212.

[81] Can. 223, § 1, n. 4.

[82] Can. 223, § 2.

[83] Vermeersch-Creusen, *Epitome*, I, 224.

[84] Abbo-Hannan, *The Sacred Canons*, I, p. 290, footnote 5.

[85] Beste, *Introductio in Codicem*, p. 235.

[86] Can. 224, § 1.

B. Administrative Aspects of the Executive Power

1. Authority over Provinces and Religious Houses

The common law grants the supreme moderator jurisdiction over all provinces, houses and members within his Institute, which is to be exercised, however, according to the provisions of the Constitutions.[87] This general and unrestricted grant of authority by the Code makes it impossible for the supreme moderator to receive any further powers through the common law. Consequently, as would be expected, the Code refrains from legislating concerning the exercise of his power in particular cases. In a very few canons, however, attention is called to a specific function reserved to the office of the supreme moderator, and, at times, his obligation to co-operate with the chapter or the council in grave matters is also mentioned. Practically all other determinations of his power must be sought in the Constitutions of his Institute, a task which is outside the scope of this study.

Although the supreme moderator may appoint a provincial and his consultors [88] as well as accept their resignations,[89] he is, nevertheless, incapable of founding new provinces, of uniting them or otherwise changing their boundaries, or of suppressing existing provinces, all of which is reserved by law exclusively to the Apostolic See.[90] In practice, however, even in these grave matters, the supreme moderator exercises considerable power and influence. As the highest superior within the Institute he is best aware of its needs and of the means most suitable to provide for them. Hence, he retains the right to petition the Holy See for a favorable decision in a problem for whose solution he contributes suggestions based on his diligent and serious study. Customarily the Holy See empowers him and his council with the necessary faculties to deal with the problem of the establishment, suppression and change of provinces, subject to its own approval.[91] The

---

[87] Can. 502.

[88] Pejška, *Ius Canonicum Religiosorum,* p. 234.

[89] Can. 187, § 1.

[90] Can. 494, § 1.

[91] The faculty to establish a new province is generally given in rescript form by the Sacred Congregation of Religious. If some complicated problem arises, or if there be need either of the suppression of provinces or of terri-

mechanics of the procedure are invariably left to the discretion of the general superior.

Upon the suppression of a province, the Code authorizes the general chapter to dispose of its erstwhile property, unless the Constitutions provide otherwise, and, if the chapter is not in session, this power devolves upon the supreme moderator and his council.[92] The question arises immediately: must the general superior seek the consultative or the deliberative vote of his council to effect the proper disposal of the property? Some canonists, basing themselves on the fact that matters of admittedly grave importance are here considered and that the general council is acting as a substitute for the general chapter, find implied the need of a deliberative vote.[93] The phrasing, however, of the canon, which simply states that "the supreme moderator with his council" is to settle the property affairs of the extinguished province, seems to imply that only a consultative vote of the council is necessary. A phrase which adverts to the imposing of an obligation upon the general superior should by rule of law be interpreted strictly and, hence, a simple consultation seems the most that can be demanded. Coronata also sees canons 11 and 15 as militating against the opinion of those who demand a deliberative vote.[94]

Without interfering in the internal government of the province, the supreme moderator exercises a supervisory authority over the provincial. The general visitation, made by himself or by his delegate, informs him of the status of the province and, should any violations of the religious life be discovered, he is to make provision for their immediate eradication. Culpable superiors, including provincials, are to be admonished and, if his removal from office is at stake, he is previously to be warned. Since the higher

---

torial changes, the Holy See is wont to issue an Apostolic Letter to this effect in which it requests the supreme moderator and his council to examine the situation and to present their findings for the apostolic approval. Cf. Pius XII, Apostolic Letter *Quae paterna*, 27 dec. 1945—*AOFM*, LXV (1946), 9–1.

[92] Can. 494, § 2.

[93] Schaefer, *De religiosis*, p. 151; Vermeersch-Creusen, *Epitome*, I, 348-349; Blat, *Commentarium*, Vol. II, Lib. II, p. 538; Cocchi, *Commentarium*, II, p. 33; Augustine, *Commentary*, III, 80.

[94] *Institutiones*, I, p. 619, footnote 3.

superior can appoint the provincial to office, by the same token he can remove him for a just cause. No prescribed procedure for removal from office is found in the common law of the Church, but upon the removal the Code provides for a possible recourse *in devolutivo* to the Holy See.[95]   In practice, the particular Constitutions or processual norms of the Institute determine the manner in which a provincial may be suspended or removed from office. The gravity of the cause usually indicates that the supreme moderator should not proceed summarily, but should at least consult his *definitorium*.[96]

The canonical establishment of a religious house, which is the establishing of a moral personality pertaining to their religious state in a place where the community has a permanent residence, is a complex process in which several authorities concur. Ordinarily, the initial decision to establish a new house rests with the provincial, who must also undertake the gathering of all preliminary information before he presents a formal petition for approbation by the competent ecclesiastical authority.[97]   For authorization to establish an exempt religious house, either one that is to exist fully organized or one that is only partially evolved, the approval of the Holy See and the written consent of the local ordinary are required.[98]   In practice, the provincial obtains the written consent of the local ordinary and petitions the supreme moderator to seek the approval of the Holy See.[99]   Once canonically established, the exempt religious house cannot be suppressed

---

[95] Can. 192, § 3.

[96] Cf. *Regula et Constitutiones Ordinis Fratrum Minorum*, art. 385. Opportunity is to be given to the provincial to resign from Office. If he declines, the minister general may remove him from office upon consultation with the members of his council, whose opinions are to be given by way of secret ballot. See also the *Modus Procedendi in Causis Disciplinaribus, Contentiosis, Criminalibus Ordinis Fratrum Minorum Capuccinorum auctoritate Capituli Generalis LXXII Promulgatus* (Romae, 1945), art. 37.

[97] Flanagan, *The Canonical Erection of Religious Houses*, The Catholic University of America Canon Law Studies, No. 179 (Washington, D.C.: The Catholic University of America Press, 1943), pp. 33–34.

[98] Can. 497, § 1.

[99] *Regula et Constitutiones Ordinis Fratrum Minorum*, art. 340, § 1.

by the supreme moderator without the permission of the Apostolic See.[100]

In view of his universal power over all the provinces and religious houses of the Institute, the supreme moderator can exempt a religious house from the jurisdiction of the provincial and make it immediately subordinate to himself. It is customary for general superiors to reserve to themselves the jurisdiction over religious houses destined for international purposes, such as universities, research academies and institutes.

The establishment of the limits of the cloister within the religious house is left to the major superiors of the Institute or to the general chapter, as determined by the Constitutions.[101] It is unlikely that this power will be reserved to the general chapter in any Institute, for the long intervals between chapters make it inadvisable.[102] As a rule, in addition to the faculty exercised through the Constitutions or by the general chapter, which may order to be left open some parts of the religious house, which the Code prescribes to be enclosed, the defining of the limits of the cloister is principally vested in the provincial. The supreme moderator's rôle is practically reduced to that of supervision to be exercised at the time of the general visitation.

2. Authority over the Members of the Religious Community

a. Admission to Novitiate and Profession

The admission of lay brother postulants and clerical candidates to the novitiate was always a right reserved to the major superiors of exempt Institutes, and not infrequently it was restricted by special law to the supreme moderator.[103] In the present law the right to admit candidates to the novitiate and to subsequent profession, either temporary or perpetual, belongs to the major superiors in union with the vote of their council or of their

---

[100] Can. 498.

[101] Can. 597, § 3.

[102] Schaaf, *The Cloister*, The Catholic University of America Canon Law Studies, No. 13 (Washington, D.C.: The Catholic University of America, 1921, p. 72, footnote 78.

[103] A historical survey of the pre-Code legislation regarding the reception of novices is given by O'Brien, *The Provincial Superior*, pp. 87–88.

chapter, according to the particular Constitutions of the respective Institutes.[104]   Although major superiors as such receive this faculty through the common law, the Constitutions of all Mendicant Orders attribute its exercise to the provincial superiors without any intervention on the part of the supreme moderator.[105] The vast territorial expansion of these exempt Institutes and their tremendous numerical growth make it unfeasible to expect the direct and immediate intervention of the general superior.[106]

It can be noted immediately that the special law is given extensive powers and must be consulted for supplementary legislation in this regard.   The Constitutions will, as a rule, determine specifically which of the major superiors, exclusively or cumulatively, have the authority to grant admission to the novitiate and to profession.   Secondly, the Constitutions will indicate which chapters or councils are to cast their vote for admission to the novitiate, and which have electoral rights regarding admission to temporary or perpetual profession.   Finally, special law will define the requisite nature of this vote, whether it be deliberative or consultative, with its resultant effect upon the validity of the novitiate or the profession.[107]

In abstraction from special legislation, however, several important factors in the common law must be considered.   According to the Code the admission to the novitiate or to the various professions is not reserved to the same major superior, nor is the vote of the same chapter or council prescribed, nor is the same type of vote required in all instances.[108]   The common law simply states that the right to admit a candidate to the novitiate and to profession resides in the major superiors in union with the vote of their council or of their chapter.   Hence, for validity, a vote of one of these bodies is necessary; the Constitutions retain only the right to determine which of these two is to be approached by the major

---

104 Can. 543.

105 Larraona, "Commentarium Codicis," *CpRM*, XIX (1938), 8–9.

106 There is no canonical foundation for the opinion of Chelodi, who contended that the admission of a novice to temporary profession frequently is reserved to the Provincial, while the perpetual profession is made into the hands of the supreme moderator.—*De personis*, p. 428.

107 Larraona, "Commentarium Codicis," *CpRM*, XIX (1938), 8.

108 Larraona, "Commentarium Codicis," *CpRM*, XVIII (1937), 319.

superior. Furthermore, since the Code does not speak of "counselors or capitulars" but of "councils or chapters," it is clear that the fixed and stable constitutional bodies, voting as a group, and not simply the individual constituent members, are to cast their votes.[109] This voting must follow the rules enacted in canon 105. Larraona is of the opinion that the major superior could not designate a body of counselors whose only duty would be the deliberation concerning the fitness of the candidates for admission to the novitiate or to profession.[110]

The general superior may obtain either the deliberative or the consultative vote of his chapter or of his council for the valid admission to the novitiate according to the norm established in the Constitutions of his Institute. For the admission, however, to the first temporary profession, the deliberative vote is required, although a mere consultative vote is sufficient with reference to the perpetual profession.[111] Since only the major superiors have the right to admit to the novitiate and to profession, the chapter or the council does not have and cannot be given this faculty by the Constitutions. Even after obtaining an affirmative vote from these bodies, the major superior is not obliged to follow the result of their voting. In fact, if he considers the candidate unworthy of reception he need not even bring him under scrutiny for possible admission.[112] Canonists differ on the validity of admission to the novitiate or to profession apart from the previous vote of the council or the chapter.[113] In the light of the strong arguments adduced by both sides, and in view of the lack of a definite pronouncement from the Holy See, the nullity of the act performed without the consultation of the chapter or the council need not be upheld.

In connection with the admission to profession an incidental question arises. In reference to it the supreme moderator is the

---

[109] Coronata, *Institutiones,* I, 703; Larraona, "Commentarium Codicis," *CpRM,* XVIII (1937), 326.

[110] "Consultationes," *CpR,* I (1920), 368.

[111] Can. 575, § 2. Cf. Larraona, "Consultationes," *CpR,* I (1920), 367.

[112] Coronata, *Institutiones,* I, 703.

[113] De Carlo (*Jus Religiosorum,* pp. 81–82) and Goyeneche ("Consultationes," *CpR,* III [1922], 265) provide a summary of the argumentation for both opinions.

sole superior authorized to act. According to canon 569, § 1, the novice must freely and for the duration of his vows dispose of his goods, but should need arise for him to change this disposition he cannot undertake it without the permission of the supreme moderator.[114]

b. Dismissal of Religious

1) The *Ipso Facto* Effected Dismissal of Members of a Religious Community

The three causes or delicts which precipitate the *ipso facto* effected dismissal of a religious are public apostasy from the Catholic faith, flight with a person of the other sex, and attempted or contracted marriage, even the so-called civil marriage.[115] A dismissal is incurred even if the religious is ignorant of the law, for it is not conditioned by any degree of knowledge as is the case for the contracting of *latae sententiae* penalties, i.e., of penalties which are incurred *ipso facto*.[116] In these three delicts no special solemnities are required for dismissal. It suffices that the major superior with the chapter or his council make a declaration of the fact as prescribed by the Constitutions. He must also take care to preserve in the registers of the house the collected evidence of the fact.[117] The Pontifical Commission for the Authentic Interpretation of the Code has, however, stated that this declaration is not necessary for validity.[118]

Since the Code uses the unrestricted term "major superiors," the authorized superior who can make the declaration of the fact of dismissal is the one defined in canon 488, n. 8.[119] The Consti-

---

[114] Can. 580, § 3.

[115] Can. 646, § 1.

[116] Can. 2229. Cf. Pfaller, *The Ipso Facto Effected Dismissal of Religious,* The Catholic University of America Canon Law Studies, No. 259 (Washington, D.C.: The Catholic University of America Press, 1948), pp. 107–158, for an analytic discussion of these delicts and a critical evaluation of the circumstances accompanying the commission of each of them.

[117] Can. 646, § 2.

[118] *Responsum,* 30 iulii, 1934—*AAS,* XXVI (1934), 494; Bouscaren, *Digest,* II, 175. Cf. Maroto, "De Religiosis Dimissis," *CpR,* XV (1934), 352.

[119] It must be noted that there is question here, not of a *sententia declaratoria,* but simply of a *declaratio facti.* In the pre-Code legislation a true

tutions of the Institute should determine which major superior, the immediate or the supreme, is competent in this matter. If the Constitutions do not make any express determination, then it seems that the provincial, as the immediate major superior, should act without any need of intervention on the part of the supreme moderator.[120]

Before proceeding to the declaration of the fact of dismissal, the superior must institute an investigation whereby he becomes informed of the pertinent facts, namely, that the given delict was indeed committed by the religious in question.[121] Having diligently gathered the evidence, usually the testimony of two or three witnesses, a civil document or affidavit, or any other extra-judicial source of information, the superior must confer with the chapter or his council. The Constitutions of the Institute must indicate which of the two is to concur with the major superior in the declaration of the dismissal.[122] If, however, they are silent, it suffices for the major superior to act with his personal council, since it is more convenient than to await the convocation of the chapter. The Constitutions should likewise determine the nature of the vote of the participating chapter or council.[123] If in this matter also the Constitutions maintain silence, a consultative vote should be sufficient, for the major superior thereby fulfills his obligation to act with the chapter or his council as prescribed by law. The opinion of some canonists, namely, that the Constitutions may designate which body, the chapter or the council, is to participate in the declaration of dismissal when it is not entrusted to the major superior alone by law, leads them to conclude that the designated body must participate with a deliberative vote.[124]

---

sententia declaratoria was demanded. Cf. Tabera, "De Dimissione Religiosorum," *CpR,* XI (1930), 419.

[120] Pfaller, *op. cit.,* p. 169.

[121] Coronata, *Manuale Practicum Iuris Disciplinaris et Criminalis Regularium* (Taurini-Romae, 1938), p. 110 (hereafter cited as the *Manuale Fracticum*); Toso, *Commentaria Minora,* V, 248.

[122] Coronata, *Institutiones,* I, 851, footnote 6.

[123] Schönsteiner, *Grundriss des Ordensrechtes* (Wien-Donauwörth-Basel, 1930), p. 627.

[124] Pfaller, *op. cit.,* p. 174; Villien, "La Procédure Canonique pour l'Expulsion des Réligieux," *Le Canoniste Contemporain,* XXXVI (1913), 214.

This, however, seems to be too demanding and without foundation in the text of the law.

The text of the canon, furthermore, imposes upon the major superior the duty to declare the fact of dismissal. Although the Pontifical Commission for the Authentic Interpretation of the Code stated in one of its Responses that the declaration is not necessary for the effecting of the dismissal, it certainly did not intend to free the superiors from this obligation, for that would then be tantamount to the abrogation of the law itself.[125] The official Response of the Commission must be construed to mean that the dismissal is not conditioned on the declaration of the fact, but follows automatically and immediately (*ipso facto*) upon the commission of the delict. Hence, no suppression of the superior's obligation to make a declaration to this effect was intended.[126] In fact, the phrasing of the canon indicates that it is not merely a power which is possessed by the superior, but that it is an obligation, and indeed one that he must fulfill personally without delegating it to another.

Since no method or form of procedure is indicated in the Code, the manner in which the declaration is to be made is left to the discretion of the superior.[127] Consequently, since no formal decree is required, a simple declaration is sufficient.[128]

Lastly, the evidence that has been gathered must be preserved by the superior in the archives. Some canonists, adhering strictly to the text of the canon, are of the opinion that only the preservation of the proofs is intended by the Code.[129] It seems logical, however, that the intent of the law is for the official statement containing the declaration of the fact of dismissal to be likewise preserved for the record.[130]

---

[125] Maroto, "Annotationes," *CpR*, XV (1934), 355; Jombart, "De Religiosis Dimissis," *Nouvelle Revue Théologique*, LXI (1934), 1081.

[126] Pfaller, *op. cit.*, p. 175.

[127] Coronata, *Institutiones*, I, 851.

[128] Goyeneche, "Studia Canonica," *CpR*, XIII (1932), 103–104; Bastien, *Directoire Canonique a l'Usage des Congrégations à Voeux Simples* (5 ed., Bruges, 1951), p. 129.

[129] Augustine, *Commentary*, III, 386; Eichmann, *Lehrbuch des Kirchenrechts* (4 ed., 2 vols., Paderborn, 1934), I, 257.

[130] Coronata, *Manuale Practicum*, p. 111; Toso, *Commentaria Minora*, V, 249.

2) Dismissal of Religious in Temporary Vows

According to the Code, the dismissal of a religious in temporary vows in a religious Order or a pontifical Institute is effected by the supreme moderator with the consent of his council manifested by secret ballot.[131] Since the consent and not merely the advice of the council is required by law, its vote is deliberative, so that it must be followed by the general superior for the valid dismissal of the religious.[132]

Although no formal canonical process is prescribed, the general superior must ascertain the existence of serious reasons warranting the dismissal, either on the part of the institute or on the part of the religious.[133] The gathering of these data is usually incumbent upon the provincial, but the supreme moderator should see to it that the evidence is recorded in writing, so that it may be forwarded to the Sacred Congregation of Religious in case the dismissed religious seeks redress from the Holy See.[134] The reasons for the dismissal must be made known to the religious, who must be allowed to answer the charges brought against him. A written record of the charges and of their refutation should be made and then be given to the religious to read, correct and sign.[135] Should he refuse to do so, this refusal should be attested in writing.

The supreme moderator seeks the consent of his council to effect the dismissal of the religious after the second admonition proves to be of no avail. He must present to the council the proofs of the reasons adduced for the dismissal, indicate that the administered admonitions and salutary penances failed, and pre-

---

[131] Can. 647, § 1.

[132] Schaefer, *De religiosis*, p. 990.

[133] Can. 647, § 2, nn. 1 and 2. An exhaustive study and an enumeration of the serious causes sufficient for dismissal are made by O'Neill, *The Dismissal of Religious in Temporary Vows, The Catholic University of America Canon Law Studies*, No. 166 (Washington, D.C.: The Catholic University of America Press, 1942), pp. 107–143. Cf. also Coronata, *Manuale Practicum*, pp. 112–115; Tabera, "De Dimissione Religiosorum," *CpR*, XII (1931), 369–372.

[134] Bouscaren-Ellis, *Canon Law* (2 ed., Milwaukee, Wis.: Bruce, Reprint, 1953), p. 313.

[135] Can. 647, § 2, n. 3.

sent the refutation by the religious of the charges made against him. After a mature discussion and deliberation of these matters, the council proceeds to a secret vote, with the majority deciding whether or not to authorize the general superior to effect the dismissal. The secrecy of the ballot is required only for the licitness of the procedure, and not for its validity.[136]

3) Dismissal of Religious in Solemn Vows

A canonical trial is usually required by the Code for the dismissal of men religious professed with solemn vows.[137] The supreme moderator with his council or the chapter, acting as a tribunal of at least five judges, issues the sentence of dismissal. If a sufficient number of judges is not available, he must choose, with the consent of the others, a sufficient number of religious to supplement the lack.[138] As is usual in all judicial processes, the presence of a notary is required and that of a promoter of justice, both of whom are appointed by the supreme moderator.[139] The sentence passed by this tribunal does not take effect until it has been confirmed by the Sacred Congregation of Religious, to which the general superior is obliged to forward as soon as possible the verdict and all the official acts of the judicial process.[140]

Since the common law designates the supreme moderator together with his council or the chapter as the authority competent to render a sentence of dismissal of a religious in solemn vows, the explanation previously given in this study of the interrelationship existing between the superior and his council or the chapter, and the nature of their vote in the effecting of the dismissal, is to be kept in mind.[141]

The judicial process of dismissal is not to be undertaken unless three conditions are fulfilled, namely, the commission of grave external crimes either against the common law or against the

---

[136] Coronata, *Institutiones,* I, 853.

[137] Can. 654. Possible exceptions are the provisions of canon 646, which involves cases of an *ipso facto* effected dismissal, and can. 668, which provides for a summary dismisssal in urgent cases.

[138] Can. 655, § 1.

[139] Canons 503 and 655, § 2.

[140] Can. 666.

[141] Cf. pp. 167–170.

special law of the Institute, the giving of admonitions, and the lack of amendment.[142] The immediate major superior is burdened with the pre-judicial inquisition concerning the fulfillment of these required conditions and the implementation of the admonitions. When the fact of a lack of amendment is ascertained, it is his duty to draw up the case of dismissal personally or through a delegate, and then to forward the findings to the supreme moderator.[143] Incidentally, the prescribed canonical warnings may also be made either by the supreme moderator himself or by his delegate.[144] Upon receipt of these data, the general superior must deliver them to the promoter of justice, who examines the pertinent material and makes further opportune investigations before filing the accusation with the duly constituted tribunal. This tribunal then proceeds to conduct the trial, *mutatis mutandis*, in accordance with the provisions of the fourth book of the Code.[145]

For distant countries, even amid normal and ordinary contingencies, the supreme moderator may, with the consent of his council or the chapter, delegate the faculty of dismissing his subjects. He may delegate at least three trustworthy and prudent religious, who must conduct the trial in accordance with the provisions of canons 663–666.[146] A delegated tribunal in distant lands may be granted this faculty even habitually.[147] If special circumstances warrant it and the supreme moderator and his council deem it advisable, the tribunal may be increased to five members.[148] Upon completing the trial, the supreme moderator and his tribunal proceed to issue the sentence of dismissal. The execution, however, of the sentence is deferred until confirmation is received from the Sacred Congregation of Religious. In other words, the sentence of the tribunal is not the final act of dismissal sentence (*sententia definitiva*).[149] In view of this, the opinion of

---

[142] Can. 656.

[143] O'Brien, *The Provincial Superior*, p. 161.

[144] Can. 659.

[145] Can. 664, § 1.

[146] Can. 667.

[147] Coronata, *Manuale Practicum*, p. 131.

[148] Can. 1576, § 2.

[149] Can. 1868.

Vermeersch-Creusen, who state that the religious is truly dismissed in consequence of the unconfirmed sentence, is untenable.[150]

c. The Reservation of Sins

Since the administration of the sacraments is a highly personal activity, which involves personal contact between the recipient and the minister, the common law concedes the sacramental functions to the local superior and the provincial, who are the immediate superiors of religious. The supreme moderator, in virtue of the highest authority which he possesses in the exempt Institute, exercises a remote power of supervision and, if special law so designates, an immediate intervention in the administration of the sacraments by the granting or the withholding of faculties and the imposing of restrictions. In only one instance, namely, with regard to the reservation of sins, does the Code grant the power to the supreme moderator exclusively.

A reservation signifies a withholding to oneself of a determined power, thus excluding others from the exercise of that power. The radical power to absolve from sin as received in ordination requires in addition a possession of jurisdiction for its exercise. By reserving a sin, the ordinary or the superior limits the possession of this jurisdiction to himself. Prior to the time of Clement VIII (1592–1605) all major superiors of clerical exempt Institutes possessed extensive powers for the setting up of reservations, but the Clementine reforms limited prospective reservations to eleven specific sins.[151] The law of the Code introduced further changes in the previous legislation.

Among the superiors of a clerical exempt Institute only the superior general with his council is authorized to reserve sins in their nature of sins (*ratione sui*) in regard to his subjects, but without prejudice to the provisions of canons 518, § 1 and 519.[152] The opening words of the canon, "among the superiors," raise the question of the general chapter's possible deprivation of this power. According to some canonists the phrase has reference to other individual superiors, thus leaving intact the power of the

---

[150] *Epitome*, I, 498.

[151] Clemens VIII, decr. *Sanctissimus*, 26 maii, 1593—*Fontes*, n. 177.

[152] Can. 896.

general chapter in this matter.[153] It seems, however, an unwarranted determination of the general term "superior" and an unnecessary distinction introduced into the law, which is to be understood as expressing what its words signify.

Another difficulty in the canon arises concerning the force of the injunction that the supreme moderator reserve sins "with his council." The law definitely does not indicate the degree or the kind of co-operation between the superior and his council. Some canonists are of the opinion that the council must be consulted for validity, otherwise the superior could not be said to reserve sins "with his council." It would seem, however, to be more in accordance with the rules of law to regard the supreme moderator free from following his council's opinions, since the Code itself does not hold him to this obligation.[154] *A pari* an argument may be deduced from the preceding canon, wherein the procedure prescribed for the local ordinaries in reserving sins imposes upon them the obligation only of "hearing their cathedral chapter" (*audito Capitulo cathedrali*).[155]

No longer can the supreme moderator reserve the eleven sins enumerated in the Decree *Sanctissimus* of Clement VIII, for the common law prescribes that only a very few cases should be reserved, i.e., three or at most four of only the more serious and heinous external and specifically determined crimes. This reservation is not to remain in effect longer than is necessary for the extirpation of some deep-rooted public vice and the preservation of a possibly lapsed Christian standard of morality.[156] Among these reserved sins cannot be included those which already are reserved to the Apostolic See, even by reason of censure, or those for which a censure, even though not reserved to anyone, is imposed by law.[157]

Much of the import of the power to reserve sins is lost in the legislation of the Code prescribing the authorizing of confessors

---

[153] Vermeersch-Creusen, *Epitome,* II, 104.

[154] Jone, *Commentarium,* II, 138; Cappello, *Tractatus Canonico-Moralis de Sacramentis* (5 vols., Taurini-Romae, 1943–1950), II, 325.

[155] Can. 895. Cf. Vermeersch-Creusen, *Epitome,* II, 106.

[156] Can. 897.

[157] Can. 898.

of the institute to absolve from the sins so reserved [158] and the granting of this faculty to all confessors who, having jurisdiction from the local ordinary, hear the confessions of religious who come to them for peace of conscience.[159]

d. The Prohibition of Books

The Code grants the power to the supreme moderator of clerical exempt religious to prohibit the reading of books judged to be harmful to the spiritual welfare of his subjects.[160] This power is analogous to that of the local ordinary; the only canonical difference is that the authority of the local ordinary is territorial, while that of the superior general is personal. Ordinarily the supreme moderator assisted by the chapter or his council prohibits his subjects from reading a specific book whenever a just cause arises, namely, the danger to faith and morals arising for a person exposed to pernicious literature. The Church deems it so important to forestall this danger that provision is made, if delay should prove harmful, for the provincial with his council to exercise this same power, with the obligation, however, of notifying the supreme moderator of their decision as soon as possible. If a book is prohibited by the supreme moderator, his subjects may not read it even though they have obtained a general permission from the Apostolic See to read prohibited books.[161]

Any prohibition of books in accord with the ruling of canon 1395, § 3, is an exercise of the power of jurisdiction possessed by the major superiors of exempt religious Institutes. In virtue of their dominative power, however, all superiors, including the local superior, can forbid their subjects to read a specific book which they deem harmful to their subjects' spiritual welfare.[162]

The supreme moderator, being an ordinary in the eyes of the Code, is not bound by the ecclesiastical prohibition of books, provided of course that the necessary precautions are employed.[163]

---

[158] Can. 518, § 1.

[159] Can. 519.

[160] Can. 1395, § 3.

[161] Can. 1403, § 1.

[162] Vermeersch-Creusen, *Epitome,* II, 452; Goyeneche, "Consultationes," *CpR,* IX (1928), 427.

[163] Can. 1401.

It is important to keep in mind that he is exempt only from the ecclesiastical law, which does not forbid him to read prohibited books. He is always prohibited by the divine law from reading those books which would expose him to the proximate occasion of sin.

Permission to read books that are forbidden by the law of the Code or by a decree of the Apostolic See may be given to his subjects by the supreme moderator, but for individual books only and in urgent cases exclusively.[164] If he has obtained a general faculty from the Holy See to permit his subjects to keep and read forbidden books, he must be discreet in the use of this faculty and grant such permissions only for a just and reasonable cause.[165] Since this power stems from his ordinary jurisdiction, he may delegate others to grant these permissions.

e. The Supervision of Studies

The establishment of major and minor seminaries in the Provinces, and the implementation of the *ratio studiorum* and of norms for the intellectual life of teachers and students in religious communities are governed by the particular Constitutions and the *Statuta pro Studiis Regendis* commonly introduced among the religious Institutes. In the five canons of Title XII of the Tract on Religious in the Code, only the most general of legislation is included, with a great deal of freedom left to the "judgment of superiors," the "approval of superiors and the general chapter" and the "provisions of the Constitutions." Since their future fruitful sacred ministry depends upon the proper training and education of the clerics and the teachers, the conscientious fulfillment of the provisions of the Code and of the Constitutions is incumbent upon the major superiors. Special law is usually very incisive in laying down the norms governing studies in the religious Institute. If, however, it is silent on some points, the matter of education is of such major importance that consultation with the supreme moderator and his council is indicated as a matter of prudence.

Of primary importance for the present study is the legislation

---

[164] Can. 1402, § 1.

[165] Can. 1402, § 2.

of canon 589, § 2, which insists that professors and students be granted sufficient time for study, and provides for exemption from community exercises, so that they may devote a complete and constant attention to their studies.[166] In other words, the second paragraph of this canon has a twofold purpose: first, to remove obstacles to studies by prohibiting the assignment of offices to teachers and students if they be incompatible with study; secondly, to grant to the supreme moderator and, under certain conditions, to other superiors as well, the faculty to relax the common exercises of the community if they are not conducive to the furthering of studies in the Institute.

The incompatibility of certain offices with the scholarly life of teachers and students was realized early in the history of the Church, particularly at the time of the rise of the Universities in the Middle Ages. Benedict XII (1334–1342) permitted teachers in the Cistercian Order to enjoy the services of a cleric to free them for scholastic activities. He also prescribed that houses inhabited by students should be provided with four servants to take care of the domestic chores.[167] Clement VIII (1592–1605) forbade the clerics and teachers to preach; they were to leave this task to others within the Institute who were free from studies.[168] Coronata concludes that the Code, in view of these historic precedents, prohibits students from actively exercising the sacred ministry involving the care of souls, from hearing confessions, and from performing other external offices of religion.[169] Students, however, may, once or twice, perform these functions, since the occasional hearing of confessions or delivery of a sermon is not to be construed as a habitual exercise of the pastoral office.[170]

---

[166] "Studiorum tempore magistris et alumnis officia ne imponantur quae a studio eos avocent vel scholam quoquo modo impediant; supremus autem Moderator et in casibus particularibus alii quoque Superiores possunt pro sua prudentia eos a nonnullis communitatis actibus, etiam a choro, praesertim nocturnis horis, eximere, quoties id studiis excolendis necessarium videatur."

[167] Oesterle, "De ratione studiorum in religionibus clericalibus," *CpR*, VI (1925), 315.

[168] Decree *Nullus omnino*, 25 iulii, 1599—*Fontes*, n. 187.

[169] *Institutiones*, I, 764. Cf. also the Instruction of the Sacred Congregation of Religious, October 27, 1923—*AAS*, XV (1923) 549.

[170] Shaefer, *De religiosis*, p. 648; Vermeersch, Annotationes," *Periodica de Re Morali, Canonica, Liturgica*, XII (1923), 156.

In virtue of the express declaration of canon 589, § 2, the supreme moderator may, in the interest of studies, exempt his subjects from some communal exercises, even from choir, particularly from the nocturnal recitation of the divine office. While the granting of this general, habitual exemption is reserved to the supreme moderator, in particular cases this exemption may also be prudently granted by other religious superiors.[171] Canonists agree that such a dispensation may be given to teachers and students not only while they are actively engaged in preparation for lectures or for attendance at class, but also while they are enjoying a vacation from studies.[172] As Pope Pius X, however, pointed out in his letter to the Master General of the Order of Preachers, all abuses in this regard must be sedulously avoided.[173]

f. The Affiliation of Tertiaries

The establishment of a new congregation of tertiaries living in common requires not only the securing by the bishop of the apostolic *beneplacitum* from the Sacred Congregation of Religious, but also the sending of a petition for affiliation to the First Order, which petition is to be directed to the supreme moderator of said Institute.[174] Such aggregation can be granted only by the general superiors of those Orders which have the right or the privilege of affiliating Third Orders.[175] Among these are the supreme moderators of the three Franciscan families, of the Order of Friars Preachers, of the Augustinians, of the Carmelites, and of the Servites. It is doubtful if the abbot primate of the Benedictines possesses this right.[176] Until, however, the Holy See decrees otherwise, some canonists assert this right for the monastic abbots of the Benedictines.[177]

---

[171] Vermeersch-Creusen, *Epitome*, I, 441; Fanfani, *De iure religiosorum*, p. 313.

[172] Cf. Prümmer, *Manuale Iuris Canonici*, p. 289, who also names other canonists of note who favor such a benign interpretation; cf. also Vermeersch-Creusen, *Epitome*, I, 441; De Carlo, *Jus Religiosorum*, p. 260.

[173] *AAS*, V (1913), 389.

[174] Can. 492, § 1.

[175] Can. 703, § 1.

[176] Coronata, *Institutiones*, I, 613.

[177] Augustine, *Commentary*, III, 69.

The request for affiliation may be made as soon as the Holy See has given its initial permission for the foundation of the religious Institute of Tertiaries.[178]   This aggregation is not to be effected until the new congregation is actually existing, but if it is granted prior to this moment it obtains its force from the moment of the completed establishment.[179]

The basis of affiliation or aggregation presupposes a certain spiritual affinity and a similarity in the mode of life existing between the Institute of tertiaries and the First Order. In many instances the similarity is not restricted to the community of spirit, but extends to such externals as mode of dress and official designation.[180]   In the case of Franciscan Tertiaries, for example, it consists in the adoption of the Third Order Rule especially designed for them by the founder of the Franciscan Order. The primary effect of affiliation is the participation in the indulgences and the spiritual favors of the First Order, but it does not in itself confer any jurisdiction upon the supreme moderator of the First Order over the affiliated congregation.[181]

With the rise and growth of Secular Institutes, the Holy See saw fit to extend the legislation of canon 492, § 1, to embrace them as well as the Third Orders Regular. In the Instruction on Secular Institutes a special concession is granted for them to be helped by religious Orders and to be morally guided by them, but not to an extent that would seem to detract from the autonomy of government in the Secular Institutes.[182]

---

[178] Abbo-Hannan, *The Sacred Canons,* I, 498.

[179] Coronata, *Institutiones,* I, 613.

[180] Schönsteiter, *Grundriss des Ordensrechtes,* pp. 54–56.

[181] Beste, *Introductio,* p. 320.

[182] S. C. de Religiosis, instr. 19 martii, 1948—*AAS,* XL (1948), 293–297; Bouscaren, *Digest,* III, 147–157. "Etsi nihil impediat quominus, ad normam iuris (can. 492, § 1), Instituta Saecularia Ordinibus aliisque etiam Religionibus, ex speciali concessione, aggregari, et ab ipsis diversimode adiuvari et etiam aliquo modo moraliter dirigi valeant, tamen aliae strictioris dependentiae formae, quae Institutorum Saecularium regiminis detrahere viderentur ipsamve tutelae plus minus strictae subiicere, etiamsi ab ipsis Institutis, mulierum speciatim, desiderentur et invocentur, non nisi difficulter, bono Institutorum attente considerato, atque spiritu et apostolatus cui incumbere debent natura ac ratione ponderatis, opportunisque adhibitis cautelis, concedi poterunt."

CONCLUSIONS

In our common experience we realize that human institutions and institutes are never wholly static and permanent, and hence movement and change take place. Canonically, an Order is an organized religious body of men living according to a strictly defined and approved Rule and governed by Constitutions, confirmed by the Holy See, under the authority of one Supreme Moderator. It would be anachronous to conceive of a religious Order fulfilling these conditions prior to the twelfth century. Indeed, the office of a supreme moderator is not the result of an instantaneous, well-rounded conception, but has historical and juridical precedents going back to the very foundations of monasticism in the early ages of the history of the Church. In tracing the origin and development of the concept of the supreme moderator the following conclusions have been reached:

1. Invariably the founder of a religious community acted as its supreme head during his lifetime and, more often than not, appointed his own successor either directly or indirectly.

2. Oriental monasticism, particularly the Pachomian monks, achieved a high degree of centralization and hierarchical organization equivalent to the stage of development reached by Cluny and Citeaux in the West. Elsewhere cenobitic groups were established independently of one another and were loosely held together by the personal influence of the founder, eminent for virtue and governing ability, rather than by a centrally constituted authority.

3. The great Benedictine fraternity was not an Order, and St. Benedict did not write his Rule for a specific organization but for monks in general. Each abbey had its own supreme moderator in the person of the monastic abbot, who was the absolute and independent head of the community regardless of its size. Many, however, of the prerogatives and obligations of the modern supreme moderator have their origins in the historical interpretation of the office of the monastic abbot.

4. The Cluniacs introduced the idea of a mother-house with its dependent filial foundations, thereby strengthening and increas-

ing the power of the abbot who assumed authority over a regional, even supra-national, community. General chapters and monastic visitation were introduced, not so much to curtail the absolutism of the abbot-general, as to aid in the governance of a numerically and territorially increasing community.

5. As a reaction to the reforms of Cluny, the Cistercian system maintained the autonomy of its daughter-abbeys, but provided an effective authority capable of promulgating and enforcing some laws affecting each member of the organization. Whereas the supreme moderator under the Cluniac system exercised personal and direct rule over all the abbeys and individuals of his organization, the Cistercian system established a just equilibrium between the central power, the abbot of Citeaux, and the representation of the entire community at the general chapter, thus eliminating the evils of the Cluniac centralization of all power in the hands of one man.

6. With the rise of the Mendicant Orders in the thirteenth century came the perfection of the hierarchical monastic organization, with its clearly defined divisions of the religious community on the local, provincial and general levels, with their respective local, provincial and general superiors. Legislative contributions of the past were amalgamated with the juridic innovations answering the needs of the day, and the content and scope of the office of the supreme moderator, ultimately reaching the zenith of its development, was fully delineated in the special legislation. Institutes of later origin than the Mendicants adhered, with minor modifications, to the juridic concept of the general superior as realized in the communities of the thirteenth century.

To the excluding of the possible variant enactments introduced by particular Constitutions in their treatment of the office of the supreme moderator, the following conclusions, based on the legislation of the Code, are offered as a summary of the canonical commentary found in the present study:

1. In keeping with the frequent concessions granted by the Code to the Constitutions and Chapters of respective Institutes of exempt religious, far more legislation on the supreme moderator is to be found in special legislation than in the common law of the Code. The great number of Institutes with their individual purposes and the diverse means of attaining their ends are an

insurmountable obstacle for providing common legislation suitable for all. Consequently, the barest minimum is to be found in the tract of law for religious in the Code.

2. The quasi-episcopal powers enjoyed by the supreme moderator are radically the same as episcopal jurisdiction. With the exemption of certain religious from the jurisdiction of local ordinaries came the gradual increase in jurisdictional powers on the part of the major superiors.

3. In the government of his subjects, the supreme moderator may make use of his dominative power and of the power of jurisdiction. The former is always exercised in the direction of the religious to the particular end of the institute; the latter serves to direct his subjects to the end of the ecclesiastical society. Consequently, acts of dominative power are of a private nature; acts performed through the exercise of jurisdictional power are of a public nature.

4. In virtue of his universal authority over the Institute and its members, the supreme moderator may restrict temporarily, if the common good warrants it, the constitutional powers of the provincial superior.

5. The supreme moderator, though radically possessed of legislative authority, usually has his legislative competence circumscribed by the Constitutions, which reserve to the general chapters the power to enact laws.

6. The general superior may dispense individuals, even habitually, from any disciplinary laws contained in the Constitutions. He cannot, without a special grant from the Holy See, dispense from the laws which govern elections and regulate the general chapters.

7. Whenever the Code or the Constitutions fail to specify the nature of the vote enjoyed by the supreme moderator's council, the consultative vote suffices to fulfill the legal requirement that the supreme moderator act jointly with his council.

8. The general chapter has evolved from a purely consultative institute into a deliberative body of representatives possessing a decisive vote regarding the grave matters of the Institute. Any curtailment of the governmental powers of the supreme moderator usually operates in favor of the general chapter.

BIBLIOGRAPHY

SOURCES

Acta Apostolicae Sedis, Commentarium Officiale, Romae, 1909–

Acta Ordinis Fratrum Minorum, Ad Claras Acquas, Quaracchi, 1882–

Acta Sanctae Sedis, 41 vols., Romae, 1865–1908.

Acta Sanctorum, quotquot toto orbe coluntur, vel a catholicis scriptoribus celebrantur quae ex latinis et graecis, aliarumque gentium antiquis monumentis collegit, digessit, notis illustravit Joannes Bolandus . . . servata primigenia scriptorum phrasi. Operum et studium contulit Godefridus Henschenius . . . Editio novissima, curante Joannes Carnondet, 71 vols., Parisiis: V. Palmé, 1863–1940.

Bouscaren, T. Lincoln, *The Canon Law Digest,* 3 vols. and Supplements through 1953 and 1954, Milwaukee: Bruce & Co., 1934–1949–1953–1954–1955.

Bullarium Franciscanum, Prima series, Tom. I–III, ed. J. Sbaralea, Romae, 1759–1764; Tom. IV, ed. A. Rossi, Romae, 1768; Secunda series, Tom. V–VIII, ed. C. Eubel, Romae, 1897–1904; Nova series, Tom. I, ed. U. Hüntemann; Tom. II–III, ed. J. M. Pou y Martí, Ad Claras Acquas, Quaracchi, 1929–1949.

Bullarium Ordinis FF. Praedicatorum, ed. a T. Ripoll, recognitum a A. Bremond, 8 vols., Romae, 1729–1740.

Bullarum Diplomatum et Privilegiorum Sanctorum Romanorum Pontificum Taurinensis Editio, 24 vols. et Appendix, Augustae Taurinorum, 1857–1872.

Codex Iuris Canonici Pii X Pontificis Maximi iussu digestus, Benedicti Papae XV auctoritate promulgatus, Praefatione, Fontium Annotatione et Indice Analytico-Alphabetico ab Emo Petro Card. Gasparri Auctus, Romae, Typis Polyglottis Vaticanis, 1917.

Codicis Iuris Canonici Fontes, cura Emi Petri Card. Gasparri editi, 9 vols., Romae (postea Civitate Vaticana) : Typis Polyglottis Vaticanis, 1923–1939 (Vols. VII–IX, ed. cura et studio Emi Iustiniani Card. Serédi).

Constitutiones Fratrum S. Ordinis Praedicatorum, Parisiis, 1886.

Corpus Iuris Canonici, ed. Lipsiensis secunda, post Aemilii Richteri curas . . . instruxit Aemilius Friedberg, 2 vols., Lipsiae, 1879–1881.

Decretales D. Gregorii IX usu cum Glossis restitutae, Romae, 1582.

Decretum Gratiani emendatum et notationibus illustratum, una cum Glossis, Gregorii XIII Pont. Max. iussu editum, 2 vols., Romae, 1582.

Holstenius, Lucas, *Codex Regularum Monasticarum et Canonicarum quas*

SS. *Patres Monachis, Canonicis et Virginibus Sanctimonialibus serv-
andas praescripserunt. Collectus olim a S. Benedicto Anianensi
Abbate: nunc autem auctus, amplificatus et in sex Tomos divisus.
Observationibus critico-historicis a R.R.P. Mariano Brockie, S.T.D.,
Priore ac Seniore Monasterii S. Jacobi Scotorum Ratisbonae illus-
tratus*, 6 vols., Augustae Vindelicorum, 1759.

Mansi, J. D., *Sacrorum Conciliorum Nova et Amplissima Collectio*, 53 vols.
in 60, Parisiis, 1901–1927.

Regula et Constitutiones Generales Ordinis Fratrum Minorum, Romae, 1953.

Schroeder, H. J., *Canons and Decrees of the Council of Trent: Original
Text with English Translation*, St. Louis: B. Herder Book Co., 1941.

REFERENCE WORKS

Abbo, John—Hannan, Jerome, *The Sacred Canons*, 2 vols., St. Louis: B.
Herder Book Co., 1952.

Acta Congressus Iuridici Internationalis, 5 vols., Romae: Apud Custodiam
Librariae Pont. Instituti Utriusque Iuris, 1935–1937.

Albers, Paulus, *S. Pachomii Abbatis Tabennensis Regulae Monasticae
accedit S. Orsiesii ejusdem Pachomii Discipuli Doctrina de Institutione Monachorum*, Florilegium Patristicum, Band XVI, Bonn, 1923.

Alvissenet, *De privilegiis Ordinum Regularium*, Venetiis, 1653.

Appeltern, V., *Compendium Praelectionum Juris Regularis*, editio altera
aucta et emendata, Parisiis, 1913.

Augustine, Charles, *A Commentary on the New Code of Canon Law*, 8
vols., Vols. III and VIII, 3. ed., St. Louis: B. Herder Book Co., 1922
and 1931.

Barker, E., *The Dominican Order and Convocation*, Oxford, 1913.

Bastien, P., *Directoire Canonique a l'Usage des Congrégations à Voeux
Simples*, 5. ed., Bruges: Abbaye de Maredsous, 1951.

Baumann, L., *Les Chartreux*. Collection "Les Grands Ordres Monastiques"
chez Bernard Grasset, 1928.

Bennett, R. F., *The Early Dominicans*, Cambridge, 1937.

Bertinato, P., *De Religiosa Iuventutis Institutione in Ordine Fratrum
Minorum*, Romae, 1954.

Beste, U., *Introductio in Codicem*, 3. ed., Collegeville, Minn.: St. John's
Abbey Press, 1946.

Biederlack, J.—Führich, M., *Jus Ecclesiasticum Privatum*, Romae, 1909.

—————. *De Religiosis*, Oeniponte: Rauch, 1919.

Billot, J., *Tractatus de Ecclesia Christi*, 4. ed., Romae, 1921.

Blaher, D., *The Ordinary Process in Causes of Beatification and Canonization*, The Catholic University of America Canon Law Studies, n. 268,
Washington, D.C.: The Catholic University of America Press, 1949.

Blat, Albertus, *Commentarium Textus Iuris Canonici*, 6 vols., Vol. II, Lib.
II, 2. ed.. Romae, 1921.

Boehmer, H., *Analekten zur Geschichte des Franciskus von Assisi*,
Tübingen-Leipzig, 1904.

Bouix, D., *Tractatus de Jure Regularium*, 3. ed., 2 vols., Parisiis, 1883.

Bouscaren, T.—Ellis, A., *Canon Law*, 2. ed., Milwaukee: Bruce, Reprint, 1953.

(Boutrais), *The History of the Great Chartreuse*, London, 1934.

Butler, C., *Benedictine Monachism*, London, 1919.

————, *The Lausiac History of Palladius*, Texts and Studies, VI, 2 vols., Cambridge, 1898–1904.

Cambridge Medieval History, ed. by J. R. Tanner, C. W. Previté—Orton, Z. N. Brooke, 8 vols., Vols. VI and V, Cambridge, 1929 and 1943.

Campbell, G. A., *The Knights Templars: Their Rise and Fall*, New York, n.d.

Capobianco, P., *Privilegia et Facultates Ordinis Fratrum Minorum*, Salerno, 1946.

Cappello, F., *Tractatus Canonico-Moralis de Sacramentis*, 5 vols., Vol. I–II, 5. ed., Vol. V, 6. ed., Taurini-Romae: Marietti, 1947 and 1950.

————, *Summa Iuris Publici Ecclesiastici*, 2. ed., Romae: Marietti, 1928.

Cappiello, Linus, *De Ordinariorum Dispensandi Facultate ad normam can. 81*, The Catholic University of America Canon Law Studies, n. 323, Washington, D.C.: The Catholic University of America Press, 1952.

Chelodi, J.—Ciprotti, P., *Ius Canonicum de Personis*, 3. ed., Vicenza-Trento, 1942.

Christ, Joseph, *Dispensation from Vindicative Penalties*, The Catholic University of America Canon Law Studies, n. 174, Washington, D.C.: The Catholic University of America Press, 1943.

Chronologia Historico-legalis Seraphici Ordinis Fratrum Minorum Sancti Patris Francisci, 4 vols., Neapoli-Venetiis-Romae, 1650–1796.

Cicognani, Amleto, *Canon Law*, 2. ed., Westminster, Md.: The Newman Press, Reprint, 1949.

Clancy, P., *The Local Religious Superior*, The Catholic University of America Canon Law Studies, n. 175, Washington, D.C.: The Catholic University of America Press, 1943.

Clarke, W. K., *St. Basil the Great. A Study in Monasticism*, Cambridge, 1913.

Cocchi, Guidus, *Commentarium in Codicem Iuris Canonici*, 8 vols. in 5, Vol. IV, 2. ed., Taurinorum Augustae: Marietti, 1926.

Coronata, Matthaeus Conte a, *Institutiones Iuris Canonici*, 5 vols., Vol. I, 4. ed., Vol. III–IV, 4 ed., Taurini-Romae: Marietti, 1950 and 1956.

————, *Manuale Practicum Iuris Disciplinaris et Criminalis Regularium*, Taurini-Romae: Marietti, 1938.

————, *Ius Publicum Ecclesiasticum*, 3 ed., Taurini-Romae: Marietti, 1948.

Creusen, J., *Religieux et Religieuses l'après le Droit Ecclésiastique*, 4. ed., Louvain, 1930.

Currier, C. W., *The History of Religious Orders*, New York, 1914.

Cuthbert, Fr., *Life of St. Francis of Assisi*, London, 1927.

De Carlo, Camillus, *Jus Religiosorum*, Parisiis-Tornaci-Romae: Desclee, 1950.

De Gubernatis, D., *Orbis Seraphicus*, 6 vols., Romae-Lugduni, 1682–1689.

Delatte, Paul, *The Rule of St. Benedict*, tr. by Justin McCann, London, 1921.

Donatus, Hyacinthus, *Rerum Regularium Quadripartita Praxis Resolutoria*, 4 vols., Neapoli, 1652–1661.

Dugdale, Wm., *Monasticon Anglicanum: A History of the Abbies and other Monasteries, Hospitals, Friaries, and Cathedral and Collegiate Churches with their Dependencies in England and Wales*, edited by J. Caley, H. Ellis and B. Bandinel, 6 vols. in 8, London, 1817–1830.

Eichmann, E., *Lehrbuch des Kirchenrechts*, 4. ed., 2 vols., Paderborn: F. Schoeningh, 1934.

Emmanuel a Conceptione, *Enchiridion Judiciale Ordinis Fratrum Minorum*, Ulyssiponae, 1693.

Evans, Joan, *Monastic Life at Cluny, 910–1157*, London, 1931.

Fanfani, Ludovicus, *De Jure Religiosorum ad Normam Codicis Iuris Canonici*, e. ed., Taurini-Romae: Marietti, 1925.

Ferroglio, G., *La Condizione Giuridica degli Ordini Religiosi*, Torino, 1931.

Flanagan, Bernard, *The Canonical Erection of Religious Houses*, The Catholic University of America Canon Law Studies, n. 179, Washington, D.C.: The Catholic University of America Press, 1943.

Galbraith, G. R., *The Constitution of the Dominican Order, 1216 to 1360*, Manchester, 1925.

Gasquet, F., *Monastic Life in the Middle Ages*, London, 1922.

Gerardus de Fracheto, *Vitae Fratrum Ordinis Praedicatorum*, ed. by B. Reichert, *Monumenta Fratrum Praedicatorum Historica*, Vol. I, Romae, 1896.

Grandi, G., *Dissertationes Camaldulenses*, Lucca, 1707.

Grundmann, H., *Religiöse Bewegungen im Mittelalter*, Berlin, 1935.

Gwynn, Aubrey, *The English Austin Friars in the Time of Wyclif*, Oxford, 1940.

Hefele, Carolus—Leclercq, Henricus, *Histoire des Conciles*, 11 vols. in 21, Paris: Letouzey et Ané, 1907–1952.

Heimbucher, M., *Die Orden und Kongregationen der katholischen Kirche*, 3. ed., 2 vols., Paderborn, 1933–1934.

Helyot, P.—Badiche, L., *Dictionnaire des Ordres Religieux ou Histoire des Ordres Monastiques, Religieux et Militaires, et des Congrégations Séculières de l'un et de l'autre Sexe, qui ont été etablies jusqu'a a Présent*, 4 vols., Paris, 1847.

Hermann, J., *Institutiones Theologiae Dogmaticae*, 7. ed., 2 vols., Lugduni, 1937.

Heussi, Karl, *Der Ursprung des Mönchtums*, Tübingen, 1936.

Holzapfel, H., *Manuale Historiae Ordinis Fratrum Minorum*, Friburgi, 1909.

Huber, R. M., *A Documented History of the Franciscan Order, 1182–1517*, Milwaukee-Washington, D.C., 1944.

Humbertus de Romanis, *Opera de Vita Regulari,* 2 vols., Romae, 1888–1889.

Janauschek, Leopoldus, *Originum Cisterciensium Tomus I,* Vindobonae, 1878.

Jone, Heribertus, *Commentarium in Codicem Iuris Canonici,* 3 vols., Paderborn: Schöningh, 1950–1954.

Kazenberger, K.—Iglesias, A., *Liber Vitae seu Regulae S. Francisci Expositio,* Romae, 1948.

Kindt, G., *De Potestate Dominativa in Religione,* Parisiis: Desclée, 1945.

Knowles, D., *The Monastic Order in England. A History of its Development from the Times of St. Dunstan to the Fourth Lateran Council, 943–1216,* Cambridge, 1941.

——————, *The Religious Orders in England,* Cambridge, 1948.

Kybal, V., *Die Ordensregeln des heiligen Franz von Assisi und die ursprüngliche Verfassung des Minoritenordens,* Beiträge zur Kulturgeschichte des Mittelalters und der Renaissance, Band 20, Leipzig-Berlin, 1915.

Ladeuze, P., *Etude sur le Cénobitisme Pakhomien pendant le IV siècle et la Prémiere Moitié du V,* Louvain, 1898.

Le Couteulx, C., *Annales Ordinis Cartusiensis ab anno 1084 ad annum 1429,* 8 vols., Monstrolii, 1887–1891.

Lega, Michael, *Praelectiones in Textum Iuris Canonici, De Iudiciis Ecclesiasticis,* 4 vols., Romae, 1896–1901.

——————, —Bartoccetti, V., *Commentarius in Iudicia Ecclesiastica iuxta Codicem Iuris Canonici,* 2. ed., 3 vols., Romae: Anonima Libreria Cattolica Italiana, 1950.

Lewis, Gordian, *Chapters in Religious Institutions,* The Catholic University of America Canon Law Studies, n. 181, Washington, D.C.: The Catholic University of America Press, 1943.

Lezana, Joannes, *Mare Magnum Ordinum Praedicatorum, Minorum, Eremitarum Sancti Augustini, Carmelitanorum cum ipsorum Regula, Servitarum et Minimorum,* Venetiis, 1653.

Linderbauer, B. S., *Benedicti Regula Monasteriorum.* Florilegium Patristicum, Fasc. XVII, Bonn, 1928.

Mahn, J. B., *L'Ordre Cistercien et son Gouvernement des Origines au Milieu du XIII siècle (1098–1265),* Paris, 1945.

Mandić, P. D., *De Legislatione Antiqua Ordinis Fratrum Minorum,* Mostar, 1924.

Mandonnet, P., *St. Dominic and His Work,* St. Louis: B. Herder Book Co., 1944.

Marchesi, F., *Summula Iuris Publici Ecclesiastici,* Neapoli: M. D'Auria, 1948.

Mayer, H. S., *Benediktinisches Ordensrecht in der Beuroner Kongregation,* 3 vols., Beuron, 1929–1936.

Mazon, C., *Las Reglas de los Religiosos. Su Obligación y Naturaleza Jurídica,* Analecta Gregoriana, Series Iuris Canonici, Vol. xxiv, Romae, 1940.

Micheletti, A. M., *De Superiore Communitatum Religiosarum, Manuale Asceticum, Canonicum ac Regiminis,* Romae, 1911.

Michiels, Gommarus, *Principia Generalia de Personis in Ecclesia,* Lublin: Universitas Catholica, 1932.

————, *Normae Generales Juris Canonici,* 2 vols., Lublin: Universitas Catholica, 1929.

Migne, J. P., *Patrologiae Cursus Completus, Series Graeca,* 161 vols., Parisiis, 1857–1866.

————, *Patrologiae Cursus Completus, Series Latina,* 221 vols., Parisiis, 1844–1855.

Miranda, Ludovicus, *Manualis Praelatorum Regularium,* 2 vols., Placentiae, 1616.

Modus Procedendi in Causis Disciplinaribus, Contentiosis, Criminalibus Ordinis Fratrum Minorum Capuccinorum auctoritate Capituli Generalis LXXII promulgatus, Romae, 1945.

Molitor, R., *Aus der Rechtsgeschichte Benediktinischer Verbände, Untersuchungen und Skizzen,* 3 vols., Münster, 1928–1933.

————, *Religiosi Iuris Capita Selecta,* Ratisbonae, 1909.

Morison, E. F., *St. Basil and His Rule. A Study in Early Monasticism,* Oxford, 1912.

Mortier, R. P., *Histoire des Maîtres Généraux de l'Ordre des Frères Prêcheurs,* 8 vols., Paris, 1903–1920.

Mothon, J. P., *Institutions Canoniques,* 3 vols., Paris, 1922.

Müller, K., *Die Anfänge des Minoritenordens und der Bussbrudenschaften,* Freiburg, 1885.

Neukirchen, Marinus a, *De Capitulo Generali in Primo Ordine Seraphico,* Bibliotheca Seraphico-Cappucina, Sectio Historica, Tom. XII, Romae, 1952.

Noval, Josephus, *Commentarium Codicis Iuris Canonici,* Liber IV, *De Processibus,* 2 vols., Augustae-Taurinorum-Romae: Marietti, 1920–1932.

O'Brien, R., *The Provincial Religious Superior,* The Catholic University of America Canon Law Studies, n. 258, Washington, D.C.: The Catholic University of America Press, 1947.

Ojetti, Benedictus, *Commentarium in Codicem Iuris Canonici,* 4 vols., Romae, 1927–1931.

Onclin, Gulielmus, *De Territoriali vel Personali Legis Indole,* Gemblaci, 1938.

O'Neill, Francis, *The Dismissal of Religious in Temporary Vows,* The Catholic University of America Canon Law Studies, n. 166, Washington, D.C.: The Catholic University of America Press, 1942.

Ottaviani, Alaphridus, *Institutiones Iuris Publici Ecclesiastici,* 2. ed., 2 vols., Romae: Typis Polyglottis Vaticanis, 1935.

Pejška, Josephus, *Ius Canonicum Religiosorum,* 3. ed., Friburgi Brisgoviae, 1927.

————, *Ius Sacrum Congregationis SS. Redemptoris,* Hranice, Moravia, 1923.

Pfaller, Benedict, *The Ipso Facto Effected Dismissal of Religious,* The

Catholic University of America Canon Law Studies, n. 259, Washington, D.C.: The Catholic University of America Press, 1948.

Piatus Montensis, *Praelectiones Iuris Regularis*, 3. ed., 2 vols., Paris, 1906.

Pourrat, P., *Christian Spirituality from the Time of our Lord till the Dawn of the Middle Ages*, tr. by W. H. Mitchell and S. P. Jacques, 3 vols., London, 1922.

Prümmer, Dominicus, *Manuale Iuris Canonici in Usum Scholarum*, 6. ed., Friburgi Brisgoviae: Herder, 1938.

Raggi, Jacobus, *De Regimine Regularium*, Genevae, 1653.

Raymundus de Peñafort, *Summa de Poenitentia*, ed. nova, Veronae, 1744.

Reichert, B., *Acta Capitulorum Generalium Ordinis Praedicatorum ab anno 1220 usque ad annum 1303*, Monumenta Ordinis Fratrum Praedicatorum Historica, Vol. III, Romae, 1898.

Reiffenstuel, A., *Jus Canonicum Universum*, 3. ed., 4 vols., Ingolstadii, 1739.

Reilly, T., *The Visitation of Religious*, The Catholic University of America Canon Law Studies, n. 112, Washington, D.C.: The Catholic University of America, 1938.

Reilly, E., *The General Norms of Dispensation*, The Catholic University of America Canon Law Studies, n. 119, Washington, D.C.: The Catholic University of America Press, 1939.

Robinson, P., *The Writings of Saint Francis of Assisi*, Philadelphia, 1906.

Rodericus, Emmanuel, *Nova Collectio et Compilatio Privilegiorum Apostolicorum Regularium Mendicantium et Non-Mendicantium, praesertim in quibus ipsae Religiones communicant*, Venetiis, 1611.

————, *Quaestiones Regulares et Canonicae*, 3 vols., Antuerpiae, 1628.

Roelker, Edward, *Precepts*, Paterson, N.J.: St. Anthony Guild Press, 1955.

Ryan, J., *Irish Monasticism. Origins and Early Development*, Dublin, 1931.

Schaaf, Valentine, *The Cloister*, The Catholic University of America Canon Law Studies, n. 13, Washington, D.C.: The Catholic University of America, 1921.

Schaefer, Timotheus, *De Religiosis ad Normam Codicis Iuris Canonici*, 3. ed., Romae: Herder, 1940.

Scheeben, H., *Die Konstitutionen des Predigerordens unter Jordan von Sachsen*, Quellen und Forschungen zur Geschichte des Dominikanerordens in Deutschland, Band 38, Köln, 1939.

Schmalzgrueber, Franciscus, *Ius Ecclesiasticum Universum*, 5 vols in 12, Romae, 1813–1845.

Schmitz, P., *Histoire de l'Ordre de Saint Bénoît*, 8 vols., Maredsous, 1942.

Schönsteiner, Ferdinand, *Grundriss des Ordensrechtes*, Wien-Donauwörth-Basel: Verlag Ludwig Auer, 1930.

Smith, L. M., *The Early History of the Monastery of Cluny*, London, 1920.

————, *Cluny in the Eleventh and Twelfth Centuries*, London, 1930.

Spreitzenhofer, E., *Die Entwicklung des alten Mönchtums in Italien von seinen ersten Anfängen bis zum Auftreten des h. Benedikt*, Wien, 1894.

Synoptica Instructio pro Visitatore Generali et Praeside Capituli Provincialis, Quaracchi: Ad Claras Acquas, 1923.

Tamburini, Ascanius, *De Iure Abbatum et Aliorum Praelatorum,* 3 vols.,
    Lugduni, 1650.
Tanquerey, A., *Synopsis Theologiae Dogmaticae,* 23. ed., 3 vols., Paris-
    Tournay-Rome, 1930.
Thompson, E. M., *The Carthusian Order in England,* London, 1930.
Toso, A., *Ad Codicem Iuris Canonici Commentaria Minora,* 5 vols. in 2, Vol.
    I, 2. ed., Taurini-Romae, 1921–1927.
Valuy, B., *Le Gouvernement des Communautés Religieuses,* 8. ed., Paris,
    1925.
Van Hove, A., *Commentarium Lovaniense in Codicem Iuris Canonici,* Vol.
    I, Tom. I, *Prolegomena,* Mechliniae-Romae: Dessain, 1928; Vol. I,
    Tom. II, *De Legibus Ecclesiasticis,* Mechliniae-Romae: Dessain, 1930;
    Vol. I, Tom. V, *De Privilegiis, De Dispensationibus,* Mechliniae-
    Romae: Dessain, 1939.
Vermeersch, A., *De Religiosis Institutis et Personis Tractatus Canonico-
    Moralis ad Recentissimas Leges Exactus,* 2 vols., Romae-Ratisbonae,
    1902.
————, —Creusen, J., *Epitome Iuris Canonici cum Commentariis ad
    Scholas et ad Usum Privatum,* 4. ed., 3 vols., Mechliniae-Romae:
    Dessain, 1929–1931.
Victor a Iesu Maria, *De Iurisdictionis Acceptione in Iure Ecclesiastico,*
    Romae, 1940.
Vromant, G., *De Bonis Ecclesiae Temporalibus,* Louvain, 1927.
Waddingus, Lucas, *Annales Minorum seu Trium Ordinum S. Francisci.*
    Editio tertia auctior et emendatior ab an. 1208–1622 (25 vols., Quarac-
    chi, Ad Claras Aquas, 1931–1934). *Continuatio eorumdem Annalium*
    exarata a P. Aniceto Chiappini, vols. 26–30 (Quaracchi, Ad Claras
    Aquas, 1933–1951).
Walz, A. M., *Compendium Historiae Ordinis Praedicatorum,* Romae, 1930.
————, edidit *Acta Canonizationis S. Dominici,* Monumenta Ordinis
    Fratrum Praedicatorum Historica, Vol. XVI, Romae, 1935.
Wernz, Franciscus, *Ius Decretalium ad usum praelectionum in Scholis
    Textus Canonici sive Iuris Decretalium,* 6 vols. in 10, Romae-Prati,
    1898–1914.
————, —Vidal, Petrus, *Ius Canonicum ad Codicis Normam Exactum,* 7
    vols. in 8, Romae: apud Aedes Universitatis Gregorianae, 1923–1938.
Williams, W., *Monastic Studies,* Manchester, 1938.
Zeumer, K., *Leges Visigothorum Antiquiores,* Fontes Iuris Germanici Anti-
    qui in usum scholarum ex Monumentis Germaniae Historicis separatim
    editi, Hannoverae-Lipsiae, 1894.
Zumkeller, A., *Das Mönchtum des heiligen Augustinus,* Cassiciacum, Band
    XI, Würzburg, 1950.

ARTICLES

Bastien, P., "Conspectus historico-juridicus de regimine monasterii in ordine sancti Benedicti," *Jus Pontificium,* IX (1929), 296–305; X (1930), 44–55.

Ciprotti, P., "Il fine della Chiesa e il diritto," *Archivio di Diritto Ecclesiastico,* IV (1942), 36–40.

Crisci, G., "De delegatione a iure in iure canonico vigenti," *Apollinaris,* X (1937), 513–535.

———, "Evolutio historica delegationis a iure," *Apollinaris,* IX (1936), 270–299.

Denifle, H., "Die Constitutionen des Predigerordens vom Jahre 1228," *ALKM,* I (1885), 165–227.

———, "Die Constitutionen des Predigerordens in der Redaction Raimunds von Peñafort," *ALKM,* V (1889), 530–564.

Ehrle, F., "Die ältesten Redactionen der Generalconstitutionen des Franziskanerordens," *ALKM,* VI (1890), 87–138.

Gallen, J., "Canonical Visitation of Higher Superiors," *Review for Religious,* XII (1953), 21–35.

Goyeneche, S., "De Transitu ad aliam religionem," *CpR,* I (1920), 217–226.

———, "Consultationes," *CpR,* III (1922), 53–58; 217–219; 263–272; VI (1925), 203–208; IX (1928), 427; XIII (1932), 103–104; *CpRM,* XVII (1936), 247; XXII (1941), 199–205.

Heston, Edward, "Some Aspects of Government of Religious Communities," *The Jurist,* X (1950), 35–51.

Hilling, N., "Über den Gebrauch des Ausdrucks *iurisdictio* im kanonischen Recht während der ersten Hälfte des Mittelalters," *Archiv für katholisches Kirchenrecht,* XCVIII (1938), 165–170.

Jombart, E., "Le lecture de certains decrets," *Nouvelle Revue Théologique,* XLVIII (1921), 364–365.

———, "De religiosis dimissis," *Nouvelle Revue Théologique,* LXI (1934), 1080–1082.

———. "Questionnaire pour les superieures générales ou provinciales en visité," *Revue des Communautés Religieuses,* VI (1930), 15–21; 70–74.

Kerckhove, M. Van de, "De Notione Jurisdictionis in Jure Romano," *Jus Pontificium,* XVI (1936), 49–65.

———, "De Notione Jurisdictionis apud Decretistas et priores Decretalistas (1140–1250)," *Jus Pontificium,* XVIII (1938) 10–14.

Lambot, C., "L'Influence de Saint Augustin sur le Règle de Saint Bénoît," *Revue liturgique et monastique,* XIV (1929), 320–337.

Larraona, A., "De potestate dominativa publica in Iure Canonico," *Acta Congressus Iuridici Internationalis,* IV (1937), 145–180.

———, "Consultationes," *CpR,* I (1920), 81–82; 365–372; II (1921), 340–342.

———, "Commentarium Codicis," *CpR,* III (1922), 133–138; IV (1923), 39–46; 72–76; VI (1925), 425–431; VII (1926), 30–36; 239–248; VIII (1927), 164–176; 354–358; *CpRM,* XVIII (1937), 233–237; 319–327; XIX (1938), 8–12.

Ledwolorz, A., "De superiorum potestate dispensandi in iure particulari

Ordinis Fratrum Minorum," *Antonianum*, XIII (1938), 33–58.

————. "De potestate Superiorum O.F.M. dispensandi a legibus Constitutionum Generalium Ordinis," *Antonianum*, XXX (1955), 245–256.

————, "Illegitimität und Irregularität als Hindernisse für Bestellung zu bestimmten Ordensämtern in klösterlichen Genossenschaften," *Ephemerides Iuris Canonici*, XI (1946), 255–267.

Lefebvre, C., "Pouvoir judiciare et pouvoir administratif en droit canonique," *Ephemerides Iuris Canonici*, V (1949), 339–353.

Maroto, P., "Regulae et Particulares Constitutiones singularum Religionum ex Iure Decretalium usque ad Codicem," *Acta Congressus Iuridici Internationalis*, IV (1937), 207–299.

————, "Annotationes," *CpR*, I (1920), 99–102; XV (1934), 352–356.

Neukirchen, Marinus a, "Constitutionum Generalium Primi Ordinis Seraphici Series Chronologica," *Collectanea Franciscana*, XII (1942), 377–396.

Oesterle, G., "De ratione studiorum in religionibus clericalibus," *CpR*, VI (1925), 296–323.

————, "De relatione inter forum externum et internum," *Apollinaris*, XIX (1946), 73–86.

Roelker, E., "The Use of the Term *dispensatio* in the Code of Canon Law," *The Jurist*, X (1950), 138–151.

Tabera, A., "De Dimissione Religiosorum," *CpR*, XI (1930), 277–285; 411–420; XII (1931), 140–148; 369–375.

Toso, A., "De Conceptu Legis iuxta Aquinatis Doctrinam," *Jus Pontificium*, IV (1924), 31–36.

Vermeersch, A., "Annotationes," *Periodica de Re Canonica et Morali utilia praesertim Religiosis et Missionariis*, XII (1923), 156.

Villien, A., "La Procédure Canonique pour l'Expulsion des Réligieux," *Le Canoniste Contemporaine*, XXV (1912), 713–718; XXVI (1913), 129–142; 211–222.

Volta, P., "De monasteriis vel domibus sui iuris et superioribus majoribus," *Periodica de Re Canonica et Morali utilia praesertim Religiosis et Missionariis*, X (1922), 7–10.

PERIODICALS

Acta Ordinis Fratrum Minorum, Florentiae, 1882—

Antonianum, Romae, 1926—

Apollinaris, Romae, 1928—

Archiv für katholisches Kirchenrecht, Innsbruck, 1857–1861; Mainz, 1862—

Archiv für Litteratur- und Kirchengeschichte des Mittelalters, Berlin, 1885–1900.

Collectanea Franciscana, Romae, 1931—

Commentarium pro Religiosis, Romae, 1920–1934; ab anno 1935: *Commentarium pro Religiosis et Missionariis*.

Canoniste Contemporaine, Le—Paris, 1878–1922; ab anno 1924 ad annum 1926: *Le Canoniste.*

Ephemerides Iuris Canonici, Romae, 1945—

Jurist, The, Washington, D.C., 1941—

Jus Pontificium, Romae, 1921–1940.

Nouvelle Revue Théologique, Paris, 1869—

Periodica de Re Canonica et Morali utilia praesertim Religiosis et Missionariis, Brugis, 1905–1926; ab anno 1927: *Periodica de Re Canonica, Morali, Liturgica.*

Review for Religious, Topeka, Kansas, 1942—

Revue des Communautés Religieuses, Enghien, 1925—

Revue liturgique et monastique, Maredsous, Belgium, vol. I–XII, 1899–1910; second series, 1911—(suspended 1915–1918): *Revue liturgique et bénedictine.*

INDEX

Abbas primas,
  residence of, 127
Abbot, 16, 20, 23
  of Camaldoli, 26
  of Citeaux, 32
  of Prémontré, 35
Advice,
  of council, 130
Affiliation of tertiaries, 160–161
Age, canonical, 84
Alienation, 134
Anthony, St., 4, 6
Apices, 113
Appeal, 120
  court of, 122
Appointment of Supreme moderator,
    86
Ascetics, 3
Authority,
  of general chapter, 133

Beatification process, 123
Benedict of Aniane, St., 23
Bernard, St., 31
Bonaventure, St., 49
Books, prohibition of, 157
Bruno, St., 27

Caesarius of Arles, 14
Camaldolese, 26
Canonization process, 123
Canons,
  Augustinian, 14
  Regular, 34
Canons,
  Commentary on,
    c. 196, 61
    c. 197, § 1, 61
    c. 501, § 1, 67

    c. 502, 74–77
    c. 504, 82–85
    c. 1312, § 1 and 2, 67
    c. 1579, § 2, 117
    c. 1594, § 4, 120
Carta Caritatis, 32, 33
Carthusians, 27
Cassian, 14
Censures,
  inflicted by superiors, 114
Chapter, general,
  according to St. Basil, 12
  at Grande Chartreuse, 30
  at Prémontré, 35
  convocation of, 133
  distinct from general council, 128
  Dominican, 52
  Franciscan, 44
  generalissimum, 54
  holding of, 132
  jurisdictional powers of, 132
  legislative authority of, 133
  of military orders, 40
  suppresses provinces, 143
Cistercians, 32
Cloister,
  limits of, 146
Cluny,
  origin of, 22
Communion, frequent
  decree on, 140
Confession of religious,
  decree on, 140
Consent
  of council, 130
  of community, 131
Constitutions,
  definition of, 107
  designate major superior, 80

determine the judge, 118
provisions of, 74
restriction of power by, 90
Constitutiones Narbonnenses, 49, 115
Consuetudines, 28
Consultation,
of council, 130
Council, definitorial, 128
Council, ecumenical
participation in, 142
Council, general
and reservation of sins, 156
consent of, 75
distinct from general chapter, 128
of military orders, 40
number of members, 129
vote of, 130
Court of the first instance, 117
Curia, generalitial, 127

Daughter-houses, 20, 24
Decrees,
of general chapter, 135
of Holy See, 138
execution of, 139
Definitorium, 128
Definitors, 29, 53
Delegation,
as judge, 119
Delicts,
dispensation from, 104
for *ipso facto* dismissal, 149
Dismissal of religious, 116
by declaratory sentence, 117
in solemn vows, 153
in temporary vows, 152
ipso facto effected, 149
Dispensation,
definition, 95
from community acts, 109
from general law, 98
from impediment of illegitimacy,
74
from special law, 106
of entire community, 100
of students and teachers, 160

Documents, papal
reading of, 139
Dominic, St., 50
Dominicans, 50–55

Excommunication, 114, 116
Exemption,
privilege of, 98–99
Exercises, community
dispensation from, 102
Expulsion from Order, 117

Francis, St., 44
Franciscans, 44

Generalissimum Chapter, 54
Gilbert of Sempringham, St., 36
Gilbertine Order, 36
Goods,
disposition of, 134
Grand Master, 40
Grande Chartreuse, 27
Great Dom, 29
Guigo, 28

Harding, St. Stephen, 31, 32
Hermits, 4, 27
House, religious
canonical establishment, 145
cloister of, 146
definition of, 76
Humbert of Romans, 53

Institutes, secular, 161
Irregularities,
dispensation from, 104
Isidore, St., 15

Judge of first instance, 118
Jurisdiction,
concept of, 59
definition of, 61
delegated, 64
extent of, 74–77
of general chapters, 132

Knights Templars, 39

Law,
  and precepts, 91
  dispensation from, 98
Legislation,
  particular, 75
Legitimation, 84

Maior abbas, 32
Manifestation of conscience,
  decree on, 140
Martin of Tours, St., 14
Master General, 52
Minister General, 47–49
Moderator, supreme,
  admission to novitiate by, 146
  adumbrations of office of, 5
  among the Camaldolese, 26
  and affiliation of tertiaries, 160
  and common good, 92
  and dismissal of religious, 149–154
  and expulsion, 117
  and his council, 129
  and preceptive power, 94
  and reservation of sins, 155
  and the general chapter, 132
  appointment of, 86
  as judge of first instance, 118
  at ecumenical council, 142
  authority of, 59, 71–77
  authority over provinces, 143
  canonical visitation by, 135
  competency of, 78–80
  dispensatory powers of, 95, 100
  Dominican, 52
  executive power of, 125
  Franciscan, 45
  judicial power of, 112
  judicial rights and duties of, 120
  legislative power of, 89
  obligations to accept office, 87
  of mendicant Orders, 42
  person of, 81
  prohibition of books by, 157
  residence of, 126
  rôle according to St. Anthony, 7
  rôle according to St. Basil, 13
  rôle according to St. Benedict, 19
  rôle according to St. Pachomius,
    10
  supervision of studies by, 158
  term of office, 86
  qualifications of, 81–85
  quinquennial report by, 141
Monks,
  in Egypt, 6
  Cluniac, 23
Monasticism,
  African, 17
  Basilian, 11
  Celtic, 16
  early, 4
  French, 14
  in twelfth century, 31
  Italian, 13
  Pachomian, 8
  Spanish, 15
  St. Francis and, 49
Mother-abbey, 25

Norbert, St., 34
Notary, 120
Novitiate,
  admission to, 146

Office,
  obligation to accept, 87–88
  term of, 86
Orders,
  mendicant, 31, 42
  military, 38
Oath, 121
  against modernism, 126

Pachomius, St., 4, 7
Pactum, 16
Patrick, St., 16
Penalties,
  latae sententiae, 149
Peter the Venerable, 31
Postulator, 123
Power,

dominative, 65–67
  source of precepts, 92
judicial
  definition of, 112
  extent of, 114
Precepts,
  and law, 91
  common, 93
  definition of, 90
  jurisdictional, 93
  obligation of, 94
  power to issue, 90
Premonstratensians, 34
Prior of all, 37
Procurator general, 127
Profession,
  formula of, 54
  legitimation by, 84
  of faith, 124
Property,
  disposal of, 144
Province,
  controversy between, 118
  definition, 75–76
  subject to supreme moderator, 143
Provincial,
  dispensatory power of, 100
  judicial power of, 115
  non-monastic office, 5
  removal of, 48
  supervised by supreme moderator, 144

Qualities of superior general, 81–85
Quinquennial report, 140

Ratio studiorum, 158
Raymond of Penafort, St., 51
Reform,
  at Cluny, 23, 34
  by Council of Trent, 115
Regula bullata, 47
Regula Prima, 45
Religious, 77
Religious state,
  divine institution, 3

Report, quinquennial, 140
  made by supreme moderator, 141
Reservation of sins, 155
Residence, 126
  absence from, 127
Rimulae, 113
Romuald, St., 26
Rule,
  definition of, 107
  obligation of, 108
  of St. Anthony, 6
  of St. Basil, 11
  of St. Benedict, 18
  of St. Fructuosus, 15
  of St. Pachomius, 7

Seminaries,
  establishment of, 158
Statuta antiqua, 28
Statuta nova, 28
Statuta pro Studiis regendis, 158
Students, 159
Studies,
  supervision of, 158
Superiors,
  competency of, 78
  general, 79–80
Suspension, 114

Teachers, 159
Tertia compilatio, 28
Tertiaries,
  affiliation of, 160
Trials, 119

Visitation,
  according to St. Pachomius, 9
  canonical, 135
  delegation of, 137
  of Grande Chartreuse, 30
  revelation during, 114
  scope of, 137
Vote,
  of general council, 130
Vows,
  matter of, 69

BIOGRAPHICAL NOTE

Maurice J. Grajewski, O.F.M., was born on March 25, 1916, in Milwaukee, Wisconsin. After completing his elementary education at St. John Cantius parochial school in the same city, he attended St. Bonaventure High School in Sturtevant, Wisconsin. He entered the novitiate of the Franciscan Order at Pulaski, Wisconsin, where he made his religious profession on August 15, 1934. His classical and philosophical studies he made at St. Francis College, Burlington, Wisconsin; his theological studies at the Athenaeum Pontificium Antonianum in Rome, Italy. After ordination to the priesthood on June 20, 1940, he studied philosophy at the Catholic University of America, where he received his doctorate in 1944. In 1953 he entered the School of Canon Law at the same University, where he received the degree of Bachelor of Canon Law in June, 1954, and the Licentiate in June, 1955.

CANON LAW STUDIES *

368. Bockstie, Rev. Richard, C.SS.R., J.C.L., The principal oratory of religious.
369. Grajewski, Rev. Maurice J., O.F.M., M.A., Ph.D., J.C.L., The supreme moderator of clerical exempt religious institutes.
370. Havlik, Rev. Bernard, A.B., J.C.L., The cessation of rescripts.
371. Olkovikas, Rev. Albert William, S.T.L., J.C.L., The *instantia* of the lawsuit.
372. Poblete, Rev. Elias Olarte, J.C.L., The plenary council.
373. Sokolich, Rev. Alexander F., S.T.L., J.C.L., Canonical provisions for universities and colleges.
374. Sullivan, Rev. Jordan J., O.F.M.Cap., B.A., J.C.L., Fast and abstinence in the First Order of St. Francis.
375. Kennedy, Rev. David W., J.C.L., Canon law and liturgical music.

* For a complete list of the available numbers of this series apply to the Catholic University of America Press, 620 Michigan Ave., N.E., Washington (17), D.C., for a general catalog.